The Quest for Civil Order

Politics, Rules and Individuality

Chor-yung Cheung

imprint-academic.com

Copyright © Chor-yung Cheung, 2007

The moral rights of the author have been asserted.
No part of this publication may be reproduced in any form
without permission, except for the quotation of brief passages
in criticism and discussion.

Published in the UK by
Imprint Academic, PO Box 200, Exeter EX5 5YX, UK

Published in the USA by
Imprint Academic, Philosophy Documentation Center
PO Box 7147, Charlottesville, VA 22906-7147, USA

ISBN-13: 978184540 089 7

A CIP catalogue record for this book is available from the
British Library and US Library of Congress

Contents

Acknowledgements   vi

Chapter I: Introduction   1

Chapter II: Gellner on Civil Society:
Pluralism, Modular Man and the Separation
of State and Economy   13
1. Introduction   13
2. Plural Society of a Particular Kind   15
3. Man of a Particular Kind: The Modular Man   20
4. Modular Man as an Individualist   25
5. Separation of State and Economy   28
6. Politics vs Economics   35
7. Centralisation, Decentralisation and Pluralism   37
8. Civil or National Society?   42
9. Conclusion   46

Chapter III: Hayek on 'The Great Society':
Knowledge, Abstract Rules and the
Dethronement of Politics   51
1. Introduction   51
2. Social Practices: The Result of Human Action, Not Human Design   55
3. Co-ordination of Dispersed Knowledge: Abstract Rules as Multi-Purpose Instruments   61
4. 'The Great Society' and the Functional Nature of the Obligatory Rules   69
5. Unity of Rules and Plurality of Ends: 'The Great Society' and Pluralism   73
6. Individualism: True and False   75
7. State-Society Distinction   78

8.	'The Dethronement of Politics' or the Indispensability of the Political?	83
9.	'The Great Society' and the Inadequacy of Negative Values	86
10.	Conclusion	92

Chapter IV: Habermas on Discursive Democracy: Communicative Reason, Law, Private and Public Autonomy, and the Politics of Rational Consensus — 97

1.	Introduction	97
2.	Communicative Action and Communicative Rationality	98
3.	Communicative Reason and Social Integration	102
4.	Positive Law and Social Integration	104
5.	Law and Morality	106
6.	The Co-originality of Private and Public Autonomy	112
7.	The Co-originality Thesis: Political, Not Moral	116
8.	Constitutional Patriotism as the Political Bond in the Age of Post-traditional Society	120
9.	The Individual as an End and the Need for Mutual Respect	128
10.	Political Participation, Rational Consensus and Majority Rule	130
11.	Communicative Power, Legitimate Law and Administrative Power	135
12.	Communicative Power and Authority	138
13.	Proceduralist Democracy: Between Radicalism and Resignation?	142

Chapter V: Oakeshott on Civil Association: Moral Agency, Law and Politics — 145

1. Introduction: Philosophical Understanding and Civil Association — 145
2. Free Agents and Civil Association — 152
3. Transactional Association and Enterprise Association — 154
4. Practice and Purpose in Human Conduct — 159
5. Morality and Civility — 161
6. Civil Rules as Non-Instrumental and Authoritative Assertions — 165
7. Civil Association and Its Institutions — 169
8. Civil Association as the Rule of Law — 172
9. Civil Association: Conservatism vs Radicalism — 176
10. Politics and Civil Association — 181
11. Freedom, Diversity and Autonomy — 186
12. Conclusion — 194

Chapter VI: Conclusion — 197

Bibliography — 213

Index — 221

Acknowledgements

This book originated from my PhD thesis of the same title, which was submitted to and accepted by the University of Hull in 2005. My first and foremost acknowledgement must go to Professor Noel O'Sullivan, my thesis supervisor, for without his unfailing support and most inspiring guidance I do not think that this book could have been completed.

I became very interested in the idea of civil association in Western political theory in general and the philosophy of Michael Oakeshott in particular in the second half of the 1990s when I was a lecturer at the City University of Hong Kong. At about the same time, I discovered that at Hull there were two very distinguished professors in its Department of Politics who were accomplished experts in this area: the retired Professor Bhikhu Parekh, and Professor O'Sullivan, who was then the Director of Postgraduate Studies. I decided to join the Department of Politics for my study immediately after my first visit to the university. Although I had gone to Hull expecting just to have some initial exchanges on my study plan on civil association, what persuaded me to join the department was Professor O'Sullivan's generosity at our first meeting, spending the whole afternoon with me discussing my proposal in detail.

What struck me most was that the professor was not only very knowledgeable about Western political philosophy, but also patient enough to always relate the relevant political and philosophical issues to their proper historical context, so that a non-European like me would be able to appreciate the deeper meaning of those issues in their proper context in Western civilisation. I must admit that the quality of the conversation with Professor O'Sullivan at that meeting was unmatched by any previous intellectual exchanges that I had experienced, and I am most grateful for the seriousness shown by him to my then half-baked ideas.

Throughout my study from 1998 to 2005 (which had to be part-time owing to my full-time teaching commitment at the City University of Hong Kong), Professor O'Sullivan's advice, guidance and patience were essential to keep me on track. There were times when I was obliged to concentrate less on my study due to the passing away of close family members or the need to take up some duties to fulfil the responsibilities of being a public intellectual in Hong Kong, and I was most fortunate to have a supervisor who never lost confidence in me. What I am extremely grateful for and miss most are the long and interesting conversations we had in the O'Sullivans' place in Newland Park, the good food prepared by Mrs O'Sullivan, and the after-meal classical music that we listened to in their house. Their warm hospitality to me and my family made us feel at home. Furthermore, the efforts made by Professor O'Sullivan to make my thesis publishable after its acceptance by the university, are an intellectual debt to this remarkable teacher that I do not know how to pay back.

Over the years, I have inevitably incurred a lot of intellectual debts to many friends and colleagues. Thanks are due to Nicholas J. Rengger and Colin Tyler for their valuable comments on an earlier version of this work that I greatly benefited from. A draft chapter on Hayek in this book was presented to a graduate seminar at Hull, and I am grateful to the graduate students there for their comments on my presentation. The interest of Andy and Mabel in my study was a constant morale booster; and my detours to their place in Newcastle whenever I could after my study visits to Hull were always most enjoyable.

I am also grateful to the City University of Hong Kong for granting me leaves and providing me with financial subsidies for my study. I am indebted to members of an informal political theory study group in Hong Kong for the interesting intellectual discussions we had during 1999–2001. In particular, I would like to thank Y.K. Shih, Joseph Chan, Hong-yee Chen and Hon-lam Li for their intellectual guidance. Ming Sing commented on an earlier version of the Gellner chapter of this book and I am very grateful for his generous remarks. Tony Mok, apart from offering his comments on some draft sections of this book, has been a good intellectual companion of mine since we studied political theory together for our MPhil degrees at the Chinese University of Hong Kong. Indeed, it was Tony who first alerted me to the importance of Habermas's absorbing works some twenty years ago.

My daughter Helier Ying-wah Cheung, who is studying English Literature at the University College of London University, has constantly offered me good advice on how to polish my English in my academic writings and I must thank her for that. Gordon Tolley's very generous assistance in helping me to proof read this book during the last stage of its production is also gratefully acknowledged. Needless to say, without the care and love of my wife Anne and the charm and good humour of my son Yan-lap, I cannot imagine how I was able to cope with all the duties that I had to attend to while endeavouring to continue my intellectual pursuit for a better understanding of the quest for civil order by some great political theorists.

Hong Kong, March 2007

1
Introduction

In this book four notable thinkers in the field of modern social and political theory will be examined, with a view to determining how far it is possible to create and maintain a non-coercive but sustainable political order under conditions of diversity in contemporary Western societies. The four thinkers to be considered are Ernest Gellner, whose thought focused on the concept of civil society; Friedrich Hayek, whose principal concern was with a market-centred spontaneous social order; Jürgen Habermas, whose ideal is a discursive democracy; and Michael Oakeshott, whose model of a free society is based on a non-instrumental conception of civil association.[1]

It should come as no surprise that the thinkers examined here do not share a common approach or methodology. However, there are two reasons for grouping them together in one systematic study. The first is that, from a historical point of view, their theories are all inspired by a common concern with the threat of totalitarianism that continued to haunt European political thinkers in the decades after 1945. In fact, three of the thinkers studied—Gellner, Hayek, and Habermas—came from either Eastern or Central Europe, where the violent experiences of communism and Nazism

[1] If asked to name one work each from these thinkers that represents the most systematic and/or profound treatment of their respective social and political theory, the answer would be Gellner's *Conditions of Liberty: Civil Society and its Rivals*, London: Penguin Books, 1994; Hayek's *Law, Legislation, and Liberty*, Vols. 1–3, Chicago: The University of Chicago Press, 1973, 1976 and 1978; Habermas, *Between Facts and Norms: Contributions to a Discourse Theory of Law and Democracy*, Cambridge: Polity Press, 1996, trans. William Rehg; and Oakeshott's *On Human Conduct*, Oxford: Clarendon Press, 1991.

were both real and horrendous. While the intellectually sceptical Oakeshott had the good fortune to spend his whole life in Great Britain, he and his country nevertheless had to fight against Nazi Germany during the Second World War. In this sense, all four social and political theories can be interpreted as intellectual attempts to set limits to state power not only to prevent the emergence of a total state, but also to defend vigorously the freedom of the individual. Thus Gellner, for example, endorses a vibrant non-political concept of civil society to balance the coercive power of the state, while Hayek argues that state central planning is doomed to failure because it can never produce vital social and economic institutions. Such institutions, which are exemplified above all by the market, are never the product of planning but are always the unintended outcome of the spontaneous actions of individuals. Likewise, the more normatively oriented discursive theory of Habermas contends that regulative legislation of a democracy is legitimate only if the citizens concerned can at least become co-authors of its law. Finally, Oakeshott's ideal of civil association rests on a qualitative distinction between an enterprise state (in which all members have to serve the same collective goal) and a civil understanding of the state, for which all politically obligatory rules must be non-instrumental.[2]

---

[2] For an illuminating discussion of the responses of Hayek and Oakeshott to totalitarianism, see Noel O'Sullivan's 'Visions of Freedom: The Response to Totalitarianism', in *The British Study of Politics in the Twentieth Century*, eds Jack Hayward, Brian Barry and Archie Brown, Oxford: Oxford University Press, published for the British Academy, 1999, pp. 63–88. O'Sullivan's article also covers the visions of Isaiah Berlin and Karl Popper in this connection. It is sometimes pointed out that unlike the other three, Habermas is sympathetic to the teachings of Karl Marx, particularly in the early part of his academic career, and that his attitude towards totalitarianism is therefore somewhat different. On p. 283 of *Another Country: German Intellectuals, Unification and National Identity*, New Haven and London: Yale University Press, 2000, Jan-Werner Müller suggests that Habermas, probably because of his sympathy for Western Marxism, has been reluctant to adopt the Cold War vocabulary of totalitarianism in his critique of communism and Nazism. But this appears to be refuted by Habermas's admission of

The second reason for considering the four thinkers together, from a broader cultural and theoretical perspective, is that they have all taken the challenges of modernity seriously, in the sense that not only are their theoretical undertakings committed to the pursuit of some kind of civil order and constitutionalism (in which personal freedom and the obligation to follow the imperatives of the state are not regarded as incompatible), but they also, each in their own way, attempt to secure their respective defence of civil order on a theoretically plausible and non-arbitrary ground. They are all working in the shadow of Friedrich Nietzsche, who proclaimed the death of God in a human world where 'a common faith anchored in a common set of experiences can no longer secure and protect itself from widespread revisionism, scepticism, doubt and unbelief'.[3]

In other words, the enchanted world of harmonious human values, together with the belief that God gives universal meaning to the human world, has now disappeared. In this modern world of disenchantment, it is alleged that no values can be discovered objectively. Human values can only be chosen, and it is for the individual concerned to make a personal choice in matters of faith or systems of belief in order to give meaning to human life.[4] It is therefore no exaggeration to say that whether we like it or not, questions about freedom, individuality and the possibility or impossibility of a non-arbitrary social order are forced upon man by the advent of modernity, and serious social and political thinkers cannot but respond to this modern condition. As a result, the nature of the self, the relationship between personal freedom and political authority, and

---

the 'totalitarian integration of society' by fascism and Stalinism in his 'Conceptions of Modernity: A Look Back at Two Traditions'. See the *Postnational Constellation: Political Essays*, trans., ed. and with an intro. by Max Pensky, Cambridge: Polity Press, 2001, p. 140.

[3] William E. Connolly, *Political Theory and Modernity*, Oxford: Basil Blackwell, 1988, p. 9.

[4] Michael H. Lessnoff has given a good introductory account of the Weberian predicaments—disenchantment and rationalisation—of modernity in 'Max Weber and the Politics of the Twentieth Century', in *Political Philosophers of the Twentieth Century*, Oxford: Blackwell, 1999, pp. 8–36.

whether a legitimate social order is possible in view of the diversity (and incompatibility) of individual values, have become first-order political and philosophical questions.

In this book, it will be suggested that the sociological-functional approach adopted by Gellner in constructing his model of civil society, the spontaneous development of social institutions proposed by Hayek in defending the market and individual freedom, the communicatively rational framework presupposed by Habermas to justify positive legislation regulating the conduct of citizens in a deliberative democracy, and the anti-reductionist and radically non-instrumental nature of civil association conceived by Oakeshott to preserve the integrity of autonomous moral agents are the four most thought-provoking recent theoretical attempts to defend the possibility of civil order and to provide answers to first-order philosophical questions asked by students of social and political theory.

While the different answers provided by these theorists, along with their different approaches and theoretical perspectives, may with some justification be labelled as either 'liberal' (in the case of Gellner and Hayek), 'conservative' (in the case of Oakeshott), or 'socialist' (in the case of Habermas), Jeremy Waldron has made a valid point when he writes that

> Locke did not write the *Two Treatises* in order to *be* a liberal, any more than Burke wrote *Reflections on the Revolution in France* in order to *be* a conservative. Rather, each was developed as *a* theory of government, *a* theory of society, or *a* theory of political economy, and was intended to be judged as a contribution to a debate that knew no ideological frontiers and in which almost all thinking people of the time were interested.[5]

In what follows, therefore, the social and political theories of Gellner, Hayek, Habermas and Oakeshott will be treated not as variants of some political ideology such as liberalism or socialism, but as significant and unique contri-

---

[5] Jeremy Waldron, 'Theoretical Foundations of Liberalism', in *The Philosophical Quarterly*, Vol. 37, No. 147, April 1987, p. 127, emphasis in the original.

butions to our descriptive and normative understanding of the social and political order.

For Gellner, the modular man who can switch professions or associations relatively easily in accordance with his own choice, as required by the complex division of labour constituting industrial society, is the answer to the question of how the conception of the modern self should be conceived.

For Hayek, a preference-maximising individual alone knows his own situation best, and is responsible for the consequences of his or her decisions in the free market, as well as in social exchanges.

For Habermas, individuals are both rational and rights bearing; through active participation in democratic politics within the community they have the capacity to shape a rational and legitimate consensus among themselves. While Habermas's conception of the self has greater normative content than Gellner's modular man and Hayek's preference-maximiser, all three put much emphasis on the values of individual choice and personal autonomy in their respective conceptions of the individual.

Likewise, Oakeshott's civil association is attractive if we are all autonomous moral agents who treasure the challenge and the space to seek, jointly or severally, our wished-for satisfactions and ways of life as far as our imagination permits, subject only to conditions prescribed by non-instrumental civil rules. While the substantive content of their respective conceptions of the individual is different and will be discussed more fully in subsequent chapters of this book, their theories all share a predominantly individualist outlook, which marks a distinctive feature in their responses to the modern predicament of disenchantment.[6]

---

[6] Frank S. Meyer in his 'Western Civilization: The Problem of Political Freedom' even goes so far as to say that the uniqueness of Western civilisation, in comparison with all other major civilisations of the world, lies precisely in the central role it gives to the individual. That is why the problem of political freedom has become its central political issue. See Meyer, *In Defense of Freedom and Related Essays*, Indianapolis: Liberty Fund, 1996, pp. 209–24.

The counterpart of individual freedom in social and political theory is social order. If individuals are free and autonomous and are required to choose their own values and preferences, what provides the social and political bond needed to establish a stable and legitimate political community? As stated earlier, all the thinkers examined in this book are, in one way or another, in pursuit of some kind of civil order in which personal freedom and the obligation to follow the imperatives of the state are not regarded as incompatible. According to Thomas Hobbes, the word civil means 'artifice springing from more than one will'.[7] In other words, the word civil, in the social context, refers to practices or institutions that arise out of the voluntary actions of individuals, and civil authority in the political realm arises out of some kind of voluntary agreement amongst these wills for governing political conduct. Edward Shils, in his discussion of the virtue of civil society, captures some very important features of the concept of civility when he says, '"Civil" [from the jurisprudential and political philosophies of classical antiquity to early modern times] was contrasted with "natural". It was the condition of men living in society, living in accordance with rules.'[8]

In this respect, the theorists examined in this chapter have by and large shared Shils' understanding of civility and argue, explicitly or inexplicitly, that civil order under modern conditions of social diversity and complexity is made possible by a certain manner of constituting the community in which the rule of law is central. Although Hayek, Habermas and Oakeshott each hold different conceptions of the rule of law that may even be at odds with each other, they all agree that law is the key to the formation and maintenance of a civil order which is essential for the harmonisation of personal freedom and political legitimacy. To them, law is not rule of just any kind; rather it must be able to obli-

---

[7] See Michael Oakeshott's 'Introduction to Leviathan', in *Rationalism in Politics and Other Essays*, new and expanded edition, Indianapolis: Liberty Press, 1991, p. 247.

[8] Edward Shils, 'The Virtue of Civil Society', in *Government and Opposition*, Vol. 26, No. 1, Winter 1991, p. 7.

gate the citizens to act in a certain manner yet at the same time preserve their freedoms unhampered. A close study of the nature and attributes of legal rules thus becomes a central theoretical issue for civil order theorists.

In this connection, Gellner is perhaps the most ambiguous amongst the four theorists examined here, for there is a conspicuous omission of any systematic discussion of the rule of law in his works on civil society. But it will be argued in the next chapter that his claim that 'individual commitment to contract not status seems to be a foundation of [the modern complex] social order', in fact requires him to rely on rules similar to those required by the rule of law if he is to make his concept of civil society more coherent.[9] This makes Gellner's position a very good starting point to demonstrate why a failure to grasp the centrality of the rule of law in civil order is highly unsatisfactory for theoretical works of this kind. A closer look at Hayek's treatment of the same topic, which will be fully discussed in Chapter 3 below, reveals that, in the end, his conception of the rule of law is in fact instrumental to his naturalistic evolutionism, thus ultimately undermining his defence of individual freedom. Hayek's case shows that if civil rules are made to serve purposes other than the maintenance of civility itself, civil order can be in danger.

Subsequent chapters of this work will also argue that the approaches adopted by Habermas and Oakeshott on this issue appear to be more satisfactory, for they have made the rule of law a central concern of civil society, and each has proposed a normatively more adequate perspective (i.e. rational-dialogic consensus for Habermas and non-instrumental and authoritative rules for Oakeshott) to tackle the difficult theoretical question of how individual freedom can accommodate political obligation in a non-coercive manner. In other words, a systematic study of these four thinkers together helps to show the strengths and potential vulnerability of civil order theory.

---

[9] Gellner, *Conditions of Liberty*, p. 78

Disenchantment, according to Weber, is only half the story of the predicament facing modernity. The other half is what he calls 'rationalisation', in which man's increasing capacity to achieve ends based on his ever greater mastery of scientific knowledge contributes not only to the loss of confidence in religious or objective beliefs that cannot be verified by the tests adopted by the physical sciences, but also to the rationalisation and manipulation of more and more aspects of human life (e.g. in economics and administration).[10] What is the place of reason in civil order and how does it impact on the realm of the political in the social and political theory of these four philosophers?

Two of the thinkers studied here, Gellner and Habermas, have adopted an explicitly rationalist outlook in their theories. Throughout his academic career, Gellner always regarded himself as an ardent adherent of enlightenment rationalism.[11] His idea of the modern individual as capable of 'lucid, Cartesian thought, which separates issues rather than conflating them and takes them one at a time',[12] is not only consistent with enlightenment optimism about the possibility of a rational understanding of the world and its impatience with tradition, mystery, awe and superstition,[13] it also presupposes the rational individual's ability to distinguish the ends from the means and to choose techniques most conducive to the realisation of ends by clearly defined criteria of effectiveness and efficiency. On the other hand, there is no doubt that reason plays a central role in Habermas' theory of modernity because, as he says, 'modernity understands itself in opposition to tradition, it seeks a foothold for itself ... in reason.'[14] For Habermas it is, however, reason of a particular kind — that is communicative rationality — that makes rational consensus in a legitimate,

---

[10] See Lessnoff, *Political Philosophers of the Twentieth Century*, p. 2 and pp. 9-21.
[11] See Ernest Gellner, *Postmodernism, Reason and Religion*, London and New York: Routledge, 1992, pp. 80-96.
[12] Gellner, *Conditions of Liberty*, p. 104.
[13] See also Waldron's 'Theoretical Foundations of Liberalism', p. 134.
[14] See Habermas, 'Conceptions of Modernity', in *The Postnational Constellation*, p. 132.

discursive democracy possible, in which all citizens participate in political deliberation and decision-making for the community's self-legislation.[15]

Hayek and Oakeshott, however, appear to have a more modest view of reason and rationality. Hayek, for instance, is highly critical of what he calls 'constructivist rationalism', which, according to him, is a direct descendant of Cartesian rationalism in that it presupposes that a comprehensive understanding or even control of the world is in theory possible. He favours instead the spontaneous evolution of the market and other social institutions (like the law, languages, etc.) and argues that one of the essential conditions for the protection of individual liberty is not to allow constructivist rationalism to become the guiding principle of state action. In this connection, Oakeshott is also very mindful of the limitations of technical and scientific reason and the indispensability of judgement (or what he also calls 'practical reason') in matters relating to human conduct and social practices.[16] Oakeshott's sceptical approach in this regard does not mean that critical evaluation of social and political practices is impossible, it only means that the tribunal of reason does not work in the abstract; instead, its workings presuppose certain historical and authoritative contexts in the first place.[17]

It should come as no surprise to note at this point that despite their different epistemological positions, none of the theorists examined here can be characterised as a believer in synoptic rationalism, in which scientific reason is regarded as the sovereign guide for a comprehensive understanding of the human as well as the physical world. The rejection of synoptic rationalism does not mean that

[15] A full exposition of this can be found in chapter 4 below. Habermas's fully developed position on reason and rationality can be seen in his impressive *The Theory of Communicative Action: Reason and the Rationalization of Society*, Vol. 1, trans. Thomas McCarthy, Boston: Beacon Press, 1981; and *Theory of Communicative Action: The Critique of Functionalist Reason*, Vol. 2, trans. Thomas McCarthy, Cambridge: Polity Press, 1981.
[16] See, for examples, Michael Oakeshott's essays in *Rationalism in Politics and Other Essays*.
[17] Please refer to chapter 5 for a detailed discussion on this.

their respective conceptions of reason do not play an important role in delimiting the boundary of politics and distinguishing it from other aspects of society in their social and political theories. Hayek, for example, while highly critical of central planning and constructivist rationalism, has a tendency to identify state action mainly as an intrusive power influenced by the fatal conceit of Cartesian rationalism, and regards most if not all political interference with the operation of the spontaneous social order as illegitimate, though he is not against the provision of some basic level of welfare benefits to alleviate hardship, provided that it does not tamper with the market mechanism. This comes out most clearly, perhaps, in his popularly acclaimed *The Road to Serfdom*, in which any move towards state planning is regarded as teetering on the edge of the slippery slope to totalitarianism.[18] Habermas, on the other hand, argues that communicative rationality is capable of transforming political discourse into rational consensus for legitimate political decisions, if the citizens concerned are interacting with each other in good faith under conditions constituting something like an ideal speech situation. While more discussion of these matters has been left for subsequent chapters of this book, it is sufficient to say here that in addition to the conception of the individual and of the rule of law, what constitutes a legitimate political sphere, as opposed to an illegitimate exercise of power, is also crucially connected to conceptions of rationality.

Equally interesting, in this respect, is whether it is possible to differentiate political power from political authority, the answer to this question is crucial to the determination of whether a modern political theory aiming at defending political freedom is coherent or not. In a political community, if there is only the vocabulary of political power without the vocabulary of political authority, or if the vocabulary of power manages in the main to override that of authority, there cannot be individual freedom, though whether the power exercised therein is benign or

---

[18] Friedrich Hayek, *The Road to Serfdom*, Chicago: The University of Chicago Press, 1944, reprinted 1972.

not is another matter. De Tocqueville's warning that people in a democracy may find it difficult to be equal and remain free at the same time for long is still relevant, because they have a tendency to 'think that they have done enough for the protection of individual freedom when they have surrendered it to the power of the nation at large'.[19] For this reason theorists of civil order must remain vigilant of the distinction between power and authority.

Gellner, Hayek, Habermas and Oakeshott are no doubt towering figures in their respective fields of study; their contributions to modern social and political thought are widely recognised. In what follows, however, there is no intention to deal with every aspect of their wide-ranging philosophies. What will be concentrated upon is their theoretical attempts to conceive and defend the kind of civil order that each thinks is most plausible. In particular, their conceptions of the individual, their ideas of the political and their theory of the rule of law will be critically examined. Other important aspects of their intellectual contributions — such as Gellner's work on anthropology and Islam, Hayek's works on pure economics, Habermas's many technical and philosophical contributions to the theory of language and communicative action, and Oakeshott's famous study of the philosophy of history and philosophical idealism — will only be touched upon if they are directly relevant to the scope of this study.

---

[19] See Alexis de Tocqueville, *Democracy in America*, trans. Henry Reeve and Rev. Francis Bowen, abridged and with an intro. by Patrick Renshaw, Hertfordshire: Wordsworth Editions Limited, 1998, pp. 359-60.

2

Gellner on Civil Society

Pluralism, Modular Man and the Separation of State and Economy

Introduction

This chapter proposes to examine critically Ernest Gellner's concept of civil society, the novelty of which consists of his theoretical-cum-sociological attempt to understand the nature and character of civil society in a way which enables him to distinguish plural from civil societies, by identifying the specific kind of pluralism required by civil society. In addition, his analysis of the distinctive relationship between faith, power and production, on the one hand, and the social order that constitutes civil society, on the other, merits attention. Finally, his thesis that the idea of civil society presupposes a particular kind of human agent —'modular man'— is of particular interest.

Another highly interesting aspect of Gellner's approach is that he tries to understand the idea of civil society from a comparative perspective. Although Gellner himself believes that preaching across cultural boundaries is fairly pointless in most circumstances, his endeavours to compare and contrast the similarities and differences between civil society, segmentary community, Islamic society and Marxist society have put the nature and character of civil society in sharper focus. Furthermore, while Gellner believes that both civil society and nation-states have emerged from the same kind of social conditions, sharing similar kinds of high culture and economic conditions, the two are, nevertheless, distinct, though under certain historical circumstances, like Europe in the nineteenth century, they might join forces as allies to pursue revolutionary changes. A closer look at what keeps them apart will help to clarify the essential elements that make the former civil and the latter not.[1]

Gellner's gallant attempt to theorise the nature and character of civil society is, however, unsatisfactory and incoherent in the end, as will be argued in this chapter. One major defect is that his imagery of the modularity of modern man does not quite capture some essential aspects of the modern individual. Another reason is that Gellner has misconceived the distinctive nature of the political realm of civil society; this can be shown by the fact that he often confuses political authority with the idea of a balance of power. Such a confusion not only shows that Gellner's understanding of the distinctive role played by the political in civil society is ambiguous, but also reveals that he fails to appreciate fully the important role performed by the rule of law in helping to maintain the plural nature of civil society, thus undermining the coherence of his idea of civil society. This is important, because by exposing Gellner's ambiguities one can pave the way for a better appreciation of why the idea of civil society requires a conception of the political that is related to, but distinguishable from, power and morality. It will be argued in subsequent chapters (particularly in the two chapters on Habermas and Oakeshott) that the theorists who take the question of legitimacy most

[1] On p. 109 of *Conditions of Liberty*, Gellner asks the following question: 'If Civil Society and nationalism are the offspring of the same forces, does this affinity turn them into political allies or enemies?' His answer to this question is twofold. At the start in the nineteenth century, they were indeed allies; both had the same enemy in the baroque absolutist state. But in due course, their paths diverged, for the individualism inherent in civil society, according to Gellner, if pushed to its logical conclusion, was hostile to the cult of community. For details, see Gellner, 'Friend or Foe?', in *Conditions of Liberty: Civil Society and its Rivals*, London: Penguin Books, 1994, pp. 109–12.

seriously are the best guides when seeking to understand this issue.

A note of caution is in order before examining Gellner's detailed arguments. When people talk about civil society, they often talk in two different senses without consciously distinguishing one from the other. Gellner, however, does not commit this intellectual error, as he clearly points out that in the broader sense of the term, 'civil society' is used to describe 'a society in which there are two quite distinct realms, the political (which is also moral) and the socio-economic (which is morally neutral and instrumental)'. In this case, civil society is to be contrasted with society of another kind, feudal society for example, in which there is only one social order, political and economic, with identical political hierarchies and economic specialisations mutually reinforcing each other.[2]

On the other hand, when civil society is used in the narrower sense, it refers to the non-political part of society in which the political realm and the socio-economic realm are regarded as distinct. In Gellner's own words, the narrower sense refers to 'that part of society which stands opposed to the political structure (in the context of a social order in which this separation has taken place and is possible).'[3] In this chapter, unless otherwise specified, I shall mainly employ the term 'civil society' in the broader sense.

Plural Society of a Particular Kind

Gellner starts with an examination of what he calls the 'intuitive definition', which equates civil society with

> that set of diverse non-governmental institutions which is strong enough to counterbalance the state and, while not preventing the state from fulfilling its role of keeper of the peace and arbitrator between major interests, can neverthe-

---

[2] Gellner, *Conditions of Liberty*, p. 55.
[3] *Ibid.*, p. 56. In 'Civil society in historical context', Gellner says, 'historically, the expression civil society has of course been used in a number of senses — as opposed to savagery and/or anarchy, as opposed to the church, or as opposed to the state.' See *International Social Science Journal*, Vol. 43, No. 3, 1991, p. 495.

less prevent it from dominating and atomising the rest of society.[4]

The problem with this definition, according to Gellner, is that such a definition is too broad, and mistakenly assumes that all plural societies are compatible with individual liberty, a central phenomenon and value that characterises the modern civil order.[5] In reality, however, man can be free from the tyranny of kings only at the cost of falling under the tyranny of cousins (a kind of pluralism between the political centre and the locality), and Gellner thinks that pre-modern segmentary community is a good illustration of this point.

Gellner contends that due to technological, geographical and other reasons, an all-embracing centralised despotism was not easy to establish in pre-modern polities. It was not uncommon to find, therefore, that there existed well-organised, self-administering and largely autonomous sub-communities within a state or an empire. However, within such sub-communities, relationships among individuals could be highly ritualised and were determined by social status, and social roles were generally conceived in kinship terms, with political, economic, ritualistic and other kinds of obligation superimposed on each other.[6] Gellner believes that while segmentary communities constitute an important social form, they nevertheless differ significantly from civil society, as the former impose an ascribed identity onto the individual, whereas the latter requires a modern conception of freedom that puts much stress on the individual being able to choose his or her own identity.[7] In other words, what is crucial in this regard is not pluralism *per se*; what matters is the kind of individuals, and the particular

---

[4] Gellner, *Conditions of Liberty*, p. 5.
[5] In 'Pluralism and Liberalism', in *Political Studies*, XLII, 1994, pp. 293–305, George Crowder has argued convincingly that to equate pluralism with liberalism is theoretically untenable.
[6] Gellner, *Conditions of Liberty*, p. 7.
[7] *Ibid.*, p. 9.

conception of individual freedom presupposed in the society.[8]

The kind of pluralism that characterised civil society is closely related to the conception of freedom that, in matters of faith and morality, requires the individual to be his or her own priest and internal judge. As such, individuals in the society cannot resort to the universal church as their final arbiter; they have to turn inward to their own conscience. As a result, in matters moral and spiritual, there is no justification for imposing one's faith or virtue on others against their will; instead, consenting individuals have every justification to practise freely their shared faith or virtue.

What made this conception of individual freedom, or what Benjamin Constant calls the 'liberties of the moderns' in contrast to the group liberties of the ancients,[9] conceivable in a Europe which since the Reformation of the sixteenth century had seen an ongoing conflict between the classical religion (which appeared to be 'social, civic, this-worldly, communal, traditional, tolerant') and the world religion (which appeared to be 'egotistic, other-worldly,

---

[8] This distinction looks simple and elementary, yet it is crucial for the avoidance of many oversimplifications and misunderstandings of the idea of civil society. It is not difficult to come across scholarly works that fail to take notice of this distinction. Professor Dorothy J. Solinger's 'China's Transients and the State: A Form of Civil Society?', an occasional paper published by Hong Kong Institute of Asia-Pacific Studies of the Chinese University of Hong Kong in 1991, is one such example. In the paper, Professor Solinger attempts to assess whether the growing number of China's 'floating' population, who roam around China's more prosperous coastal cities to look for jobs or a living, always illegally and without official recognition of their residence status in those cities, could be seen as an emerging civil society in communist China. Professor Solinger employs two definitions of civil society in her analysis. The first regards civil society as standing apart from, or even against, the state, while the second, with obvious Marxist overtones, regards civil society as being inextricably ensnared within the state. Gellner would obviously not agree with the second definition. But what is revealing is that whichever definition is used in the paper, it seems that apart from the fact that the 'floating' population is no part of the state apparatus, there are no other reasons being offered to maintain the claim that this population is or is not a form of civil society in China.

[9] See Gellner, *Conditions of Liberty*, p. 9.

doctrinal and intolerant')?[10] Here, Gellner turns to David Hume's essay 'Of Superstition and Enthusiasm' for explanation, and supports Hume's claim that contrary to initial impressions, 'superstition [i.e., classical religion] is an enemy to civil liberty, and enthusiasm [i.e., world religion] a friend to it.'[11]

Gellner admits that at the initial stage, with a firm commitment to abstract religious doctrine and its serious implementation, the 'zealots of enthusiasm' (the puritans) were uncompromising, intolerant, and to that extent inimical to freedom. However, the history of seventeenth-century England witnessed the political stalemate between the puritans and the 'practitioners of superstition' (i.e. the Catholic Church, those religious sects that were hostile to the puritans and the political authorities that supported them), as neither party was in a position to achieve an ultimate and overwhelming victory over its enemy, thus leaving them with the only realistic option of accepting a political compromise:

> The enthusiasts [at first] made great inroads on the society, and in fact were for a time victorious. None the less, in the end they were defeated, though not crushed. The society as a whole favoured a compromise, a partial retention of superstition, priestly power, ritual and all, though with limited power, *and* moreover combined with a toleration of the extremists-enthusiasts, who, obliged to renounce their ambition of imposing righteousness on earth if necessary by military and political force, turn instead to pacifism and tolerance. Their efforts to impose righteousness on earth are defeated, but they are not so crushed as to be prevented from practising righteousness within their own moral ghettos, and, demanding with success toleration for their excessive but private zeal.[12]

In the process, the enthusiasts became defenders of civil or individual liberty by, initially, destroying the somewhat autocratic priestly caste and by universalising priesthood. Subsequently, with diminution of zeal forced upon them by the political stalemate, when they realised that since they

---

[10] *Ibid.*, p. 44.
[11] *Ibid.*, pp. 45–6.
[12] *Ibid.*, p. 47, emphasis in the original.

could not ensure the will of God be done on earth as it was in heaven, they turned their faith inward to their private realm, defending the right of the individual to be the final judge of their personal belief and protecting the private realm from undue political interference. In other words, the 'routinisation' of the Protestant faith, as Max Weber later describes it, created one essential condition for civil society — that is, toleration of ideological pluralism, making the separation of religion from politics conceivable and possible.

Compromised but not crushed, Gellner goes on to argue, the enthusiasts did not just stay within their private moral realm to nurture their religious commitment. They also turned outwards to productive activity, practising it with the same zeal as they showed towards their religious faith; thus engendering the kind of work ethic that is faithful to the activity itself and is largely disinterested in the material results that the activity brings. 'Only such Platonic, pure, disinterested acquisitiveness could engender that work ethic and sustained accumulation which produces a modern economy.' Gellner further observes,

> ... those who merely pursue worldly goods for worldly ends would not plough back their profits and thereby initiate the miracle of economic growth: only puritan entrepreneurs do that. Virtue not greed finds the path to true affluence.[13]

The disinterested commitment to productive activity also means that the puritans did not accumulate wealth for the sake of political ambition — thus they were no threat to the political establishment, and the power-holders then became more amicable to these budding capitalists. To Gellner, this development was also of the utmost importance for the emergence of civil society in Europe, for the separation of politics and economics provides the very condition that makes institutional pluralism possible for civil society.[14]

---

[13] *Ibid.*, p. 48.
[14] For an overview of Gellner's account of the emergence of modern industrial society from traditional agricultural society in human history, see his *Plough, Sword and Book: The Structure of Human History*,

The accuracy or plausibility of Gellner's sociological and historical account is a matter of scholarly dispute, but this is less a concern here, for what is important in his understanding of the idea of civil society is the nature of the conception of individual liberty and the kind of human agency presupposed by civil society, and how they have made the ideological and institutional pluralism of civil society possible.

Man of a Particular Kind: The Modular Man

To Gellner, 'a Protestant religious style, and egalitarian and individual relation to the deity, is the theological echo of social modularity'.[15] How is this to be explained? Two things are obvious if social modularity is analogous to Protestantism. First, each individual, through his or her own choice or consent, can enter into or withdraw from various social relationships without the need for mediation by intermediaries, ritual, social status or hierarchy, because the individual himself or herself is, in the end, his or her ultimate judge and is not dependent on social ritual or status. Second, the individuals concerned are more or less equal, in the sense that there is no predetermined hierarchy in the social relationships not formed by their consent or choices. More fundamentally, they have to subscribe to this (formally) egalitarian cultural idiom in order to be able to establish social relationships of this kind, in which each individual's decision to enter into, or withdraw from, any social relationship is equally respected. In other words, all individuals are equally replaceable and equally important in their formal relationship with others, and they believe that this is the correct state of affairs.

It is obvious that this conception of the individual is not man-as-such, for the identity of an individual in tribal or

---

London: Collins Harvill, 1988. For a good but critical discussion of Gellner's account, see Alan Macfarlane's 'Ernest Gellner and the Escape to Modernity', in *Transition to Modernity: Essay on Power, Wealth and Belief*, eds John Hall and I. C. Jarvie, Cambridge: Cambridge University Press, 1992, chapter 5. Macfarlane's chapter also appears in *The Social Philosophy of Ernest Gellner*, eds John A. Hall and I.C Jarvie, Amsterdam-Atlanta, GA: Rodopi, 1996, pp. 207–20.

[15] Gellner, *Conditions of Liberty*, pp. 105–6.

feudal society is very much constituted by his or her social status, and his or her position in the society is normally predetermined by the general social hierarchy, which is beyond the reach of most, if not all, individuals for modification.[16] If the conception of the individual presupposed by civil society requires a particular conception of the human agent, it is important to look at the character of this agent carefully, and Gellner, by drawing an analogy with the agglutinative modular furniture whose parts can be combined and recombined at will without rendering the piece of furniture incoherent, describes such an agent as a modular man.

By now, it should be quite clear that the modular man presupposed by Gellner's idea of civil society is a separate and distinct individual who is capable of exercising his or her own judgement in choosing his or her purposes and actions, or in forming his or her own opinions and beliefs. As such, he or she must, in the first place, have the intellectual capacity for 'lucid, Cartesian thought, which separates issues rather than conflating them and takes them one at a time'.[17] This capacity allows the modular man to distinguish the ends from the means, and to choose techniques most conducive to the realisation of ends by clearly defined criteria of effectiveness and efficiency, and of nothing else.[18]

The ability to separate issues and to pursue them one at a time by the most efficient method available, together with the disposition to form one's own purposes and to establish or join specific associations with like-minded individuals in a joint pursuit of shared purposes, gives rise to a social order in which the structure is readily adjustable and responsive to rational criteria of improvement. This order is also made possible by two further requirements. First, the individuals concerned are 'capable of undertaking and honouring, and deeply internalising commitments and obligations by a single and sober act'.[19] This is important not only because

---

[16] *Ibid.*, p. 13 and pp. 97-108.
[17] *Ibid.*, p. 104.
[18] *Ibid.*, p. 99.
[19] *Ibid.*, p. 103.

modular man does not just rely on elaborate rituals to establish commitments, but also on trust, which is essential even for the pursuit of *ad hoc*, voluntary and specific commitments among modular men. More fundamentally, however, social order is made possible among men of this kind by the moral order presupposed in such a society, which is such that it 'has not committed itself either to a set of prescribed roles and relations, or to a set of [substantive] practices'.[20] Instead, a man is allowed to freely join any association for the pursuit of shared specific purposes, and to leave an association when he comes to disagree with its purpose or policy, without being open to an accusation of treason or betrayal. In other words, 'the associations of modular man can be effective without being rigid'.[21]

However, Gellner is careful not to fall into the trap of abstract individualism by claiming that the existence of these separate and distinct modular men is prior to any social institutions or cultures. In order for the individualistic, self-conscious, aim-pursuing and aim-satisfying modular man seriously to engage in social co-operation with other individuals of similar nature, Gellner believes that a moral consensus, which supports the preconditions of civil society among these individuals, must exist first. It would be wrong, he maintains, to regard such a consensus as the product of a collective act of will such as a social contract, for the best strategy for a purely aim-satisfying individual would be to enter into social co-operation and receive the benefits from such co-operation without fulfilling his or her share in the co-operation whenever possible. And the question is begged if one tries to argue that the individuals concerned should honour his or her share in social co-operation because he or she is obliged by the contract (which is said to be the product of a collective act of will among individuals), unless a moral consensus about the importance of honour-

---

[20] *Ibid.*, p. 100.
[21] *Ibid.*

ing a contract and respecting individual choice is presupposed.[22]

Within such a consensus, the individual is his or her own final judge. Sovereignty of individual inquiry, both in matters of faith, opinion and interests, is a necessary part of this consensus. There is no guarantee that the individuals in such a society will share many of their most fundamental beliefs, and it is far more plausible to find that conflicting interpretations in matters of fundamental concern are the norm rather than the exception. This is why Gellner believes that such a social order is, in the end, based 'not on true and firm conviction, but on doubt, compromise and doublethink'.[23] In other words, in matters of ethical conviction, conceptions of the good and religious belief, individuals in civil society, according to Gellner's understanding, regard these matters largely as personal or private concerns applicable only to those who voluntarily join each other for such pursuits. That is, such matters do not define their public identity. Conflicts about these convictions are no longer regarded as conflicts of ultimate truth or values in which compromises are impossible without losing one's identity or undermining the salvation of one's soul.

In addition to what has been said above, looking at modernity from the vantage point of technological and economic developments on which much of modern society depends, Gellner further argues that a free and economically vibrant social order 'require[s] pluralism among cognitive explorers as well as among producers, and it is consequently incompatible with any imposition of a social consensus'.[24] The disposition to seek one's own aims, to form one's own beliefs, to respect individual judgement, to honour one's commitment in social co-operation in the pursuit of shared, albeit transient, purposes, to separate issues and take them one at a time by adopting the method most instrumental to its efficient resolution — all these tendencies

---

[22] *Ibid.*, p. 98 and p. 186.
[23] *Ibid.*, p. 94. See also Ernest Gellner, *Postmodernism, Reason and Religion*, London and New York: Routledge, 1992, pp. 91–4.
[24] Gellner, *Conditions of Liberty*, p. 95.

are not only incompatible with an imposition of social consensus, but also require that citizens are more or less equal in their social status and that the society concerned is not burdened with elaborate and parochial rituals or cultural differentiation. Instead, citizens must be able to communicate in a context-free manner in which expressions and symbols are standardised and easily comprehensible, and the kind of works engaged in by members of the society, though diverse, must, likewise, be translatable from one to the other, without which mass scale voluntary social co-operation in accordance with clearly defined efficient criteria would not be possible. As Gellner says, '[modern man] is modular because he is capable of performing highly diverse tasks in the same general cultural idiom, if necessary reading up manuals of specific jobs in the general standard style of the culture in question'.[25] In other words, modular men share a homogeneous high culture in which 'spheres have become sufficiently disentangled for the mind to move without constantly bumping into wider obstacles created by impenetrable barriers whether of religion, kinship or politics'.[26]

Pluralism of ideological convictions, diversity in cognitive explorations, the disposition to disentangle ends from means, and the willingness to adopt means most instrumental to the realisation of one's chosen end are all essential elements constitutive of the modularity of modern man. Gellner argues that the political consequences of this modularity are of real significance, for it is the emergence of modular man that makes institutional pluralism in modern society possible:

[25] *Ibid.*, p. 102. Gellner also makes the following remark on p. 105: 'The standardisation of idiom is in any case imposed on this kind of society by the nature of work within it, which ceases to be physical and becomes predominantly semantic: work is now the passing and reception of messages, largely between anonymous individuals in a mass society, who cannot normally be familiar with their interlocutors and their idiosyncrasies. Communication occurs, if not with man as such, then at any rate with man-as-standard-specimen-of-a-codified-culture.'

[26] See MacFarlane's 'Ernest Gellner and the Escape to Modernity', p. 123.

Society is still a structure, it is not atomized, helpless and supine, and yet the structure is readily adjustable and responds to rational criteria of improvement. Modularity of man is the main answer to the question: how can there be countervailing institutions or associations which at the same time are not also stifling?[27]

To Gellner, modern modular man is individualistic and formally egalitarian, capable both of effective cohesion against the state and of performing an amazing diversity of social tasks.[28]

Modular Man as an Individualist

So, Gellner's modern modular man is an individualist. But the imagery of modularity does not sit comfortably, to say the least, with the concept of individuality, for the former, like modular furniture, is replaceable at will for convenience and other functional purposes, while the latter is intrinsically related to the uniqueness of the human individual.

No doubt, modular man, according to Gellner, is full of initiatives to determine his personal convictions, to set his own goals, to choose his own career(s). No doubt he is also capable of lucid Cartesian thought in disentangling means from ends, private pursuits from public undertakings, and of making use of instrumental reason to achieve effective and efficient outcomes for his chosen objectives. However, the dominant imagery of modularity appears to suggest that all these are significant only to the extent that they help to create a readily adjustable social structure responsive to the rational criteria of economic and technological improvements. Unlike the modularity in segmentary societies, whose members were only transplantable and replaceable from one tribal society to another (i.e. a slave or a peasant expelled by one tribe would still be a slave or a peasant if he or she was subsequently accepted by a neighbouring tribe), 'real modularity' for modern modular man, Gellner argues, hinges on his capability of 'performing highly diverse tasks

[27] Gellner, *Conditions of Liberty*, p. 100.
[28] *Ibid.*, p. 102.

in the same general cultural idiom', suggesting that while modern modular man is conversant with a wide range of social and economic activities in the standardised idiom of work in modern society, he, as an individual, is also easily replaceable, for the tasks he is capable of performing can also be readily done, with a little bit of adaptation if necessary, by other modular individuals.[29]

It is not to be denied that modern individuals' ability to engage in multiple and diverse tasks in society is remarkable. The kind of division of labour made possible by such ability, moreover, is also essential to the exponential growth witnessed by modern industrial society.[30] No one should denigrate the achievements of Gellner's modular man in this regard. However, there is a danger that if modular man is only functionally oriented, he will become an anonymous member of the mass instead of being a unique individual. Civil society will then lose a lot of its appeal if its individuals are mainly replaceable and functional 'modules' for social development. The kind of diversity and pluralism implied in civil society points beyond a merely functional understanding of the concept of individuality.[31] As Stuart Hampshire points out,

> the notion of individuality includes the idea of being singular, or in relevant respects unique, and also of having a definite identity, that is, of having an appropriately continuous history — appropriate, that is, to the species to which the individual belongs.[32]

In other words, an individual is constituted by his singularity and the continuity of his identity: '... each person has a

---

[29] *Ibid.*
[30] See 'Industrial Society', chapter 3 of Gellner's *Nation and Nationalism*, Oxford: Basil Blackwell, 1983.
[31] It has been pointed out time and again that Gellner's sociology is essentially functionalist in nature. For a good criticism of Gellner's functionalism, see Kenneth Minogue's 'Ernest Gellner and the Dangers of Theorising Nationalism', in *The Social Philosophy of Ernest Gellner*, pp. 113–28. For Gellner's reply, see 'Reply to Critics', in *ibid.*, pp. 630–6.
[32] See chapter 4, 'Individuality and Memory', in Stuart Hampshire's *Innocence and Experience*, London: The Penguin Press, 1989, p. 115.

unique history', says Hampshire.[33] The singularity of the human individual is valuable partly because, according to Hampshire, among the animals, only the human individual displays the salient capacity 'to develop idiosyncrasies of style and of imagination, and to form specific conceptions of the good', and partly because such individual style and imagination, like works of art or the emotion attached to sexual love, is mostly unrepeatable, as '… the leaps and swerves of a person's imagination do not follow any standardised routes' and defy the prediction of rational and general rules and is therefore irreplaceable.[34] 'If this individual essence is destroyed when the individual is destroyed', says Hampshire, 'the world is to that degree impoverished.'[35] It is therefore not only unfortunate that Gellner employs the imagery of modularity, which is both mechanical and conformist in tone and in substance, to describe the individuals in civil society, but, more fundamentally, it indicates that Gellner fails to look beyond the functionality of the individual and to appreciate the kind of rich and non-functional pluralism allowed for in civil society if the individuals therein are encouraged to develop their respective moral and autonomous being. This is perhaps one of the major defects in Gellner's theory of civil society.

Modular man, according to Gellner, is also a nationalist.[36] Later in this chapter the relationship between civil society and national society is considered. Given the singularity of the individual in modern society, Hampshire argues that the diversity in conceptions of the good is 'an irreducible diversity'.[37] How this irreducible diversity is to be accommodated, and a civil order established, remains to be discussed. For the moment, it must be pointed out that Gellner's conception of modular man, as he himself has admitted, is bought at a price, which is that the modern world provides no warm, cosy habitat for man. The isola-

---

[33] Gellner, *Conditions of Liberty*, p. 119.
[34] *Ibid.*, pp. 118, 126.
[35] *Ibid.*, p. 117.
[36] *Ibid.*, chapter 13.
[37] Hampshire, *Innocence and Experience*, p. 118.

tion of one activity from another, he writes, 'leaves each activity unsustained by the others, cold and calculated by its own clearly formulated end, rather than part of a warm, integrated, "total" culture'.[38] While some may consider this 'disenchantment' or 'alienation' a price too high to pay, Gellner believes that the modularity of modern man, as pointed out before, is not only the precondition of civil society, but also most likely the precondition of industrialisation. From here, Gellner goes on to analyse another major characteristic of the kind of plural society that constitutes civil society: the separation of economics from politics in the miraculous growth of wealth under industrialism and capitalism.

Separation of State and Economy

The emergence of modular man and the transition of society in the northwestern part of Europe from aristocratic to commercial at the Enlightenment was a phenomenon closely watched by many thinkers of the time, and some of them were very anxious about its possible consequences. The Scottish Enlightenment thinker Adam Ferguson, the author of *An Essay on the History of Civil Society*, is the one whom Gellner regards as the most illuminating, for it was Ferguson, according to Gellner, who rightly perceived the central puzzle of civil society.

To Gellner, Ferguson is interesting not because he is acutely aware of the fact that 'by having separated the arts of the clothier and the tanner, we are the better supplied with shoes and with cloth';[39] rather, it is Ferguson's reflection on the implications of the kind of division of labour presupposed in civil society that is most revealing; for the division of labour in civil society does not just happen in the economic realm alone, it also separates the rulers/warriors from the civilians (who are concentrating on productive activities). 'By this separation', Ferguson contends, 'we in effect deprive a free people of what is necessary for their

---

[38] Gellner, *Conditions of Liberty*, p. 104.
[39] Adam Ferguson, *An Essay on the History of Civil Society*, quoted from Gellner, *Conditions of Liberty*, p. 62.

safety; or we prepare a defence against invasion from abroad, which gives a prospect of usurpation, and threatens the establishment of military government at home'.[40]

Ferguson's worries, however, did not materialise in civil societies in his part of Europe, though societies in the traditional world of Islam as described by Ibn Khaldun, a Muslim scholar greatly admired by Gellner, did produce a politically helpless commercial class oppressed by their military counterparts. The puzzle for Gellner, then, is, why was civil society able to escape this predicament?

Gellner proposes three kinds of reasons in his attempt to explain this escape. The first is economic affluence. The second is the rise of a new division of labour in modern society, in which social and productive activities, including military activities, have become not only more distinct and professional, but also more mobile. And the third reason is the political and ideological stalemate that brings with it the privatisation of virtue.[41] Economic affluence will be considered first.

Gellner believes that Ferguson's worries did not materialise partly because he failed to anticipate the fact that the kind of liberties constitutive of civil society were in fact made possible by economic affluence.[42] The industrial and scientific revolutions of eighteenth-century Europe brought with them an apparently unending perpetual and exponential increase in productive powers that endowed the new social system with an unlimited 'social bribery fund' to buy its way out of any external and internal threat.[43] As Gellner says when commenting on the advent of early capitalism under the influence of the Protestant ethic,

> [the] abstention from further political ambition ... made the puritans acceptable to the power-holders, for they are no danger to them, or at any rate are no longer such, and so they need not be and are not segregated in a social ghetto like earlier pariah capitalists. The old rulers can marry

[40] Quoted from Gellner, *Conditions of Liberty*, p. 63.
[41] *Ibid.* See also 'Conditions of the Exit', in Gellner's *Plough, Sword and Book*, pp. 154–70.
[42] Gellner, *Conditions of Liberty*, p. 65.
[43] *Ibid.*, p. 73.

rather than confiscate the new wealth, an altogether more amiable arrangement, and one which aids the general commercialisation of society. This option is all the more attractive if the old land- and honour-oriented ruling class practises primogeniture, so that its younger sons are not averse to acquiring wealth by other means, such as marriage or even work.[44]

Under this new situation, production becomes a better path to wealth than domination. Indeed, according to Gellner, it is quite possible to make money without acquiring or bothering too much with power.[45] Furthermore, in this society, 'law protects wealth, independently of whether one has formed special alliances or groups of followers for its protection. Wealth leads to power, more than the other way round.'[46]

In other words, economic and technological development not only helps to tame the power-holders of the society, but also the economic and political spheres become increasingly separate and distinct, for it is possible to engage in money-making without involvement in politics. It is indeed the economic sphere that seems to become increasingly distinct and prominent, because the law protects individuals in their productive activities regardless of how powerful they are within the society. In fact, Gellner even goes so far as to say:

> the splendid thing about Civil Society is that even the absent-minded, or those preoccupied with their private concerns or for any other reason ill-suited to the exercise of eternal and intimidating vigilance, can look forward to enjoying their liberty. Civil Society bestows liberty even on the non-vigilant.[47]

The separation of the economic sphere from power politics and the recognition that law is non-instrumental are highly significant in terms of understanding the character of civil society, and it will be argued shortly that Gellner

---

[44] *Ibid.*, p. 48.
[45] *Ibid.*, p. 74.
[46] *Ibid.*, p. 75.
[47] *Ibid.*, p. 80.

fails fully to appreciate the importance of these factors when it comes to grasping the nature of the social order.

The perpetual and exponential economic growth mentioned earlier has been made possible not only by the industrial and scientific revolutions; it is also the result of the increasing specialisation in the division of labour in the new society. What is really fundamental, according to Gellner, is neither the separation of clothier and cobbler that has improved the supplies of shoes and cloth, nor, as observed by Ferguson, the separation that has now reached beyond the economic realm and distinguishes citizens from soldiers. What is really crucial is the fact that it is the manner in which different activities, social or economic, are separated that has changed, and Gellner regards this as 'supremely important'.[48]

What is so special about this manner of separation? On the one hand, there are more separate and distinct jobs; the division of labour in industrial society has gone further than before. But on the other hand, there is far more homogeneity in the way we do things:

> every job is carried out in the same style and in much the same spirit. The manuals and the rules are articulated in a publicly shared and accessible idiom, for there is a mobility between jobs ... Occupational mobility is the norm ... specialisms are inter-locking, specialists are obliged to communicate with and understand other specialists, they have to 'speak the same language.'[49]

This homogeneity amounts to a common high culture shared by members of the society, and a generic education fitting a man for all the specialisms is essential. A man of this kind, according to Gellner, naturally wishes to protect his culture and the kind of education in which he has invested so much. Here lies the origin of modern nationalism.[50] As was stated earlier in this chapter, while Gellner

---

[48] *Ibid.*
[49] *Ibid.*, pp. 75-6.
[50] See chapter 13 of *Conditions of Liberty* for a fuller elaboration of this. Also consult Gellner's posthumous work, *Nationalism*, London: Widenfeld & Nicolson, 1997, for his definitive statement on nationalism. For Gellner's earlier works on nationalism, see his

believes that nationalism and civil society did share the same social conditions that were conducive to their emergence, the two are, by nature, quite distinct. In the section entitled 'Civil or national society?' in this chapter, this distinction will be examined, in order to see how a civil order is different from a national order, at least according to Gellner. For the moment, what is important when considering the division of labour is that while there are more and more separate and distinct jobs and activities, mobility among them is perfectly feasible and normal. Movement into, and out of, any profession is not restricted. As Gellner observes,

> Modern societies have farmers not peasants: agriculture is an occupation like any other, which can be both entered and left without crossing legally and ritually sanctified borders of an estate or a caste. It has soldiers but not a warrior caste. The same holds true of politics and the profession of arms: the Black and the Red are not legally or sacramentally distinguished from the rest of society. Off duty they generally dress in civilian garb.[51]

While Gellner is right to emphasise this new manner of division, what seems to have escaped his attention is the nature of the kind of obligatory rules associated with it. When people can freely move in or out of various social, economic, political and even military professions, the rules regulating human conduct in such a society can no longer be prohibitive in respect of any of these pursuits. At the same time, obligatory rules (i.e. laws) are no longer directly instrumental to the pursuit of any of the professions or purposes, for binding instrumental rules are applicable only if the specific pursuits concerned are made compulsory,

---

Thought and Change, Chicago: The University of Chicago Press, 1964, chapter 7; 'Scale and nation', in Ernest Gellner, *Selected Philosophical Themes: Vol. II Contemporary Thought and Politics*, eds I. C. Jarvie and J. Agassi, London and New York: Routledge, 1974, chapter 11; and *Nations and Nationalism*. For a good collection of critical studies on Gellner's theory of nationalism, see *The State of the Nation: Ernest Gellner and the Theory of Nationalism*, ed. John A. Hall, Cambridge: Cambridge University Press, 1998. See also Part 2, 'Nations and Nationalism', in Minogue, *The Social Philosophy of Ernest Gellner*, pp. 71–189.

[51] *Ibid.*, p. 76.

which is contrary to the kind of social and economic division of labour required in civil society. What needs to be regulated is not, therefore, any individual specific pursuit *per se*, but the manner in which these pursuits are conducted. Hobbes perhaps captures the nature of this best when he says,

> [f]or the use of laws, which are but rules authorised, is not to bind the people from all voluntary actions; but to direct and keep them in such a motion, as not to hurt themselves by their own impetuous desires, rashness or indiscretion; as hedges are set, not to stop travellers, but to keep them in their way.[52]

In other words, what is required to make pluralism in civil society possible is neither common pursuits nor common faith, but a common set of non-instrumental rules that applies equally to all in their separate and diverse pursuits, without judging the validity of those pursuits as such.

The law-making authority in civil society, therefore, should not impose any specific purposes on the people, but is there to formulate and promulgate general and non-instrumental (i.e. relative to specific individual purposes) rules to keep them from standing in each other's way in their own pursuit of individual purposes. This is not only compatible with the character of Gellner's modular man, who is, at the end of the day, his own judge when it comes to matters moral and spiritual, but in fact is what is required if men are allowed to seek their own separate and distinct purposes in diverse ways within the same spatial-temporal dimension. More and fuller discussions on the nature, character and implications of the kind of non-instrumental rules at issue here will be further examined when the theories of Hayek, Habermas and Oakeshott in subsequent chapters are examined. It is, however, crucially important to note that the non-instrumental nature of this common set of obligatory rules, regulating the kind of social and economic division of labour in a civil order, has a number of corollaries that are highly relevant to Gellner's idea of civil society.

---

[52] Thomas Hobbes, *Leviathan*, ed. John Plamenatz, Collins/Fontana, 1978 (9th impression), p. 304.

First, since the obligatory rules are not there to impose any specific purposes on the individuals, the validity of the law in general does not depend on the successful achievement of those specific purposes.

Second, although obligatory rules are not instrumental to the fulfilment of individual voluntary pursuits, they are highly important to those pursuits by acting as 'hedges' to protect people from treading on each other in the course of each and every individual's distinctive pursuit. In other words, law is important in ensuring the plural nature (i.e. separate and different pursuits by all individuals for their own specific purposes) of civil society, although the success or failure of any individual's pursuit in it is not a direct consequence of the law concerned.

Third, while it is reasonable to suppose that given our understanding of the human condition, law will not be effective without some kind of coercive penalties affixed to it against contraventions, it would be wrong to conclude that the validity of the law is based on coercion. As the above-mentioned quote from Hobbes says, laws are 'but rules authorised'. The validity of the law is, in this view, based on authority, not brute force or coercion. You are rightly kept within the 'hedges' not because you are coerced to do so, but because the authentic authority so prescribes. The key conceptual question to be asked, therefore, in understanding the political nature of civil society, is not whether the balance of brute force or power in the society is favourable to the protection of individual liberty, but what is the nature of political authority in civil society and why is it compatible with individual liberty?

These points are not only important in their own right; a better appreciation of them would also help us to understand why Gellner's idea of civil society is inadequate, and why his views on the nature and character of civil society are, although highly illuminating, misconceived in some major respects, as will be argued in the following sections.

Politics vs Economics

In the last section, two of the reasons offered by Gellner to explain why Ferguson's worries about a military takeover of society did not happen in civil society were examined. One major deficiency in Gellner's account was his failure to appreciate the significance of the non-instrumental nature of law in such a society. This will be elucidated further in the hope that it will indicate how Gellner has, in some major respects, misconceived the nature of pluralism in civil society. Before that Gellner's third reason will be examined. This concerns the need for political and ideological compromise, due to the privatisation of virtue, to which he also attributes the failure of Ferguson's worries.

Gellner convincingly argues that due to some contingent political and historical factors, free merchants in the northwestern part of Europe in the eighteenth century not only survived, but also managed to establish the kind of social order that we now call 'civil society'. One of the factors that contributed to this was the fact that Europe was a multi-state system. 'In a multi-state system', Gellner contends, 'it was possible to throttle Civil Society in some places, but not in all of them.'[53] In other words, because at least some of the civil societies in Europe were left in peace to operate the new economy in accordance with the new social and economic division of labour mentioned above, they eventually demonstrated that they were in general far superior to traditional societies both economically and militarily.

While the diversified and conflict-laden nature of the international arena of Europe was a blessing in disguise, the internal political stalemate between different classes or vested interests, and the ideological stalemate between the 'zealots of enthusiasm' and 'practitioners of superstition', mentioned above in countries like England, were other factors that Gellner regards as equally significant; for the former not only encouraged tolerance and diversities, but also 'led to a unique perfection of the rule of law', while the latter

---

[53] *Ibid.*, p. 74.

led to mutual tolerance and confined many controversial moral issues to the private realm of personal judgement.[54] This plurality of personal values joined forces with the pursuit of commercial interests by the first modern capitalists—a unity which in turn made the civil social order highly successful commercially.

In order to command the respect of all the parties concerned in such a political and ideological stalemate, the law must not be instrumental to the pursuit of one sector's particular interest or faith at the expense of others', rather it should stay above the fray of all potentially conflicting substantive ends and provide a framework in which all are satisfied that the regulative rules they have to observe in their personal pursuit are just. In other words, it seems that internal political stalemate might be a favourable historical condition for the development of the kind of non-instrumental rules for the regulation of individual behaviour that was required for the emergence of civil society. However, it appears that Gellner does not fully appreciate the distinctive nature of these rules. Instead, his analysis mainly concentrates on how the industrial and scientific revolutions enabled the society to acquire an unlimited 'social bribery fund' to bribe its way out of any external or internal threat, and allow both the stalemate and the conditions favouring the development of civil society to become more permanent and stable.[55] Nowhere in Gellner's works on civil society can we find his views on how the rule of law helps to constitute the kind of pluralism required by civil society, and it must be pointed out that Gellner's historical and sociological explanation of the emergence of some social conditions favourable to the development of civil society is no substitute for the need to come up with a better conceptual understanding of the normative nature of such a society.

While Gellner is probably correct to say that the disinterested pursuit of wealth is beneficial economically as well as politically (for those who pursue wealth in civil society do not use their wealth for the acquisition of power, and thus

---

[54] *Ibid.*, p. 78.
[55] *Ibid.*, pp. 73, 79.

have broken through the vicious circle in the past that obliged power-holders to suppress the rich as an imminent political menace to their power), what he fails to examine further, however, is that such a situation requires more than just mutual tolerance between the power-holders and the rich.[56] Such a situation may also imply that the political realm should not interfere with the economic realm, and vice versa, if the growth of the market is not going to be harmed, so rules governing the economic realm should be recognised as distinguishable from those instrumental rules for the pursuit of power.

All these considerations, however, have escaped Gellner, who views the plural nature of civil society as ultimately inseparable from the perspective of the balance of power between the political realm and the economic realm, and his misconception becomes all the more manifest when he tries to argue that one major characteristic about the pluralism of civil society is political centralisation and economic decentralisation.

Centralisation, Decentralisation and Pluralism

Gellner gives two reasons to support the claim that civil society requires economic decentralisation. First, he argues that economic pluralism is indispensable for economic efficiency and economic growth, for it requires 'the existence of genuinely independent productive and property-controlling units in society' to engage in all sorts of innovative and economic ways of doing things to keep the economy going.[57] Gellner believes that the reason for the inefficiency and final collapse of the communist economies is precisely because they followed the law of political hierarchies, not of the market, in their productive activities, which regarded the maintenance of the positions of the different sections within those hierarchies as paramount, regardless of whether they were productive or not.[58]

---

[56] *Ibid.*, p. 78.
[57] *Ibid.*, p. 88.
[58] *Ibid.*, pp. 88–9.

Second, Gellner thinks that while civil society is impossible without pluralism, such pluralism, which contains countervailing forces and balances, should be located in the economic sphere 'precisely because effective political-coercive centralisation is a necessary pre-condition of its functioning'.[59] In other words, 'political pluralism in terms of independent or autonomous coercive units is *out* ... Liberty, on the other hand, is impossible without pluralism, without a balance of power. As it cannot be political, it must be economic.'[60]

While Gellner is quite right to point out that the existence of 'independent or autonomous coercive units', each with its own loyalty to its unit within the political realm of civil society, would not be conducive to economic growth and efficiency, it would be quite wrong to put the emphasis on coercion rather than on sovereignty in terms of the so-called 'requirement of political centralisation' in civil society. For one thing, there is no guarantee that centralised coercion would protect economic pluralism, and history is littered with many examples of this kind, and Gellner's own criticism of communism has in fact demonstrated this point well.

More fundamentally, authority would only become sovereign if there is one recognised supreme office to make final decisions that obligate the people in the society. These decisions are authoritative not because they are coercive, though non-compliance might be punished, but because they are properly enacted by the recognised office to whose authority all members of the society concerned subscribe. Further, this final and supreme authority would be conducive to social and economic pluralism only if it authorises its rules in the manner consistent with those 'hedges' commended by Hobbes to keep individuals 'in their way' in their pursuit of wealth or social goals; however, those 'hedges' also require an office to act as a final arbiter to resolve disputes and differences among individuals in

---

[59] *Ibid.*, p. 87.
[60] *Ibid.*, p. 88, emphasis in the original.

order to ensure fair application and consistent observance of the rules concerned.

Thus political centralisation in the sense of recognition of a final and supreme authority to enact non-instrumental rules to regulate social and economic behaviour is what is required in civil society; but this Gellner has failed to see. What he comes up with is the misconceived idea of the centralisation of coercive political power balanced by a powerful and vibrant economy to help to maintain freedom and pluralism in civil society. This comes out most clearly in his discussion of the relationships between the political and the economic realms of civil society. Take the following paragraph from Gellner as an example:

> The simplest formula for Civil Society, then, is political-coercive centralisation with accountability, rotation and fairly low rewards for those manning the political apparatus, and economic pluralism ... The economic pluralism however ... puts limits on political centralism, compelling it to remain within the bounds of its prescribed and restricted role.[61]

The first question for this formulation is, what are the bounds of the prescribed and restricted role for the so-called 'political centralism'? In the absence of a full discussion of the concept of political authority and the kind of obligatory rules that are most appropriate for civil society, such a formulation is, to say the least, ambiguous and incomplete. In *Legitimation of Belief*, Gellner does briefly touch upon the question of sovereignty and legitimacy.[62] There, however, he was mainly arguing that social scientists from Western democracies tend more and more to use the word 'legitimacy' in a non-committal manner in their discussion of the question of the right to rule in developing countries, and avoid using the more value-loaded word 'sovereignty'. We still fail to find a detailed discussion on the nature and character of these two concepts. Likewise, in *Plough, Sword and Book*, Gellner says,

---

[61] *Ibid.*, p. 93.
[62] See Ernest Gellner, *Legitimation of Belief*, Cambridge: Cambridge University Press, 1974, pp. 24–7.

... the capacity to assign a place without being challenged is the paradigm of legitimacy. Coercers and legitimators are complementary. Legitimators are underwritten by a given power situation; but equally, the balance of power depends on the nature and size and position of groupings, which in turn are built up by the humble daily activities of the ushers and usherettes of each society, who lead men to their places.[63]

This formulation of the question of legitimacy (the capacity to hold an office without being challenged because of the right kind of balance of power) again depends very much on the context of the balance of power instead of on the idea of authority.

Further, when Gellner says that economic pluralism 'compels' political centralism to remain within its bounds, it is quite clear that for him the relationship between the two realms is part of the balance of power, and the kind of pluralism he has in mind is sustained by the right balance of power between the economic and the political realms, which if left on their own are, apparently, neither intrinsically friendly nor complementary to each other.[64]

Of course it is always empirically possible that the rich or the powerful might foolishly, inadvertently or deliberately subvert the delicate 'balance' and undermine the kind of pluralism enjoyed by civil society. But the error of Gellner's balance of power interpretation is conceptual rather than empirical, for it blurs the distinctive and separate role played by the various kinds of social and economic division of labour required by civil society, and renders his whole conception incoherent, because in the end it reduces the whole nature of pluralism in civil society to power, as all divisions and separations in it are nothing but a function of the right kind of balance of power being maintained between the two realms.

Gellner's formulation of the nature of the pluralism inherent in civil society is therefore misconceived. Given

---

[63] See Gellner, *Plough, Sword and Book*, p. 18.
[64] Gellner also uses words like 'countervailing forces' and 'balancing mechanisms' to describe the kind of pluralism he has in mind. See *Conditions of Liberty*, p. 87.

the nature of modular man and the separation of professions required by civil society, and given also that virtues have been confined to the private realm and that politics is to be stripped of many of its ideological contents (the so-called 'ideological stalemate'), it makes for a more coherent doctrine to think that what is required in the political realm is the establishment of a political authority whose main function is to enact a common set of authoritative rules to govern individuals in pursuit of their goals, and that these rules act like 'hedges' to keep all concerned in their own way, rather than as a tool instrumental to the achievement of substantive ends. Thus the non-instrumental and authoritative character of the rules constituting the political realm of civil society appears to be central to the kind of pluralism required in civil society. This character is not something that can be fully explained as a balance required in order to maintain that pluralism.

Gellner's failure to grasp the distinctive role played by non-instrumental authoritative rules in the maintenance of the kind of pluralism required by civil society also leads him to applaud the so-called 'mixed economy' of modern society.[65] To him, 'the fact that so much of the economic demand is inevitably under the control of political agencies of one kind or another is that we are not dealing with a genuinely neutral market situation'.[66] However, this does not concern him, for

> the most effective modern economies are those which practise a loose state-economy co-operation, working on the basis of informal networks and pressures, without depriving productive units of their autonomy and liberty of movement, but frankly recognising the significance of the

[65] Gellner, *Conditions of Liberty*, p. 170. On pp. 106-7 in *Plough, Sword and Book*, Gellner points out that Protestantism makes men both instrumentally rational in handling things and non-instrumentally honest in dealing with each other because they become rule-followers in matters political and spiritual. However, his tendency to characterise social rules in the context of the balance of power perspective, appears to have barred him from coming to realise that power and authority could be two distinct concepts with totally different political implications.

[66] Gellner, *Conditions of Liberty*, p. 91.

state as weather-maker, and the inevitably political nature of major economic decisions.[67]

But how can the state, being at the same time an economic agent and participant, not undermine its essential role as the maker and defender of 'hedges' for civil society? From the perspective of the balance of power, would not the state have a kind of interest of its own not to respect other competing productive units' freedom of movement, property and so on? With the advent of modern technology, Gellner is perhaps right to point out that the side-effects of economic operations, if unrestrained, would disrupt our environment, our cultural heritage and so on; but when he goes on to argue that although 'the economy must be free enough to provide plural institutions with their bases, but not powerful enough to destroy our world', and must therefore be politically restrained, one cannot but ask, if the state is itself one of the economic agents, where shall we draw the line?[68] If it is all a matter of the balance of power, how can we be sure that it is not the almost all-powerful state (which is both politically coercive and economically a 'weather-maker') that is going to destroy our world?[69] And what makes pluralism in civil society conceptually stable and coherent? A balance-of-power perspective fails to provide satisfactory answers to these questions, whereas a non-instrumental conception of the state, together with a recognition that the economy should operate relatively autonomously under the framework provided by such a state, produces a more coherent understanding of the nature and character of civil society.

Civil or National Society?

Gellner believes that social modularity is the precondition of civil society. But he also thinks that his modular man can

---

[67] *Ibid.*, p. 92.
[68] *Ibid.*, p. 170.
[69] For a similar critique of the instrumental conception of the state, see Terry Nardin's 'Private and Public Roles in Civil Society', in *Toward a Global Civil Society*, ed. Michael Walzer, Providence, Oxford: Berghahn Books, 1995, pp. 29–34.

also be a nationalist. The same homogeneous high culture and the kind of generic education required for 'context-free' communication and for 'the standardisation of idiom' in which the nature of work has become semantic rather than physical not only made the rise of civil society possible in eighteenth-century Europe, but also made the emergence of nationalism possible in Europe in the nineteenth and the twentieth centuries.[70]

For Gellner, '… nationalism is a political principle which maintains that similarity of culture is the basic bond', in which the principles of authority that exist between people are dependent 'for their legitimacy on the fact that the members of the group concerned are of the same culture (or, in nationalist idiom, of the same "nation")'.[71] Like civil society, nationalism, according to Gellner, is the product of modern industrialism. Nationalism requires the congruence between the cultural and the political, meaning that nationalism requires a state to protect or to promote the shared high culture of the same nation as the prime political principle. The kind of generic education required in order to make the whole population conversant in this kind of high culture is not affordable by a single tribe or a local community in either the tribal or the agrarian age. Only a national government is able to bring it about. This, Gellner believes, makes any claims that nationalism is atavistic unsustainable, for while primitive tribes may share the same folk culture amongst themselves, '[s]mall bands of foragers can hardly be credited with a state, even if they have leaders'.[72] Without the existence of a state to unite a culture, nationalism is just impossible. Similarly, the empires in agrarian societies do provide humanity with political authorities similar to states. Their emphasis, however, on status, hierarchy, and the separation of a high culture from the various mutually

---

[70] See chapters 12 and 13 of *Conditions of Liberty*, and chapters 6 and 7 of *Nationalism*.
[71] Gellner, *Nationalism*, pp. 3–4.
[72] *Ibid.*, p. 6. For a highly interesting discussion of how the Berber tribes of the Atlas mountains had lived in anarchy until very recently, see Gellner's 'How to Live in Anarchy', in *Selected Philosophical Themes*, pp. 87–94.

incompatible folk cultures amongst the ruled in different parts of the same empire, has made nationalism highly unlikely to emerge, for the agrarian state requires different cultures to symbolise different status in the same political entity, making congruency between the cultural and the political contrary to the ethos of agrarian society.[73]

The marriage of state and culture that produces nationalism in a political community is not always virulent, as explained by Gellner in the case of Europe. In the north-western part of Europe, for example, with the major exception of Ireland, the boundaries between the cultural and the political have coincided happily ever since the dynastic states there were in power. The same culture has always been under the roof and protection of the same political authority, and the question of nation building or of fostering the same culture by political means has not, for most of the time, been a major issue.[74] Not too dissimilarly, in nineteenth-century central Europe, while there was a need for both the Germans and the Italians to unify their fellow nationals into one single nation-state, the common high culture for the Germans or for the Italians was already there. What was required for the emergence of a national society was not to build such a culture by political efforts; rather, what was needed was a common political framework to give overall political shape to the common culture that was already in existence. '[T]he fact that it was primarily unification that was at stake, rather than "liberation", that no cultural manipulation was required, and that the compactness of the territories to be unified dispensed with the need for ethnic cleansing', Gellner observes, 'all this meant that at least nineteenth-century unificatory nationalism could be relatively benign and liberal, and could act in alliance with liberalism.'[75]

In other words, when what is required is the setting up of a common political authority and a common set of obliga-

---

[73] See 'Culture in Agrarian Society', in *Nations and Nationalism*, pp. 8–18, and chapter 3 of *Nationalism*.
[74] See Gellner, *Nationalism*, pp. 49–52.
[75] *Ibid.*, p. 53.

tory and political rules, or when such a political and authoritative framework is already there and acknowledged, civil order is perfectly compatible with nationalism, as what is then primary is not which culture prevails, but how to ensure the observance of a common set of political rules by all in their different and separate pursuits of their own purposes.

However, what is catastrophic, according to Gellner, is this:

> It is the simultaneous creation of a national state and a national culture, in a social world lacking both, and endowed with an appallingly complex patchwork of linguistic and cultural differences, interspersed both on the map and in the social structure: it is this combination which is a recipe for catastrophe.[76]

In other words, when political means are used to create a particular national culture and to purge those who do not accept it, or who are for whatever reason deemed not to be acceptable by such a culture, then nationalism will turn murderously virulent.

Gellner gives a number of reasons why the same set of basic social conditions may sometimes produce a kind of benign nationalism, yet at the same time could bring about some obviously uncivil and nationalistic disasters to the history of Europe. Among his explanations is the so-called 'tidal wave of industrialism', in which late entrants to industrial development may find themselves in a highly disadvantageous position when compared with early entrants who have already occupied most of the privileged positions and are more fortunate in being able to become conversant with the new homogenous culture of the industrial world.[77] If the late entrants want to improve their position, they must either have opportunities to be assimilated by the early entrants or, alternatively, if it is possible for them to

> distinguish themselves culturally from their exploiters and oppressors, it is very much to their advantage to hive off

---

[76] *Ibid.*, p. 54.
[77] *Ibid.*, p. 35.

politically, when the opportunity arises, and to modernise their own flag, in their own sovereign territory. Hence they can protect their development from lethal competition by the more advanced, and here their own dialect is spoken with pride, as the state language, rather than muttered with shame as the badge of backwardness and rusticity.[78]

This is not the place to examine too closely the details of Gellner's thought-provoking theory of nationalism. What is crucial for civil order is the observance of a common set of non-instrumental political rules by all. If this is accepted by national society, civility is still possible there. However, when what is at issue is the purposeful establishment of a national state for the protection of a nation or a culture, or when nationalism tries to create a nation in pursuit of the political interests of the people concerned, nationalism and civil order are likely to part company, as what is required of the former is political manipulation for the realisation of some specific ends (i.e. a so-called 'common national culture'), whereas what is required of the latter is the observance of a set of common obligatory rules by all to protect individual pursuits.

Since Gellner has never adequately appreciated the important role played by the rule of law in civil society, his interesting historical and sociological explanation of the vicissitudes of nationalism as it appeared in European history has become less persuasive. Above all, one is left wondering why the balance of power as it occurred in western and central eighteenth- or nineteenth-century Europe managed to produce institutional and ideological pluralism, while the balance of power elsewhere, particularly in eastern Europe, turned out to produce just the opposite of a civil order.

Conclusion

Notwithstanding these criticisms of Gellner, he has touched upon many important questions that are inescapable if we want to enhance our understanding of the nature and character of civil society. Gellner is perfectly correct to argue

---

[78] *Ibid.* For other explanations, see pp. 61–7.

that the kind of pluralism found in civil society is qualitatively different from the pluralism of segmentary society, for while segmentary society is collectivist in nature, ideological and institutional pluralism are inherent in civil society, which entails that the autonomy of the individuals in civil society is a must and the separation of the economic realm from the political realm in such a society is also taken for granted. Furthermore, although the imagery of the modular man appears to be partial and misleading, to say the least, it has nevertheless aptly captured the versatile, self-made and malleable aspects of the individual in civil society.

The separation of faith, power and the economy inherent in the civil order is also eloquently argued by Gellner. Although Gellner has failed to grasp the essential point that it is the acceptance of a set of common non-instrumental rules that enables civil society to replace common faith, or centralised coercive power in maintaining social order, nevertheless his bold attempts to employ sociological and historical explanations to describe how, against all odds, this unique social and economic division of labour succeeded in taking root in the northwestern part of Europe under certain favourable historical conditions, are both highly interesting and intellectually thought-provoking, and it is no exaggeration to say that this idea of civil society has since become a prominent ideal for many non-Europeans.

In particular, this ideal has been eagerly pursued both before and after the collapse of communism in Europe since 1989, and in contrasting the success of civil society and the failure of communism, Gellner contends that industrialism of the latter kind failed mainly because it had ignored the kind of social, ideological and economic division of labour required to propel exponential growth, which incidentally must be complemented by respect for individual freedom.[79]

---

[79] See Michael Ignatieff's 'On Civil Society: Why Eastern Europe's Revolutions Could Succeed', in *Foreign Affairs*, March/April 1995, Vol. 74, No. 2, pp. 128–36, and John Keane, *Civil Society: Old Images, New Visions*, Cambridge: Polity Press, 1998. But also see Michael Walzer's 'The Civil Society Argument', in *Dimensions of Radical*

Communism also failed because of Marxism's 'over-sacralisation of the immanent [i.e. the over-sacredness of work and the worker]';[80] for man 'cannot stand perpetual intoxication with the sacred (even if they like it intermittently), and they need to relax in profanity'.[81] However, the story of Islam, according to Gellner, is very different. Despite the onslaught of modernity, Islam successfully refuses to secularise and preserves itself as 'an absolute moral community, which seems to work tolerably in a modern or quasi-modern context' with little individualism, pluralism and countervailing forces balanced against the state.[82]

In fact there may be at least three different kinds of modern social order which could be considered. The spectacular economic success of East Asia in recent decades has not escaped Gellner's attention, and it is not difficult to point out that this success in Confucian East Asia has little to do with individualism. Societies there, he notes, 'have not too much in common with the modular social ethos of Western Civil Society—and which, as far as one can tell, do not greatly mind this being so'.[83]

Democracy: Pluralism, Citizenship, Community, ed. Chantal Mouffe, London and New York: Verso, 1992, chapter 4, for a reminder of the limitation of the civil society argument.

[80] Gellner, Conditions of Liberty, p. 40.
[81] Ibid.
[82] Ibid., p. 28.
[83] Ibid., p. 197. The Senior Minister of Singapore, Mr Lee Kuan-yew, is perhaps the most famous representative of East Asia in this respect. He says, 'the idea of the inviolability of the individual has been turned into dogma', and claims that his government 'used the family to push economic growth'. Lee also believes that spectacular economic growth has been achieved in East Asia partly because people there are fortunate to have the cultural backdrop of 'the belief in thrift, hard work, filial piety and loyalty in the extended family, and, most of all, the respect for scholarship and learning'. See the interview with Lee by Fareed Zakaria in 'Culture is Destiny', in Foreign Affairs, March/April 1994, Vol. 73, No. 2, pp. 109–26. Henry Rosemont, Jr, has also eloquently pointed out the different nature of the Confucian conception of the individual in the following observation: 'What the early Confucian writings reflect ... is that there are no disembodied minds, nor autonomous individuals; unless there are at least two human beings, there can be no human

However, for the purpose of this study of the nature and character of civil order, Islam and Confucianism, and their relationships with modernity, will not be considered. Instead, it is time to probe further into the implications of the criticisms made of Gellner's theory and see whether other theoretical attempts will fare better in coming up with a more satisfactory account of the kind of pluralism that characterises civil order in the Western world. For instance, Gellner's tendency to rely on the balance-of-power perspective to view the separation of the political from the economic realm in civil society will be found wanting by theorists who believe that the two realms are, in some important sense, qualitatively different. In this respect, Friedrich Hayek, arguably the most distinguished theorist of the free market of the twentieth century, has developed an impressive theory of the spontaneous order not only to try to differentiate politics from the market, but also to explain how a liberal order of the most comprehensive kind is possible if only we would follow the logic of the market, respect the rule of law and contain political power as far as possible within the confines of the spontaneous order. The next chapter examines Hayek's attempt to develop an ambitious social and political theory that aspires to provide a profound justification for individual freedom and civil order.

---

beings. For the early Confucians there can be no *me* in isolation, to be considered abstractly: I am the totality of the roles I live in relation to specific others. I do not *play* or *perform* these roles; I *am* these roles.' See his 'Why Take Rights Seriously? A Confucian Critique', in *Human Rights and the World's Religions,* ed. Leroy S. Rouner, Notre Dame, IN: University of Notre Dame Press, 1988, pp. 175–7, emphasis in the original. For two interesting discussions of Japan's non-individualistic development towards industrial society, see Ronald Dore's 'Sovereign Individuals' and Shmuel Eisenstadt's 'Japan: Non-Axial Modernity'. Both articles appear in *The Social Philosophy of Ernest Gellner.* See pp. 221–36 and pp. 237–56 respectively.

3

Hayek on 'The Great Society'

Knowledge, Abstract Rules and the Dethronement of Politics

Introduction

Like Gellner, Hayek is an ardent supporter of civil society, though he prefers to use the terms 'the Great Society'and 'the extended order' to characterise the nature of that society.[1] Like Gellner, once again, Hayek is also an avid reader of Adam Ferguson's work *An Essay on the History of*

[1] For the term 'the Great Society' see Friedrich Hayek, *Law, Legislation, and Liberty: Rules and Order, Vol. I*, Chicago: The University of Chicago Press, 1973, p. 2. Here, Hayek explicitly points out that he is following Adam Smith's usage in referring to the kind of society in question as 'the Great Society'. For 'the extended order' see Hayek, *The Fatal Conceit: The Errors of Socialism*, London: Routledge, 1988, p. 19. It should be pointed out that in this last major work of Hayek, he believes that even the term 'the Great Society' is problematic, as the word 'society' presupposes that all systems of interconnection of human activities are of the same kind and implies 'a common pursuit of shared purposes [among the members of the same system] that usually can be achieved only by conscious collaboration.' (*The Fatal Conceit*, p. 112.) However, for the purpose of this study, these two terms will be treated somewhat synonymously, unless otherwise specified. The reasons for doing so are: first, readers may find the term 'the extended order' not immediately understandable. Secondly, although Hayek is right to say that the word 'society' may presuppose a common aim and interest, this is only one of the legitimate meanings of the word. According to *The Concise Oxford Dictionary*, London: Oxford University Press, p. 1154, the first

Civil Society. But unlike Gellner, the chief lesson Hayek learns from Ferguson is that civil societies are 'the results of human action, but not of human design'.[2] This observation turns out to be of profound theoretical significance, for it enables Hayek to develop a distinctive social philosophy, a philosophy that, among others, is also highly influenced by Hume's 'the three fundamental laws of nature',[3] Adam Smith's 'invisible hand'[4] and the Dutch thinker Bernard Mandeville's idea of 'private vices, public benefits.[5] It is a philosophy that depends very much on a view of epistemology that is highly sceptical of the ability of Reason with a capital R consciously to shape social and human development. This philosophy, at the same time, also places much faith in undirected, spontaneous social interaction for the satisfaction of human needs and the development of civilisation.

It is perhaps no exaggeration to say that what underpins Hayek's 'system of ideas', which crosses the boundaries of a number of major intellectual disciplines like economics, politics, philosophy, law, psychology and the history of

---

meaning of the word 'society' is 'the sum of human conditions and activity regarded as a whole functioning interdependently.'

[2] See 'The Results of Human Action but not of Human Design', in Hayek's *Studies in Philosophy, Politics and Economics*, Chicago: The University of Chicago Press, 1967, pp. 96–105.

[3] See Hayek's 'The Legal and Political Philosophy of David Hume (1711–1776)', in *The Collected Works of F A Hayek, Vol. III, The Trend of Economic Thinking*, eds W. W. Bartley III and Stephen Kresge, 1991, pp. 101–18. The three fundamental laws of nature mentioned by Hume are 'the stability of possession, of its transference by consent, and of the performance of promises', of which, Hayek thinks, the whole system of law is merely an elaboration. See also. p. 109, *The Trend of Economic Thinking*.

[4] Hayek regards Smith's 'invisible hand' as a convenient way to describe how man is led to promote an end which was no part of his intentions. See Hayek, *Rules and Order*, p. 37.

[5] Hayek observes that Mandeville's observations 'mark the definite breakthrough in modern thought of the twin ideas of evolution and of the spontaneous formation of an order'. See his essay 'Dr Bernard Mandeville (1670–1733)', in *Trend of Economic Thinking*, 1991, pp. 79–100. The quotation cited above can be found on p. 81.

ideas, is precisely his social philosophy.[6] While it is not possible to give a comprehensive critique of Hayek's social philosophy in this chapter,[7] it is nevertheless important to indicate how this philosophy helps him to argue for a kind of civil society the members of which are united not by common ends, but by common abstract rules.[8]

In what follows, it will be shown how Hayek, influenced by Ferguson's observation of the unintended consequences of human action on the development of social practices, develops his thesis by a theory of mind which permits him to argue for the relatively spontaneous nature of many of our practices in society, including the market, languages, rules of conduct and moral beliefs. This is the sphere within which the government should abstain from interfering, and this may well be the most persuasive part of Hayek's social and political theory.[9]

---

[6] John Gray, in chapter 1 of his *Hayek on Liberty*, London and New York: Routledge, 1998, 3rd edn, argues that Hayek's writings constitute 'a system of ideas, a structure of principles with the aid of which we can understand social and political life and subject it to reasoned criticism' (p. 1). For a critical reassessment of Hayek, see Gray's postscript to this book.

[7] Apart from Gray's book mentioned in note 6 above, the best recent book-length treatises on Hayek are, among others, Chandran Kukathas, *Hayek and Modern Liberalism*, Oxford: Clarendon Press, 1990; Jeremy Shearmur, *Hayek and After: Hayekian Liberalism as a Research Programme*, London and New York: Routledge, 1996; and Andrew Gamble, *Hayek: The Iron Cage of Liberty*, Cambridge: Polity Press, 1996.

[8] In Hayek's 'Great Society', 'common concrete ends are replaced by common abstract rules', for while 'enforced obedience to common concrete ends is tantamount to slavery, obedience to common abstract rules (however burdensome they may still feel) provides scope for the most extraordinary freedom and diversity'. See *The Fatal Conceit*, pp. 63–4.

[9] Gerald F. Gaus, in an essay evaluating the contributions made by liberal theorists in the twentieth century, has made this remark: 'Admittedly, faith in conscious and relatively detailed control of the economy, which was "winning recognition everywhere" in the 1930s, has been abandoned by today's liberals. This is perhaps the chief development in the liberal political theory over the past century: all liberalism is now market liberalism.' See Gaus, 'Ideological dominance through philosophical confusion: Liberalism in the twentieth century', in *Reassessing Political Ideologies: The*

There is no doubt that Hayek's idea of 'the Great Society' is subtle, profound and complex. However, it is also not immune from tensions. Ralf Dahrendorf describes Hayek as 'a ruthless theorist who does not worry about taking his argument to absurd lengths'.[10] There is more than a little truth in this comment. In the concluding parts of this chapter, it will be shown that Hayek's tendency to turn his epistemological thesis into an all-comprehensive single explanation of the social order leads him to be excessively (and is therefore unjustifiably) sceptical about the role played by the state in the development and protection of civil society. Likewise, his almost absolute faith in the spontaneous development of social practices blinds him to the danger that the market order, when placed as the predominant practice at the centre of a social order, could engulf the political realm of civil society, thus making the state not only subservient to the market, but also incapable of correcting its excesses or destructive effects.

The search for theoretical underpinnings also makes Hayek a victim of his own philosophy, for if social practices and institutions can never be the product of reason, planning alone, contrary to what Hayek fears, can never bring us to totalitarianism. Hayek not only fails to recognise this, his attempt to perceive morality mainly from a functional perspective (to be explained later in this chapter), also deprives 'the Great Society' of many of the positive values that it requires in order to sustain the loyalty of its members. In the end, in order to free the spontaneous order from any possible interference from organisational power, Hayek even proposes that only the dethronement of politics (in the sense of political power) could save his 'Great Society'. He does not seem to be bothered by the fact that in doing so he may have inadvertently crowned economic power as the sovereign in civil society, thus threatening the kind of pluralism that he wishes to defend in his 'Great Society'. Such a conse-

---

Durability of Dissent, ed. Michael Freeden, New York: Routledge, 2001, p. 21.

[10] See Dahrendorf's review of Hayek's *The Fatal Conceit*, 'Socialism's honourable exit', in *The Times*, 25 November 1988.

quence is not only morally problematic, it may also show that in the final analysis, Hayek's intellectual outlook is based on a serious disregard for the autonomy of the political, as well as the moral dimension of the social order and hence fails to appreciate Ferguson's warning against capitalism:

> By having separated the arts of the clothier and the tanner, we are the better equipped with shoes and with cloth. But to separate the arts which form the citizen and the statesman, the arts of policy and war, is an attempt to dismember the human character, and to destroy those very arts we mean to improve.[11]

Social Practices:
The Result of Human Action, Not Human Design

Ferguson's famous observation of the unintended consequences of human action is perhaps most eloquently expressed by the following paragraph:

> Like the winds, that come we know not whence, and blow whithersoever they list, the forms of society are derived from an obscure and distant origin; they arise, long before the date of philosophy, from the instincts, not from the speculations, of men. The crowd of mankind, are directed in their establishments and measures, by the circumstances in which they are placed; and seldom are turned from their way, to follow the plan of any single projector ... Every step and every movement of the multitude, even in what are termed enlightened ages, are made with equal blindness to the future; and nations stumble upon establishments, which are indeed the result of human action, but not the execution of any human design.[12]

While social establishments are seldom the results of the design of any single person, these establishments, nevertheless, originate in the interaction of the individuals in society:

> Mankind, in following the present sense of their minds, in striving to remove inconveniences, or to gain apparent and contiguous advantages, arrive at ends which even their

---

[11] See Adam Ferguson, *An Essay on the History of Civil Society*, ed. Fania Oz-Salzberger, Cambridge: Cambridge University Press, 1995, p. 218.

[12] *Ibid.*, p. 119.

imagination could not anticipate, and pass on, like other animals, in the track of their nature, without perceiving its end. He who first said, 'I will appropriate this field: I will leave it to my heirs'; did not perceive, that he was laying the foundation of civil laws and political establishments. He who first ranged himself under a leader, did not perceive, that he was setting the example of a permanent subordination, under the pretence of which, the rapacious were to seize his possessions, and the arrogant to lay claim to his service.[13]

To Hayek, Ferguson's insights here pose a number of important questions for the understanding of society. If social establishments are not the results of human rationality, in what sense are they the products of man? What is the nature and range of man's unavoidable ignorance in social interaction? Given such unavoidable or radical ignorance, how is it that individual interaction can still lead, albeit unintentionally, to all kinds of social cooperation and well-established social practices?

To tackle these problems, Hayek proposes a theory of mind to demonstrate the validity of Ferguson's insights. To begin with, he argues that far from being independent of civilisation, the development of the human mind is, in reality, very much dependent upon it:

> Man did not simply impose upon the world a pattern created by his mind. His mind is itself a system that constantly changes as a result of his endeavour to adapt himself to his surroundings ... [T]he growth of the human mind is part of the growth of civilisation; it is the state of civilisation at any given moment that determines the scope and the possibilities of human ends and values. The mind can never foresee its own advance.[14]

The fact that the growth of the human mind is part of the growth of civilisation implies that the two, in fact, evolve concurrently, with the latter providing a context for the former to acquire meaning and value, while the former, in interacting with the natural and social environments, modifies existing social practices by exploring new ones or select-

---

[13] *Ibid.*
[14] Friedrich Hayek, *The Constitution of Liberty*, London and Henley: Routledge & Kegan Paul, 1960, rpt. 1976, pp. 23-4.

ing the more successful ones to cope with the challenges human beings face.[15]

In other words, Hayek denies the possibility of a Cartesian mind that exists independently of social institutions and arrives at conclusions purely by logical deduction from explicit and demonstrable premises. Civilisation as human artefact, in Hayek's view, is artificial not because of deliberate human decision, but because of human convention.[16]

From the concurrent evolution of mind and civilisation, Hayek goes on to suggest that there are two inherent limitations of human knowledge, one circumstantial and one logical. Looking at his argument for the logical limitation of human knowledge brings us to one of the fundamental premises of his theory of mind, for the mind (or the mental order), to Hayek, is a mechanism of classification in which external stimuli we have perceived are related to other stimuli or to our past experience in accordance with the classification structure of the mental order, in relation to which we make sense of human interaction and the external environment, and derive meanings and values which guide human action.[17]

To Hayek, 'a question like "what is x?" has meaning only within a given order, and within this limit it must always refer to the relation of one particular event to other events belonging to the same order'.[18] In other words, what Hayek is saying is that meaning does not lie in the so-called 'nature' or 'essence' of the thing as such. Rather, what is meaningful is necessarily relational, and our mind can comprehend things out there only within a classification framework already established.[19] In this regard, Hayek maintains that the way to establish whether a person is colour-blind is

---

[15] Hayek, *Rules and Order*, pp. 17–19.
[16] *Ibid.*, pp. 9–11 and 20–1.
[17] For a full description of the mental order and how it classifies external stimuli in relation to its experience, see Friedrich Hayek, *The Sensory Order: An Inquiry into the Foundations of Theoretical Psychology*, Chicago: The University of Chicago Press, 1952, Midway reprint, 1976, pp. 127–31.
[18] Hayek, *The Sensory Order*, pp. 4–5.
[19] Gray, *Hayek on Liberty*, pp. 5–6.

not by ascertaining how 'red' looks to him in any absolute sense, but by ascertaining instead whether and how it differs from various other shades of 'red' and from 'green'. [20]

From such a perspective, it is not difficult to understand that Hayek does not recognise the existence of any 'absolute' qualities of sensations. Instead, he describes such a presupposition as a 'phantom-problem' in the philosophy of mind, for 'any question about the nature or character of particular sensory qualities' should necessarily arise as 'a question about the differences from (or the relations to) other sensory qualities; and the extent to which the effects of the occurrence of any other qualities determines the whole of its character'.[21] Such a conception of mind as an 'order of events' or 'a complex of relations' implies that

> all the attributes of sensory qualities (and of other mental qualities) are relations to other such qualities, and that the totality of all these relations between mental qualities exhausts all there is to be said about the mental order.[22]

The relations that constitute the mind must be abstract in nature, for to identify the differences between the sensory qualities involved means only to highlight the relevant, not all, attributes of the qualities concerned.[23] As Hayek says, 'we never act, and could never act, in full consideration of all the facts of a particular situation, but always by singling out as relevant only some aspects of it'.[24] Thus, abstraction, which necessarily involves classification, 'is not something which the mind produces by processes of logic from its perception of reality, but rather a property of the categories with which it operates—not a product of the mind but rather what constitutes the mind'.[25]

---

[20] Hayek, *The Sensory Order*, p. 31.
[21] *Ibid.*, p. 35 and pp.30-6.
[22] *Ibid.*
[23] 'Whenever a *type* of situation evokes in an individual a *disposition* towards a certain *pattern* of response, that basic relation which is described as "abstract" is present.' Hayek, *Rules and Order*, p. 30, emphasis in the original.
[24] *Ibid.*
[25] *Ibid.*

As a result, the mind, as a mental order of classification and abstraction,

> ... must possess a structure of a higher degree of complexity than is possessed by the objects which it classifies ... therefore, the capacity of any explaining agent must be limited to objects with a structure possessing a degree of complexity lower than its own ... it means that no explaining agent can ever explain objects of its own kind, or of its own degree of complexity, and, therefore, that the human brain can never fully explain its own operations.[26]

This conception of the logical limitation of the mind for complete self-explanation is supported, Hayek suggests, by Georg Cantor's theorem in the theory of sets according to which in any system of classification, there are always more classes than things to be classified, which presumably implies that no system of classes can contain itself.[27] Given the fact that mind and civilisation develop concurrently, it is only logical for Hayek to contend that it is not possible for the mind to stay outside society and shape the development of the latter in accordance with some separate and preconceived ideas of the former. It is society or civilisation, he writes, that gives the context of meaning for the mind, whose capacity to make sense of the environment is inherently dependent on many of the practices in our civilisation and society.[28] Thus the idea of a Cartesian mind is absurd, and any social engineering derived from such a conception of mind is, to say the least, extremely misconceived, since it puts the cart before the horse

While the Cartesian conception of mind is untenable, this does not mean that there is no rational or explicit knowledge. Hayek readily accepts that scientific knowledge, as knowledge explaining simple phenomena (like physics), is capable of precise and demonstrable explanation and prediction of particular events from explicit and clear

---

[26] Hayek, *The Sensory Order*, p. 6.
[27] Friedrich Hayek, *Studies in Philosophy, Politics and Economics*, Chicago: The University of Chicago Press, 1967, pp. 61-2.
[28] For a highly critical and illuminating discussion of Hayek's theory of the mind, see Murray Forsyth's 'Hayek's Bizarre Liberalism: A Critique', in *Political Studies*, 1988, XXXVI, pp. 235-50.

premises. However, in the more complex endeavour of social interaction, Hayek maintains that there is an equally important body of knowledge that is not explicit in the normal sense of the word, for this non-rational kind of knowledge, or 'tools' as Hayek loosely calls it, consists in a large measure of forms of conduct which man habitually follows without knowing why:

> They consist of what we call 'traditions' and 'institutions,' which [man] uses because they are available to him as a product of cumulative growth without ever having been designed by any one mind. Man is generally ignorant not only of why he uses implements of one shape rather than of another but also of how much is dependent on his actions taking one form rather than another. He does not usually know to what extent the success of his efforts is determined by his conforming to habits of which he is not even aware ... Concurrent with the growth of conscious knowledge there always takes place an equally important accumulation of tools in this wider sense, of tested and generally adopted ways of doing things.[29]

What is more, there also exists, apart from these 'tools,' a wide spread of particular and local knowledge that is necessarily dispersed. This is so partly because much of this is knowledge of particular circumstances of time and place, and partly because whether a piece of information is useful or not very often depends on an individual's subjective choices:

> It is with respect to this [knowledge of particular circumstances of time and place] that practically every individual has some advantage over all others because he possesses unique information of which beneficial use might be made, but of which use can be made only if decisions depending on it are left to him or are made with his active cooperation ... The shipper who earns his living from using otherwise empty or half-filled journeys of tramp-steamers, or the estate agent whose whole knowledge is almost exclusively one of temporary opportunities, or the *arbitrageur* who gains from local difference of commodity prices—are all performing eminently useful functions based on special

---

[29] Hayek, *Constitution of Liberty*, p. 27.

knowledge of circumstances of the fleeting moment not known to others.[30]

This dispersal of circumstantial knowledge, or what Hayek also calls the 'fragmentation of knowledge', which no single mind can know in toto, is the second unavoidable limitation of human knowledge.[31] Yet to Hayek, the most remarkable thing in this respect is that while the fragmentation points to the fact that each member of society can have only a small fraction of the knowledge possessed by all, and is therefore ignorant of most of the facts on which the working of society rests, 'civilisation begins when the individual in the pursuit of his ends can make use of more knowledge than he has acquired and when he can transcend the boundaries of his ignorance by profiting from knowledge he does not himself possess'.[32]

How is this possible in the light of the unavoidable limitations in human knowledge? The answer Hayek gives to this question is crucial for the understanding of the nature of 'the Great Society' that he has in mind.

Coordination of Dispersed Knowledge: Abstract Rules as Multi-Purpose Instruments

Given that our necessary ignorance makes synoptic social planning (which presupposes total knowledge of the society) impossible, the secret by means of which Hayekian social actors can overcome their constitutional ignorance and thus render successful social interaction possible is their ability to follow abstract rules even though they may not be aware of them. In the essay 'Rules, Perception and Intelligibility', Hayek makes the following remarks:

> The most striking instance of the phenomena from which we shall start is the ability of small children to use language

---

[30] Friedrich Hayek, 'The Use of Knowledge in Society', in *Individualism and Economic Order*, Chicago: The University of Chicago Press, 1948, rpt. 1980, p. 80, emphasis in the original.
[31] Hayek, *Rules and Order*, p. 14.
[32] Hayek, *Constitution of Liberty*, p. 22.

in accordance with the rules of grammar and idiom of which they are wholly unaware.[33]

And,

> Rules which we cannot state ... do not govern only our actions. They also govern our perceptions. The child who speaks grammatically without knowing the rules of grammar not only understands all the shades of meaning expressed by others through following the rules of grammar, but may also be able to correct a grammatical mistake in the speech of others.[34]

Human action and human perception, Hayek suggests, are, more often than not, rule-guided. In the realm of practical skill, for example, there are social practices or human actions that are not the products of Cartesian reasoning, but are nevertheless successful in the sense of fulfilling human expectations. One does not need to deliberate on the mechanics of cycling before one is capable of riding a bicycle. Nor does one need to know in a game of billiards how to construct mathematical formulas that would give the directions of travel of the balls the chance to score most points before one is a good billiards player.[35] These examples show that the ability to act successfully is not necessarily derived from the ability to explicitly demonstrate by 'reason' why it is successful. Or, to use Gilbert Ryle's oft-celebrated statement, there is a realm of human phenomena that is most appropriately regarded as 'knowing how' without 'knowing that'.[36]

The rules in the above examples, like the rules of language and of mathematical calculation, can be followed by us all and are essential in coordinating human interaction and communication, even though we may not be aware of them or understand the logic of them. For the functioning of a complex society, it is evident that rules of many different kinds are required in order to make spontaneous social inter-

---

[33] Hayek, *Studies in Philosophy, Politics and Economics*, p. 43.
[34] *Ibid.*, p. 45.
[35] *Ibid.*, pp. 43–5.
[36] See Gilbert Ryle, *The Concept of Mind*, England: Penguin Books, 1963, chapter 2. See also Michael Polanyi, *Personal Knowledge*, London & Henley: Routledge & Kegan Paul, 1962, chapters 4 and 5.

action possible. These include many of the rules of human conduct, such as prudential rules like saving for rainy days, moral rules like keeping promises, and rules of just conduct (i.e. laws) that prohibit murder. Given the fragmentation of knowledge and the diversity of individual ends and preferences, the rules that are capable of creating or maintaining a spontaneous social order must have the ability to coordinate the actions of separate individuals or to harmonise unknown, dispersed and even conflicting ends pursued by separate individuals or organisations.[37]

While man is to observe these rules in his actions even if he is not conscious of them, the final adoption or selection of the rules will, according to Hayek, depend on their ability to adapt to 'the solution of recurring problem situations faced by the society concerned and thereby help to make the members of the society in which they prevail more effective in the pursuit of their aims'.[38] In other words, while the characteristics of these rules help to coordinate diverse human actions, it is their long-term utility that ensures their prevalence. That is why Hayek calls many of the general rules in his 'Great Society' 'multi-purpose instruments', which, it is important to note, reveal not only the instrumental aspect of 'the Great Society', but also the requirement for these 'tools' to continually evolve and improve.[39]

What are the distinctive attributes of these abstract rules that make the spontaneous formation of a social order possible? In the first place, an order in which the ever-changing particular ends of its members can be coordinated should be an order that is capable of attaining any

---

[37] For an interesting discussion of the different roles played by social rules of conduct and by the price mechanism in Hayek's theory of spontaneous social coordination of dispersed knowledge, see Steve Fleetwood's 'Hayek III: The Necessity of Social Rules of Conduct', in *Hayek: Economist and Social Philosopher*, ed. Stephen F. Frowen, London and New York: MacMillan/St. Martin's Press, 1997, pp. 155–78. See also Fleetwood's *The Political Economy of Hayek: The Socio-economics of Order*, London: Routledge, 1995.
[38] Hayek, *Law, Legislation, and Liberty: Vol.2, The Mirage of Social Justice*, London and Henley: Routledge & Kegan Paul, 1976, rpt. 1979, p. 21.
[39] Hayek, *The Mirage of Social Justice*, p. 4.

degree of complexity.[40] As it is impossible for any individual or organisation in a complex social order to know the expectations of all the actors in their entirety, or for a single actor to know all the particular circumstances of time and place, the rules of the spontaneous order must be able to coordinate all the separate individuals and organisations pursuing diverse, dispersed and even conflicting ends without the need to resort to any central planning. The correspondence of individual ends in the social order has to be achieved by rules that can satisfy different individual expectations or guidance for further action. In other words, unlike a command or a specific instruction that aims at a specifiable result, the first distinctive attribute of these rules must be that they are end-independent (i.e. not aiming at one particular end), and are capable of forming abstract relations among individual members related in terms of these rules. The relations are abstract because the rules, unlike commands, do not apply to the here-and-now situation alone but to an unknown number of future instances, and to no specific individuals in particular but to anyone who happens to subscribe to the conditions determined by the rules.[41]

This end-independent and abstract attribute appears to apply to various kinds of rules (prudential, moral and legal) required in Hayek's 'Great Society', but perhaps the most graphic mechanism to demonstrate how abstract relations can perform the function of coordinating dispersed and fragmented information without the need to concentrate and centralise all the information involved is the highly elaborate 'multi-purpose instrument' called the 'price system'. In this mechanism, by a kind of symbol (in numerical form), only the most essential information, which aims at no specific ends but is useful for the participants to determine or adjust their own concrete ends and activities, is passed on to those concerned. It is a kind of machinery for registering change, or a system of telecommunications that enables individual producers to adjust their activities to changes of

[40] Hayek, *Rules and Order*, p. 38.
[41] Hayek, *The Mirage of Social Justice*, p. 35.

which they may never know more than is reflected in the price movement. The following is one of the most famous paragraphs among Hayek's works that illustrates this point:

> Assume that somewhere in the world a new opportunity for the use of [tin] has arisen, or that one of the sources of supply of tin has been eliminated. It does not matter for our purpose — and it is significant that it does not matter — which of these two causes has made tin more scarce. All that the users of tin need to know is that some of the tin they used to consume is now more profitably employed elsewhere and that, in consequence, they must economise [on] tin. There is no need for the great majority of them even to know where the more urgent need has arisen, or in favour of what other needs they ought to husband the supply. If only some of them know directly of the new demand, and switch resources over to it, and if the people who are aware of the new gap thus created in turn fill it from still other sources, the effect will rapidly spread throughout the whole economic system and influence not only all the uses of tin but also those of its substitutes and the substitutes of these substitutes ... The whole acts as one market, not because any of its members survey the whole field, but because their limited individual fields of vision sufficiently overlap so that through many intermediaries the relevant information is communicated to all. The mere fact that there is one price for any commodity ... brings about the solution which might have been arrived at by one single mind possessing all the information which is in fact dispersed among all the people involved in the process.[42]

To allow the price mechanism to function properly requires free competition. Free competition is required precisely because the data prevalent in a market are widely dispersed, and to utilise this data presupposes a procedure by which the individuals who are the possessors of it are placed in a position to receive signals indicating whether the information they possess is wanted. They, in turn, can also use this procedure to give their responses, to see if there is any chance for a correspondence of expectations to

---

[42] Hayek, *Individualism and Economic Order*, pp. 85-6.

occur.[43] Without free competition, it would not be possible for the individuals concerned to test whether the information they hold locally and separately is wanted. If the competition is not free it means that not all the dispersed data held by individuals are available to those who want them, in which case some people's preferences or knowledge are either ignored or not utilised, thus making the procedure less than optimal.

To protect free competition, therefore, requires the delimitation of a sphere of individual responsibility in which the individual concerned can make free and full use of his or her knowledge and skill. The institution of private property is also presupposed in a free market order, as the individuals in this order should have sufficient control over the use or disposal of the knowledge, skills and resources that each of them possesses without being obliged to follow the will of other agents or institutions who do not have a legitimate claim on these resources, and only the institution of private property can give such a control. In addition, it appears that in order to allow those prudential rules such as the price mechanism to maximise their effectiveness in communication and coordination of individual ends, Hayek's 'Great Society' would require some moral and legal laws to protect a domain in which the individual is free to act as he or she chooses.[44] This becomes a distinctive attribute of the kind of obligatory rules that are required in 'the Great Society' to protect the proper or uninterrupted functioning of both the prudential rules and the multi-purpose instruments. This implies, in turn, a conception of the individual as one who knows his or her own situation best, at least in terms of the

[43] See 'The Meaning of Competition', in *Individualism and Economic Order*, chapter 5. Also, see 'Competition as a Discovery Procedure', in Hayek, *New Studies in Philosophy, Politics, Economics and the History of Ideas*, London: Routledge & Kegan Paul, 1978, rpt. by Routledge in 1990, chapter 12. The fact that the dispersed and subjective data relevant to the market will not be known to anyone before the operation of the price mechanism makes the so-called 'perfect competition' or 'equilibrium analysis' suspect. For details, see 'Economics and Knowledge', chapter 2 of *Individualism and Economic Order*.

[44] Hayek, *The Mirage of Social Justice*, p. 36.

local knowledge provided to him or her by chance or circumstances. He or she is, in short, entitled to make choices and decisions of his or her own in order to try to satisfy his or her preferences and to facilitate better coordination of social interaction.

With the freedom to compete and the right to the full use of one's knowledge and skill secured, the price mechanism can become a very powerful tool for spreading information and matching expectations. More importantly, the price mechanism does not only bring about a mutual adjustment of individual plans, it also ensures that whatever is being produced will be produced by people more cheaply than, or at least as cheaply as, others who do not produce it, and that each product will be sold at a price lower than that at which anybody who in fact does not produce it could supply it;[45] for while 'almost any product can be produced by a great many different quantitative combinations of the various factors of production', the relative prices of these factors as shown by the price mechanism will signal to participants 'which of [the factors involved] will be the least costly'.[46]

Consequently, by the functioning of the price mechanism we can achieve a state of efficiency and orderliness, that is a state in which a correspondence of expectations is produced by the cheapest means, without the need for any central plan. All that individuals need to do is to observe the price mechanism and utilise their dispersed knowledge and skill as they see fit, provided that they also observe the obligatory rules (both moral and legal) that protect the delimited domain for the most efficient functioning of the prudential rules or tools.

Strictly speaking, the result of any particular manifestation of the market order is not foreseeable, due to the inherent limits of human rationality, for it is just impossible to know for certain in advance when and why availability of certain factors of production will change. The outcome of the spontaneous market order is, therefore, unintended, and for the same reason the price mechanism, similar to all

[45] Hayek, 'Competition as a Discovery Procedure', p. 185.
[46] Hayek, *The Mirage of Social Justice*, p. 118.

other abstract social practices, is also independent of the concrete ends pursued by individuals, for it has no preconceived preference for any of the concrete ends of any individual or for the specific dispersed knowledge or skill possessed by any market participant. Hayek would go even further and say that talk about the justice of the outcome of the market is meaningless. This is the case because, strictly speaking, since justice is only an attribute of human conduct and since nobody in the market order is in a position to determine the outcome of the order, there is, as a result, no individual or group of people against whom those whose expectations have not been satisfied in the process could make a just complaint.[47]

On the contrary, if anyone or any authority tries to hamper its self-regulative function by limiting its changes, or artificially fixing the price level or intruding into the protected domain of the individual, the mechanism will no longer be able to inform the individuals about the relative changes relevant to their respective circumstances, or indicate to them the most efficient way of utilising resources without distortion. This will not only deprive the individuals of the chance to use their knowledge in pursuit of their own ends, it will also allow interference in that part of the system of interdependent actions which is determined by information known only to the several acting persons. In this process, it will subordinate these to a directing authority, which must act on the basis of different knowledge and in the service of different ends.[48] In other words, such interference not only disrupts the spontaneous order of the market, but also interferes with individuals' freedom to exercise their skills in accordance with their free choices.

---

[47] Hayek, *The Mirage of Social Justice*, chapter 9. Hayek's argument here reverses the argument made by Rawls and others concerning the lack of justification in the natural and social lottery. Rawls believes that there is no morally valid ground to allow a person to get advantage or suffer disadvantage purely as a result of 'natural' gift or luck and argues for a redistribution of the 'natural' endowments. See John Rawls' *A Theory of Justice*, Oxford, Melbourne and Cape Town: Oxford University Press, 1972.

[48] Hayek, *Rules and Order*, p. 51.

'The Great Society' and the Functional Nature of the Obligatory Rules

The above account of Hayek's social philosophy points to two conclusions. First, the two central tenets of Hayek's social philosophy — the constitutional limitation of human rationality and the spontaneous formation of social order — not only rule out the possibility of synoptic human design for the development of society, but also oblige human beings to embrace abstract multi-purpose instruments or abstract rules in order to cope with the human and social world that, willingly or unwillingly, we have inherited. Secondly, in order to maintain the smooth functioning and maximum efficiency of these multi-purpose instruments, we also develop some abstract obligatory rules to regulate interpersonal activities. The value of these rules appears to be a function of their ability to maintain the overall spontaneous order and the better survival (e.g. in the form of greater population growth) of mankind.[49] While it is true that these obligatory rules, being end-independent, are not there to ensure the realisation of some specific results or individual ends, their functional status (i.e. their indirect utility in facilitating the long-term preservation of certain desirable consequences and outcomes) in Hayek's 'Great Society' becomes all the more apparent when we further examine their character.

Hayek points out that among the evolved and firmly established habits and traditions of human society, moral rules are the most important.[50] The observation of these must be regarded as 'a value in itself'.[51] This is so, however, not because there are any intrinsic values inherent in the moral rules as such, but because of the limitation in human rationality, as well as their long-term effectiveness in the maintenance of a spontaneous social order:

> It is unlikely that any individual would succeed in rationally constructing rules which would be more effective for

---

[49] Hayek describes the purpose of the rule of law as serving the abstract order of the whole. See *The Mirage of Social Justice*, p. 5.
[50] Hayek, *Constitution of Liberty*, p. 62.
[51] *Ibid.*, p. 67.

their purpose than those which have been gradually evolved ... We have thus no choice but to submit to rules whose rationale we often do not know, and to do so whether or not we can see that anything important depends on their being observed in the particular instance. The rules of morals are instrumental in the sense that they assist mainly in the achievement of other human values; however, since we only rarely can know what depends on their being followed in the particular instance, to observe them must be regarded as a value in itself, a sort of intermediate end which we must pursue without questioning its justification in the particular case.[52]

In other words, the values that the moral rules have are derivative, and this is so mainly due to the limitation of human rationality.

Hayek's position in this regard comes out most clearly in his critique of utilitarianism. In a nutshell, his critique aims not at utility as such, but at the 'constructivist fallacy' of the act and rule versions of utilitarianism. Given the constitutional limitation of human rationality, it would not be possible for us to ascertain the overall utility of a particular act in a particular situation, as it is not possible for us to know beforehand all the consequences of our action, thus making act utilitarianism untenable. Rule utilitarianism, likewise, is not defensible for the same reason. As society is constituted by a system of evolved rules in which the observance of a particular rule will be effective only if other rules are also observed at the same time, to judge the utility of one particular rule in this system would presuppose that the utility of the other rules is being taken for granted instead of being consciously determined, making the consistent application of utility as a general criterion for the whole system of rules impossible.[53]

However, if we take out this 'constructivist fallacy' from utilitarianism, we find that Hayek's view on moral rules can be interpreted as a kind of evolutionary utilitarianism, in the sense that the value of the moral rules depends ultimately on their long-term usefulness and effectiveness in

---

[52] *Ibid.*, pp. 66-7.
[53] Hayek, *The Mirage of Social Justice*, pp. 17-23.

promoting the spontaneous social order. This has to be evaluated on a long-term basis so that evolutionary selection can take its time about determining the usefulness of the rules concerned in actual experience, as human reason alone can never ascertain this in advance. That is why Hayek always refers to Hume's argument that rules of justice may be regarded as contrary to public interest in their particular application but must be viewed as absolutely necessary for the support of society and for the well-being of every individual in the long-term perspective.[54]

Hayek's criticism of rule utilitarianism also touches upon another aspect of the obligatory rules in his 'Great Society' — namely that the acceptability of a particular rule is to be determined by its compatibility with other rules in the same system. In other words, all valid criticisms of rules of conduct must be immanent criticisms, not to be assessed by some preconceived external concrete ends.[55] Similarly, the obligatory rules are, in the main, negative in character, in the sense that they prohibit rather than enjoin particular kinds of actions. In addition, they do not confer rights on particular persons, but only lay down the conditions under which such rights can be acquired.[56] This is so for the obvious reason that human reason is not able to know in advance what particular kinds of actions can for certain enable the individuals concerned to achieve their own concrete ends in a spontaneous social order.

While 'the Great Society' with deeply ingrained moral beliefs allows individuals to conform to the obligatory rules voluntarily most of time, 'it would be necessary, for the smooth running of society, to secure a similar uniformity by coercion, if such conventions or rules were not observed often enough'.[57] Thus, for the sake of the smooth running of 'the Great Society', some obligatory rules should be

---

[54] *Ibid.*, p. 16. For a good discussion of Hayek's evolutionary utilitarianism, see R.T. Allen, *The Political Thought of F A Hayek & Michael Polanyi: Beyond Liberalism*, New Brunswick and London: Transaction Publishers, 1998, pp. 115-34.
[55] *The Mirage of Social Justice*, pp. 24-9.
[56] *Ibid.*, pp. 36-8.
[57] Hayek, *Constitution of Liberty*, p. 62.

strengthened and supported by coercion to ensure adequate compliance. These obligatory rules are called 'laws' in the sense of enforced rules of conduct, many of which are the results of the explicit enactment of rules of conduct to avoid ambiguities or uncertainties, or to tackle urgent and unexpected circumstances or rectify past errors.[58] While laws are often articulated in nature and are the result of rational deliberation, Hayek also believes that their source and meaning are derived from the same spontaneous rules of conduct, for 'no system of articulated law can be applied except within a framework of generally recognised but often unarticulated rules of justice'.[59] Hence, legal positivism is wrong to suppose that law is derived from the will of a sovereign legislator with unlimited power, for this mistakenly assimilates law to command by the sovereign to achieve specific goals. Legal positivism's error can be further shown by the fact that in the application of law to a particular instance, the main job of the judge, unlike the head of an organisation, is to try to find out the true meaning of the law in a specific context by applying an accepted body of rules of just conduct, both articulated and unarticulated, not to enforce the command or the will of the legislator.[60]

Although law and moral rules do share such attributes of abstract rules as being end-independent, general and universal, applicable to an unknown number of future instances and prohibitive in the sense of specifying the condition whereby an individual can act freely within his or her protected domain, there are vital differences. These include the fact that legal rules are more articulated and are supported by coercion. A further important distinction, however, is the fact that while legal rules must be enacted by a recognised procedure and be enforced by an appointed authority, there are no such requirements for moral rules.[61]

---

[58] Hayek, *Rules and Order*, pp. 88-9.
[59] See Hayek's 'The Results of Human Action but not of Human Design', in *Studies in Philosophy, Politics and Economics*, p. 102.
[60] Hayek, *Rules and Order*, pp. 94-101 and 118-22.
[61] Hayek, *The Mirage of Social Justice*, p. 58.

Yet another difference is that while law is enacted with an intention for perpetual observance, Hayek thinks that non-coercive rules of conduct should be observed 'only in most instances', in order to 'allow further experience to lead to modifications and improvements' of rules if possible.[62]

Hayek's emphasis on the need for a recognised procedure for enactment of law and on an appointed authority for its implementation touches upon the question of political authority in 'the Great Society'. However, this emphasis turns out to be half-hearted, for 'in order to ascertain what in a given community is in fact the law', one ultimately has to refer not to the recognised procedure for enactment, but to the 'function' of the law, which is 'to assist the constant re-formation of a factually existing spontaneous order'.[63] Again, the functional nature of law (similar to the functional nature of the moral rules in Hayek's 'Great Society') is primarily to ensure the smooth running of the multi-purpose instruments for the reformation of the spontaneous order for better survival. In other words, Hayekian political philosophy appears not to take the questions of political authority and legitimacy seriously.

Unity of Rules and Plurality of Ends: 'The Great Society' and Pluralism

'The Great Society', then, is knitted together by abstract rules. As Hayek clearly says, 'What reconciles the individuals and knits them into a common and enduring pattern of a society is that to ... different particular situations they respond in accordance with the same abstract rules.'[64] Among the abstract rules, multi-purpose instruments like the market are for coordination and maximisation of individual preferences; as regards the moral rules, they not only create common obligations for individual members of 'the Great Society', but also regulate interpersonal conduct by ensuring that one's free sphere will not be unduly interfered with by intruders who distort the smooth running of the

---

[62] Hayek, *Constitution of Liberty*, p. 62.
[63] Hayek, *The Mirage of Social Justice*, p. 60.
[64] *Ibid.*, p. 12.

social order. Law is needed for adequate compliance with the obligatory rules, and government is there mainly to enforce the law for the maintenance of the spontaneous social order.

It is clear that at the most fundamental level, 'the Great Society' requires a common subscription to functionally effective abstract rules/instruments, and members of 'the Great Society' are united by a common system of rules the main purpose of which is the preservation of the spontaneous order. However, it is important to note at this point that the kind of social unity achieved by these functional rules is utilitarian in nature; that is, people appear to subscribe to them because in doing so they can maintain a more efficient and effective social order for the maximisation of their several and individual ends, though, due to limitations in human rationality, no one knows in advance which concrete goals or individual ends are going to be satisfied. The questions of social cohesion and political identity apparently have no direct bearing on these abstract rules, and it is assumed that whatever the consequences (even, say, the creation of acute economic inequality by the spontaneous market order), people will just have to accept the resultant social order as given or unchallenged, provided that this spontaneous order has not been deliberately tampered with.

In contrast to the unity of rules to ensure the functional effectiveness of 'the Great Society', pluralism in such a society occurs at the level of individual concrete ends or preferences. Indeed, abstract rules are necessary precisely because there is a plurality of individual ends and because human rationality is unable to know in advance how to realise them simultaneously. In this regard Hayek is more insightful than Gellner who, as shown in the last chapter, has failed to appreciate the indispensable role played by end-independent rules in ensuring the kind of pluralism that is required in modern liberal society. The plurality of individual ends and the limitation of human rationality also make it desirable for 'the Great Society' to protect individual freedom, for nobody is a better judge than the individual himself or herself of his or her own circumstances. In order to allow the social order to operate smoothly, that is, to maximise the utilisation of the fragmented knowledge and skill, individuals must be allowed to give their responses to multi-purpose instruments like price signals as freely as possible. That is why Hayek calls the condition of freedom 'a state in which the individuals are allowed to use their own knowledge for their own purposes'.[65]

Individualism: True and False

But such a state of individual freedom is allowed not because the individual in 'the Great Society' is regarded as valuable as such, but because human ignorance and the fragmentation of knowledge make it necessary to allow the individual a secure private sphere free from external interference in order to facilitate the smooth operation of the spontaneous order. That is why Hayek thinks that his conception of individualism in essence is 'primarily a *theory* of society', for, to him, it is the theoretical impossibility of synoptic rationality that makes individualism plausible.[66] Hayek is very frank in admitting this when he acknowledges that the constitutional limitation of man's knowledge and interest is 'a sufficient basis' to ground his idea of true individualism, for an individual

> should be free to make use of *his* knowledge and skill, that he must be allowed to be guided by his concern for the particular things of which *he* knows and for which he *cares*, if he is to make as great a contribution to the common purposes of society as he is capable of making.[67]

Likewise, Hayek's attacks on the so-called 'rationalistic pseudo-individualism' are mainly based on the same epistemological approaches (i.e. the constitutional limitation of human rationality and the fragmentation of practical knowledge). The error of rationalistic individualists like the followers of Descartes and Rousseau lies, according to

---

[65] *Ibid.*, p. 8.
[66] See Hayek, 'Individualism: True and False', in *Individualism and Economic Order*, p. 6, emphasis in the original.
[67] *Ibid.*, p. 14, emphasis in the original.

Hayek, precisely in the fact that they mistakenly believe that an individual planner can rely on reason alone to come up with definitive and exhaustive conclusions about the best course of social action to achieve the most rational and best results for all without the need to rely on abstract rules and other social practices.[68] This 'false' individualism, together with its erroneous social theory, will most likely 'lead to practical collectivism' because the rationalistic planner will sooner or later inevitably discover that his or her plan does not quite achieve what he or she intended, yet his or her faith in constructivist rationalism will prompt him or her not to admit defeat but instead to demand yet more power to be concentrated in his or her hands for rectifying those unintended (and hence undesirable) consequences by more coercive means, at the expense of individual freedom.[69]

Hayek is of course against coercion, except the legitimate coercion exercised by the government to stop or deter greater coercion.[70] For him, 'coercion is evil precisely because it thus eliminates an individual as a thinking and valuing person and makes him a bare tool in the achievement of the ends of another'.[71] Here, it seems that Hayek is trying to defend a non-instrumental and non-functional conception of the individual by emphasising the individual's rational and moral capacity as a value in itself that must be respected by others.

However, such an impression is contradicted by passages like the following one that can be found in many of Hayek's works: '... if the *result* of individual liberty did not demonstrate that some manners of living are more *successful* than others, much of the case for it would vanish'.[72] Likewise, in *The Constitution of Liberty*, Hayek has referred to the following passage from the work of H. B. Phillips approvingly:

---

[68] *Ibid.*, pp. 6–11.
[69] *Ibid.*, p. 6. See also chapter 3, 'Individualism and Collectivism', in Hayek's *The Road to Serfdom*, pp. 32–42.
[70] See 'Coercion and the State', in *Constitution of Liberty*, chapter 9.
[71] *Ibid.*, p. 21.
[72] *Ibid.*, p. 85, emphasis mine.

In an advancing society, any restriction on liberty reduces the number of things tried and so reduces the rate of progress. In such a society freedom of action is granted to the individual, *not* because it gives him greater satisfaction but because if allowed to go his own way he will on the average *serve the rest of us better* than under any orders we know how to give.[73]

On the whole, it is fair to say that given Hayek's conception that the idea of individualism is ultimately derived from his social theory, the kind of individualism presupposed in Hayek's 'Great Society' is primarily functional in nature, for the individual is valuable and his or her freedom should be protected to the extent that he or she is able to maximise the utilisation of his or her local knowledge for the effective and efficient functioning of the spontaneous order. As preference maximiser, the individual's value and freedom are derivative and the value of the so-called 'unlimited variety of human gifts and skills' is not a merit in itself, for *which* gifts or skills are in the end really valuable can only be known 'through a social process in which everybody is allowed to try and see what [the individuals concerned] can do'.[74] Ultimately, then, the individual treasured by Hayek is only of functional value. A.E. Galeotti is correct to point out that to Hayek, liberty in the end is only '... a procedural, methodological value'.[75] Although Galeotti tries to argue that liberty as a procedure is 'strictly linked with the needs of the species' and 'we cannot give it up for any kind of advantages', he at the end of the day has to admit, 'being a procedure, one appreciates it [i.e. liberty] on the ground of its positive results'.[76]

---

[73] This passage from H. B. Phillips's 'On the Nature of Progress', which appeared in *American Scientist*, XXXIII, 1945, p. 255, is found on the covering page of part I of *Constitution of Liberty*, emphasis added.
[74] Hayek, 'Individualism: True and False', p. 15.
[75] A. E. Galettoi, 'Individualism, Social Rules, Tradition: The Case of Friedrich A. Hayek', pp. 284-5, in *Friedrich A Hayek: Critical Assessments, Volume IV*, eds John Cunningham Wood and Ronald N. Woods, London and New York: Routledge, 1991, pp. 280-96.
[76] *Ibid.*, p. 285. For another good discussion of the problems of individualism in Hayek's philosophy, see A. P. Hamlin's 'Procedural

Individuals are of course allowed to come together and form organisations by consent in their joint pursuit of agreed ends. A proliferation of individual ends may imply a proliferation of voluntary organisations in this sense. This will enhance pluralism in 'the Great Society', but only so long as the organisations concerned all subscribe equally to the abstract rules that constitute the society. In fact, all units of 'the Great Society', including non-voluntary ones like the family and coercive one like the government, have to adhere to the abstract rules, or at least not to tamper with these rules by coercive interference, for pluralism in 'the Great Society' is made possible only by the primacy and unity of the abstract rules.

State-Society Distinction

What implication does such an understanding of pluralism in 'the Great Society' have for the famous 'state-society' distinction in civil society? In fact Hayek's theory gives this distinction a unique twist, which can be understood by considering Charles Taylor's essay 'Invoking Civil Society'.[77] Taylor gives a very good account of the factors in European history that contributed to the rise of the distinction between state and society. Among the factors mentioned by Taylor are, first, the medieval notion of society in which society was not defined in terms of its political organisation, for the latter was only one organ among others in society. Secondly, the tradition of Latin Christendom endowed Europe with an idea of the church as an independent society not subordinated, but parallel, to the state. Thirdly, the quasi-contractual relations between lord and vassal in feudal Europe (in which both had rights against, as well as duties to, each other), had imposed on the former the neces-

---

Individualism and Outcome Liberalism', in *Friedrich A Hayek*, pp. 16–29.
[77] In Charles Taylor, *Philosophical Arguments*, Cambridge, Massachusetts and London: Harvard University Press, 1995, pp. 204–24.

sity of winning consent from the latter for important changes.[78]

From these historical factors, according to Taylor, Europe developed two variant conceptions of civil society: the first stresses the pre-political (e.g. will, nation or community) or a-political (e.g. self-regulating market) nature of the non-state sectors; the second gives primacy to the political but stresses the fragmentation of the political sector itself in which checks and balances prevail.

From the perspective of Hayek's social philosophy, the main source of pluralism in civil society does not lie in the usual political and non-political distinction (the so-called 'a-political self-regulating market' notwithstanding, for organisations in the market can also undermine the market order if they impose their will on it). It lies, rather, in the categorical distinction between the spontaneous and the organisational spheres, according to which all forms of coercive power must be firmly regulated in order not to allow the latter to interfere illegitimately with the former.

Such an understanding does not fit well into the first conception of civil society described by Taylor, for the kind of pluralism presupposed by civil society lies not so much in the non-state sectors as such, but in how the abstract rules of the society facilitate the coordination of people and organisations with very different ends and goals without the need for a central command. As for the second conception, while Hayek is all for limited government under the rule of law in his 'Great Society', the essence of the distinction depends less on the checks and balances exerted by 'an interlocking mass of agencies and associations' in society against the state than on a clear understanding of the end-independent and general character of the law in civil society.[79] This delimits the reach of the state and protects a domain for the individual to act freely in accordance with his or her own separate and substantive ends. The following passage from the first volume of *Law, Legislation, and Liberty: Rules and Order*, from Hayek is perhaps the most explicit:

[78] *Ibid.*, pp. 210–12.
[79] *Ibid.*, p. 214.

> The freedom of the British which in the eighteenth century the rest of Europe came so much to admire was thus not, as the British themselves were among the first to believe and as Montesquieu later taught the world, originally a product of the separation of powers between legislature and executive, but rather a result of the fact that the law that governed the decisions of the courts was the common law, a law existing independently of anyone's will and at the same time binding upon and developed by the independent courts; a law with which parliament only rarely interfered and, when it did, mainly only to clear up doubtful points within a given body of law. One might even say that a sort of separation of powers had grown up in England, not because the 'legislature' alone made law, but because it did *not*: because the law was determined by courts independent of the power which organised and directed government.[80]

Given Hayek's categorical distinction between the spontaneous sphere and the organisational sphere, it is not surprising to see that his chief concern in 'the Great Society' is to prevent the unwarranted mingling of the two. In the economic realm, his attacks are not directed only at central planning and state intervention in the market.[81] He is equally critical of the power of the trade unions in determining wage levels and employment,[82] of corporatism in economic management, of big corporations' attempts to exert their influence on society by putting their resources in some so-called 'public interest' endeavours[83] and, to a lesser extent, of the monopolists' power to stifle free competition.[84]

Politically, Hayek is at pains to stress the differences between the coercive function of the state in maintaining the law and its role as a provider of services for the public. He is

---

[80] Hayek, *Rules and Order*, p. 85.
[81] See chapters 7-9 on the socialist calculation debate in Hayek, *Individualism and Economic Order*, for example.
[82] Hayek, 'Labour Unions and Employment', chapter 18 of *Constitution of Liberty*.
[83] Hayek, 'The Corporation in a Democratic Society', chapter 22 of *Studies in Philosophy, Politics and Economics*.
[84] Friedrich Hayek, *Law, Legislation, and Liberty: Vol. 3, The Political Order of a Free People,* Chicago: the University of Chicago Press, 1979, pp. 83-5.

highly critical of the idea of popular sovereignty, for he believes that this idea renders unlimited power to the majority without respecting the qualitative differences of the two state functions (i.e. the enactment of general laws for the observation of rules of just conduct and the making of policy decisions to achieve specific goals for the society at large).[85] Hayek is therefore ambivalent about democracy, though he accepts that democracy is so far the best means available for the peaceful transition of power between governments. He sees a great danger in pressure group politics in a democracy, for they promote a culture of political bargaining that could easily turn the law into an instrument for the fulfilment of particular, partial and sectional interests at the expense of the public good.[86] Most fundamentally, his greatest worry in this respect is the mixing up of the nomos (the law of liberty) and the thesis (the law of legislation) in modern legislature, for the former belongs to the spontaneous order in which a body of rules of just conduct, whether in articulated or unarticulated form, regulates interpersonal interaction to facilitate the pursuit of individuals' separate ends; whereas the latter embodies the particular will of the legislator or a coalition of legislators (be they the majority, the ruling elite or even a dictator) for the implementation and fulfilment of their concrete policy.[87] That is why Hayek is most eager to propose a model constitution for modern democracies in which these two kinds of law are to be strictly enacted by two separate legislative bodies in order to maintain the proper state (understood as an organisation) and society distinction in his 'Great Society'.[88]

The state, to Hayek, is always an organisation, though it is an organisation of a very special kind in a spontaneous society, for only it has the authority to enforce the abstract rules of just conduct in order to make sure that they are being

---

[85] Hayek, *Constitution of Liberty*, pp. 106–7.
[86] Hayek, *The Political Order of a Free People*, pp. 13–17.
[87] Hayek, *Rules and Order*, chapters 5 and 6.
[88] Hayek, *The Political Order of a Free People*, chapter 17.

observed.[89] 'Societies form but states are made', Hayek says.[90] As such, the state is never identical with society, for the latter is the multiplicity of grown and self-generating structures of free men whereas the 'government is of necessity the product of intellectual design.[91] While the government is there to provide an effective external framework within which self-generating orders can form, it should never be allowed to have the power to shape the society.

Unfortunately, from the welfare state to the socialist and totalitarian states, under the influence of Cartesian Rationalism, modern politics, according to Hayek, is littered with tragic examples of the organisational state overpowering society and shaping the latter after the image of the former. Hence, with the emergence of the monolithic state, the proper state-society distinction in civil society is abolished. Supreme political power has become unlimited power; legislation has turned into an instrument for the realisation of the particular interests of those in power rather than being a system of end-independent rules of conduct to coordinate and regulate interpersonal interaction in the pursuit of individuals' separate and divergent ends. In order to restore the political order of a free people, Hayek believes that it is necessary to dethrone politics in order to dismantle the monolithic state, restore the proper distinction between the state (i.e. the organisational order) and the society (i.e. the spontaneous order) and establish institutions to separate the two distinct functions of government. Government power should also be restrained by abstract rules of conduct that cannot be altered by a particular will.[92] To what extent is his argument persuasive?

---

[89] Hayek defines the state as 'the organisation of the people of a territory under a single government'. See *The Political Order of a Free People*, p. 140.
[90] *Ibid.*, p. 140.
[91] *Ibid.*, p. 152.
[92] Hayek, 'Containment of Power', in *The Political Order of a Free People*, chapter 18.

'The Dethronement of Politics' or the Indispensability of the Political?

Hayek, in fact, does not like the term 'state', for he thinks that this is a 'metaphysically charged' idea inherited from 'Hegelian thought'. Whenever possible, he prefers to use the term 'government' instead because it is more 'appropriate and precise'.[93] In Volume One of his *Law, Legislation, and Liberty*, Hayek goes so far as to say that 'it becomes particularly misleading when "the state" rather than "government" is contrasted with "society" to indicate that the first is an organisation and the second a spontaneous order', for, to be precise, it is always the organisation of government that acts or pursues policy.[94]

Hayek, however, is forced to admit that in international politics, it is more admissible to use the term 'state' to contrast with 'society'.[95] Why is this the case? Presumably, it is because in international exchanges a state does not only represent members of its government, but also the nation, the territory, the society and so on.[96] It is through the state that these latter units can acquire a political meaning, and it is also through the state that they are represented in the international arena. In this case, it would be inappropriate to equate the term 'state' with 'government', and even if we regard the former as an organisation, it is really no ordinary organisation, for it is through the state that the political identity of a nation, a territory and a society is being defined.

---

[93] Hayek, *Rules and Order*, p. 48.
[94] *Ibid*. However, Hayek himself is less than consistent in this respect, as he does not follow his own advice when he makes the following remark on p. 140 of *The Political Order of a Free People*: 'The state, the organisation of the people of a territory under a single government... is yet very far from being identical with society, or rather with the multiplicity of grown and self-generating structures of men who have any freedom that alone deserves the name of society.'
[95] Hayek, *Rules and Order*, p. 48. Also, see Hayek, *Mirage of Social Justice*, p. 61.
[96] In cases involving the Head of State who is not a member of the government of the day of the state concerned (e.g. the British Monarch), no members of the government are involved.

The case for distinguishing between state and government becomes even more compelling in the case of war and peace. When war is declared, it is the state that decides on behalf of society who its enemies are. In entering into an alliance with other states, the state then decides for the society who its friends are.[97] If you are a member of the government, you may quit the government if you find that you have difficulties in accepting its decision to declare war on another state, but that state is, formally speaking, still nevertheless your enemy. It is in the light of this that Ferguson's acute observation that 'without the rivalship of nations, and the practice of war, civil society itself could scarcely have found an object, or a form' can be readily understood.[98]

In this respect, while one can still say that it is wrong to identify the state with society, this is so not because, as Hayek claims, the former is 'only one of many organisations [in a free society]; rather, it is because without the state, civil society can scarcely acquire the political form that binds society into a coherent whole.[99]

But is this function of the state really limited to inter-state relationships, as implied by Hayek? In his discussion of emergency powers under a model constitution for the protection of the spontaneous order, Hayek says,

> ... when an external enemy threatens, when rebellion or lawless violence has broken out, or a natural catastrophe requires quick action by whatever means can be secured, powers of compulsory organization ... must be granted to somebody.[100]

---

[97] Needless to say, the classical formulation of the friend-enemy relationship as the defining characteristic of the political comes from Carl Schmitt. See his *The Concept of the Political*, trans. George Schwab, Chicago and London: The University of Chicago Press, 1996, particularly p. 26.

[98] Ferguson, *An Essay*, p. 28. In the same place, Ferguson also observes, 'he who has never struggled with his fellow-creatures, is a stranger to half the sentiments of mankind'. Notably, the sentiments of the other half of mankind are, according to Ferguson, the sentiments of affection and friendship.

[99] Hayek, *The Political Order of a Free People*, p. 140.

[100] *Ibid.*, p. 124.

Clearly, apart from the threat of an external enemy, the other two incidents, rebellion or lawless violence and natural catastrophe, which require powers of compulsory organisation to be granted, are clearly internal matters. In those cases, however, Hayek does not hesitate to admit that somebody has to assume emergency powers; he even goes out of his way to say, '… whoever has the power to proclaim an emergency and on this ground to suspend any part of the constitution is the true sovereign'.[101] This is in stark contrast to the other claim stressed time and again by Hayek that sovereignty, understood in the positive sense, has no place at all in constitutional government, since such a government is a limited government in which the supreme power must be negative in nature, in the sense that it only prohibits or restricts subordinate powers rather than exercising omnipotent control.[102] This contrast lies not so much in the fact that the sovereign holding emergency powers is claiming unlimited power as in the fact that ultimately the positive political power to declare a state of emergency and decide what powers (whether assertive or passive) are necessary to cope with that situation rests with the sovereign, whose power can never be just passive or negative.

Furthermore, the same logic should also apply to normal situations, though in a less apparent manner, for the same organisation (i.e. the state) 'is required to provide an effective external framework within which self-generating orders can form', and the decision about the nature and parameters of this 'effective external framework' is again a political one that the state has to take.[103] Renato Cristi's following remarks thoroughly endorse this point of view:

---

[101] *Ibid.*, p. 125. It is interesting to note that Hayek's position here is in agreement with Carl Schmitt's claim in his *Political Theology*: 'Sovereign is he who decides on the exception.' For a discussion of the challenges posed by Schmitt's ideal of the political to civil order theorists, see the concluding chapter of this book.
[102] Hayek, *Political Order of a Free People*, p. 123.
[103] *Ibid.*, p. 140. Andrew Gamble, in his *Hayek: The Iron Cage of Liberty*, has also mentioned a similar criticism of Hayek by John Maynard Keynes in this regard. Gamble says, '… the real disagreement between Keynes and Hayek was … the question of knowing where to

Hayek's idea of a spontaneous order presupposed civil society's capacity for self-regulation and autonomous administration. This should confirm the complete dethronement of politics within that sphere. Still, the negative tasks ascribed to the state were to be determined and sustained by the action of the state itself. It was thus positively and actively that the state ought to restrict and limit its action to a merely negative one, so that the depoliticisation of civil society could turn dialectically into the state's active preservation of its monopoly over the political as such.[104]

'The Great Society' and the Inadequacy of Negative Values

The problem with Hayek does not stop at his reluctance to admit the positive nature of the political. Equally problematic are his negative definitions of freedom and justice. When freedom is defined as the absence of arbitrary coercion and arbitrary coercion as coercion not in accordance with the rule of law, given Hayek's understanding of the function of law as the preservation of the spontaneous order, such a negative definition boils down to asking us to support freedom in the sense of supporting the smooth functioning of the spontaneous order without giving any justification for the value of freedom in itself, or describing its positive content.[105] As A. E. Galeotti rightly points out,

> ... if liberty has nothing to do with one's choice and with the shaping of one's life and personality; if liberty is limited

---

> draw the line between intervention and non-intervention. Keynes's criticism of Hayek was that he accepted that the logical extreme of no intervention at all was not possible, but gave no guidance in *The Road to Serfdom* as to where the line should be drawn ... Keynes thought that it was a matter of practical judgement, not principle. He acknowledged that Hayek would draw the line differently than he would, but criticized him for underestimating the practicability of a middle course. He also argued that since Hayek accepted that a line had to be drawn, it was disingenuous of him to imply that "so soon as one moves an inch in the planned direction you are necessarily launched on the slippery path which will lead you in due course over the precipice."' See *Hayek: The Iron Cage of Liberty*, pp. 159-60.

[104] 'Hayek contra Schmitt' in Renato Cristi, *Carl Schmitt and Authoritarian Liberalism*, Cardiff: University of Wales Press, 1998, p. 167.

[105] Hayek, *Constitution of Liberty*, chapter 1.

to the fact that we are so blind that we cannot foresee what is going to happen; in a word, if liberty is basically our miscalculation, why should we care so much about it?'[106]

Such a conception of individual freedom implies at most a functional understanding of the value of the individual. The same can be said of justice in Hayek's 'Great Society', for Hayek believes that justice is a negative virtue and that the way to ascertain the justice of a rule of conduct is by subjecting it to the test of internal consistency with the system of rules that constitutes the spontaneous order. As a result, what is just is evaluated by the spontaneous order itself; or to be more precise, what is not unjust is to be determined by internal consistency with the spontaneous order, without giving any positive content to justice itself to support this value. Given the fact that the spontaneous social order, like the market order, is not the result of human design, and also given the fact that, according to Hayek, questions of justice can arise only in relation to intentional human conduct or interference, one cannot but accept the spontaneous social order as something given and refrain from questioning its legitimacy and validity.

In adopting a negative approach to the problems of the political, freedom and justice, Hayek fails to explain why these are valuable in their own right. The question then becomes, is 'the Great Society' itself morally attractive? Why should we support or be loyal to such a society? One ready answer to the first question is, of course, that 'the Great Society' is highly efficient and is often successful in bringing prosperity to its members because of its innovative and efficient use of resources. However, efficiency is only instrumentally valuable: the most efficient machine to destroy the global environment can be justly condemned as an evil machine. As for prosperity, this also cannot stand on its own, for if prosperity is achieved at the expense of grave inequality or obvious disregard of great human suffering, many would legitimately find it difficult to support the

[106] Galeotti, 'Individualism, Social Rules, Tradition', p. 283.

results of the market order, giving rise to problems of social cohesion in the spontaneous social order. [107]

Hayek appears to appreciate the moral emptiness of his 'Great Society' when he laments, in the last chapter ('Religion and the Guardians of Tradition') of his last major work, *The Fatal Conceit*, the loss of the role played by religion in the preservation of the traditions of spontaneous order. Here, the questions of social cohesion and of the constitutive role played by beliefs and traditions in upholding such cohesion have come to the fore. In that chapter, Hayek says,

> the premature loss of what we regard as nonfactual [i.e. religious] beliefs would have deprived mankind of a powerful support in the long development of the extended order that we now enjoy, and that even now the loss of these beliefs, whether true or false, creates great difficulties.[108]

In addition, Hayek also asks the following question:

> How could traditions which people do not like or understand, whose effects they usually do not appreciate and can neither see nor foresee, and which they are still ardently combating, continue to have been passed on from generation to generation?[109]

To this question, Hayek gives two answers. The first is an evolutionary explanation in terms of group selection, for 'groups that behave in these ways simply survive and increase'.[110] The second answer is religion. In fact, the second answer is more crucial in this context, for given Hayek's idea of the constitutional ignorance (derived from his idea of the inherent inability of the human mind to fully

---

[107] In the recent 'neglected drugs' campaign, Oxfam and *Medecins Sans Frontieres*, two international humanitarian aid organisations, have pointed out that while the global drug market allows the big multinational drug companies to reap huge profits in producing expensive drugs for the rich countries, these companies just do not find there are enough material incentives to produce drugs for tropical diseases that would allow millions of people from poor countries to be cured. The means of producing such drugs already exists, of course.
[108] Hayek, *The Fatal Conceit*, p. 137.
[109] *Ibid.*, pp. 135–6.
[110] *Ibid.*, p. 136.

understand itself) of human beings, it is unlikely that the groups concerned will have adopted these practices out of a conscious understanding of their beneficial effects in advance, particularly when the practices are in conflict with some strong human feelings. So the role played by religious beliefs is crucial to Hayek in the evolution and preservation of his 'Great Society' before their beneficial effects can be widely recognised, and this may have endowed the social order with some values. But the ultimately naturalistic, and even fatalistic, nature of Hayek's defence of his 'Great Society' becomes even more apparent when we take a closer look at his answer to the above question.

Hayek acknowledges that primitive custom and tradition (mostly in the form of totem and taboo) in restraining individual action within a group may serve as signs of mutual recognition among members of the group in the first place.[111] These signs of recognition (preserved as belief in spirits that punish transgressors and restrain members' individual action) constitute the religious and political bonds that hold the group together and keep its common practices intact. Yet these bonds do not appear to have a value of their own, for if they impede the evolutionary development of the spontaneous order, Hayek will simply dismiss them as merely the atavistic echoes of an earlier stage of social development that are out of place in the modern world.[112] Only when they have subsequently succeeded in restraining individual actions within a group in ways which are conducive to the development of the spontaneous order will they be regarded as useful. This, however, is not 'sufficient', for in order to allow any real selection to occur, 'common practices must have a chance to produce

---

[111] *Ibid.*, p. 136.
[112] In dismissing nationalism as one such echo, Hayek says that 'the ideas which are changing our civilisation respect no boundaries ... The growth of ideas is an international process, and only those who fully take part in the discussion will be able to exercise a significant influence.' See *Constitution of Liberty*, p. 405. Hayek's views on nationalism are, needless to say, in stark contrast to Gellner's, who regards nationalism as a product of modernity. See Gellner, *Nationalism* etc.

their beneficial effects on a group on a progressive scale before selection by evolution can become effective'.[113] Since cultural transmission will not occur automatically, Hayek adds, 'many generations will therefore probably be required to ensure that any particular such traditions are indeed continued, and that they do indeed eventually spread', even if these beliefs or practices are seldom understood by the people and are in conflict with other treasured values like solidarity and altruism, which Hayek calls 'human instincts'.[114]

In other words, religious beliefs and the individuals who uphold them will have value only if they are instrumental to the evolutionary development of the spontaneous order; and as the beneficial effects of evolution will take a long time to take root, generations and generations of human beings are required to adhere to these practices somewhat blindly, even when they are in conflict with other human values. Generations of men are regarded as instruments in this process in order to allow evolution to yield ultimately beneficial results (mainly in terms of better survival) for mankind. Hayek's instrumental understanding of the value of the individual is perhaps most bizarre at this point. Furthermore, while some religious practices, particularly those that support property and the family, do have an historical connection with the values that have played a positive role in shaping the development of 'the Great Society', Hayek does not think that this proves that there is an intrinsic connection between the two.[115] In other words, religion only has a functional, not intrinsic, value to 'the Great Society'. Thus, Hayek's two explanations—group selection and religion—amount to nothing more than a fatalistic and

---

[113] Hayek, *The Fatal Conceit*, p. 136.
[114] *Ibid.*, p. 136. Hayek tries to rule out solidarity and altruism as human morality by classifying them as genetically developed human instincts on one hand, and by defining morality as those non-instinctive rules that enabled mankind to expand into an extended order on the other. See *The Fatal Conceit*, chapter 1. However, it is doubtful if solidarity and altruism are genetically determined rather than the products of human civilisation.
[115] *Ibid.*, p. 137.

mystical acceptance of the practices conducive to the development of the spontaneous order. In this respect, they do not go beyond his uncritical acceptance of the results of the market order, despite criticisms from defenders of social justice and social cohesion.[116]

Having deprived obligatory rules and religious beliefs of any intrinsic value or positive content, Hayek cannot avoid slipping into a position where his 'Great Society' is devoid of any persuasive moral resources which would encourage its members to develop deep commitments to the social order. In this connection, Irving Kristol is quite right to say, '[n]o merely utilitarian definition of civic loyalty is going to convince anyone that it makes sense for him to die for his country'.[117] Kristol, a prominent American critic of liberal capitalism, is also right to point out that the disestablishment of religion and morality in liberal capitalism facilitates the destruction of authority, which brings with it the threat of nihilism; for liberal capitalist society can generate more and more nihilistic products as long as there is a market for them, hence accelerating the self-destructive tendency of such a society.[118] This danger has also been identified by other critics like John Gray and Noel O'Sullivan, with the latter stressing that the unfettered market 'tends to destroy all the integrating institutions of society by encouraging attitudes which are wholly insensitive to the non-instrumental presuppositions of morality, on the one hand, and communal identity, on the other'.[119]

---

[116] For an excellent account of Hayek's 'physicalist notion of man and society', which renders his defence of liberalism in a formalistic and naturalistic manner, see Murray Forsyth's 'Hayek's Bizarre Liberalism: A Critique'.
[117] Irving Kristol, 'Capitalism, Socialism, and Nihilism', in his *Neoconservatism: The Autobiography of An Idea*, The Free Press, 1995, p. 100. Also see David Miller's *Market, State, and Community*, Oxford: Clarendon Press, 1990, for a critical discussion of the problems in Hayek's market capitalism.
[118] Kristol, 'Capitalism, Socialism, and Nihilism', p. 102.
[119] See Gray's 'Postscript' to his *Hayek on Liberty*, 3rd edn. See O'Sullivan's 'Visions of Freedom: The Response to Totalitarianism', p. 77. For an interesting discussion of how Hayek's negative conception of liberty and the political creates problems for his views

Conclusion

While it is true that one of the main purposes in Hayek's whole enterprise is to demolish Cartesian Rationalism, the character of his social philosophy is itself, in the end, highly rationalistic, for within such a philosophy all social and political action appears to be a function of epistemology. This is perhaps the greatest irony found in his social and political theory. For Hayek, the foundation of social order and social action is ultimately neither moral nor political; rather, the constitutional limitation of man's knowledge is a 'sufficient basis' to support the conclusions of his social and political philosophy.[120] Similarly, the problems he identifies with constructivism are not essentially moral or political; if constructivism is epistemologically tenable, man should simply give up his freedom:

> If there were omniscient men, if we could know not only all that effects the attainment of our present wishes but also our future wants and desires, there would be little case for liberty.[121]

Likewise, we follow the self-regulative mechanisms of the spontaneous order and of many of our rule-governed practices and allow individuals to make their choices mainly 'because every individual knows so little and, in particular, because we rarely know which of us knows best that we trust the independent and competitive efforts of many to induce the emergence of what we shall want when we see it.'[122]

---

of social rules, social cohesion and community identity, see A. E. Galeotti's 'Individualism, Social Rules, Tradition'.

[120] Hayek, 'Individualism: True and False', in *Individualism and Economic Order*, p. 14.
[121] Hayek, *Constitution of Liberty*, p. 29.
[122] *Ibid.* Irving Kristol's following critical remark on capitalism is highly relevant here. 'One of the keystones of modern economic thought is that it is impossible to have *a prior* knowledge of what constitutes happiness for other people; that such knowledge is incorporated in an individual's "utility schedules"; and this knowledge, in turn, is revealed by the choices the individual makes in a free market.' See 'Capitalism, Socialism, and Nihilism', pp. 94–5.

As 'government is of necessity the product of intellectual design'[123] and the spontaneous order is based on the epistemological thesis of the logical limitation of human reason or 'evolutionary rationalism', there is no room for politics or morality to have a place in the ultimate design of the state and in the justification of the spontaneous order.[124] Judith N. Shklar is most perceptive when remarking, 'The Rule of Law is necessary in Hayek's view, not because there are recurrent dangers of oppression and persecution ... but because of mankind's irreducible ignorance ... Everything else is derivative.'[125]

Thus, 'the dethronement of politics' by Hayek also leads to the depoliticisation of the state, making the state subsidiary to the spontaneous order, which requires that market forces be left unfettered.[126] The Hayekian state and its rule of law are not meant to create a common political bond to unite society or give it common aspirations: they exist ultimately only to prevent inefficiency and irrationality. Only secondarily do they also create social integration by preventing arbitrariness and oppression; not because this is their original aim, however, but because, Hayek believes, Cartesian rationalism creates the illusion that men do not need to follow abstract rules in a complex society to meet their expectations. But Cartesian planners, who retain their belief in the need for artificial integration, will not admit defeat. Instead, they resort more and more to totalitarian methods of control to perpetuate their disastrous rule.[127]

While Shklar is right to question whether the Cartesian error alone would lead to Nazism and communism, recent developments do seem to confirm that in many East Asian countries the market can become increasingly spontaneous without a corresponding liberalisation of the politics of the

---

[123] Hayek, *The Political Order of a Free People*, p. 152.
[124] Hayek, *Rules and Order*, chapter 1.
[125] 'Political Theory and the Rule of Law', in Judith N. Shklar, *Political Thought & Political Thinkers*, Chicago and London: The University of Chicago Press, 1998, ed. Stanley Hoffmann, pp. 27 and 29.
[126] Hayek describes the government as 'a maintenance squad' of the spontaneous order. See *Rules and Order*, p. 47.
[127] Shklar, *Political Thought & Political Thinkers*, p. 28.

state.[128] This again brings out the problem of Hayek's spontaneous order and evolutionary thesis, for it appears that the ways the spontaneous market order develops can be very different from his expectations. As Galeotti remarks, 'Hayek's account of spontaneity does not describe how things actually have happened; rather it is conjectural reconstruction.'[129] In other words, a defence of the spontaneous order is no substitute for a defence of individual freedom, whose moral and political justification cannot ultimately rely on the effective and efficient functioning of the market order.

What may now be added is that, in many instances, economic powers can be no less oppressive than political ones. If 'the dethronement of politics' inadvertently leads to the enthronement of economics, the state-civil society distinction may simply be replaced by the engulfment of the political by the economic realm. The question then becomes, if the market is supposedly there to defend civil society from the state, what is it that can defend civil society from destructive market forces?[130] Also, what moral and political resources

---

[128] *Ibid.* See, for example, David Martin Jones, *Political Development in Pacific Asia*, Polity Press, 1997, particularly chapter 3, 'Democratisation, Civil Society and the Pacific Asian Nouveaux Riches'.

[129] See Galeotti's 'Individualism, Social Rules, Tradition', p. 292. Likewise, Andrew Gamble finds that Hayek's evolutionary argument is at its weakest when he tries to use his epistemological presuppositions to argue that constructivist rationalism is not only an intellectual error, but cannot survive the test of evolutionary selection: '[Hayek's] division of liberalism into two camps, the true and the false, and his denunciation of constructivists and rationalists for being completely wrong in their perception of the world ... [belong to] an aspect of Hayek which many commentators have found difficult to accept. If the problems of modern Western civilization are due to intellectual error, how has this error arisen? Hayek's evolutionary arguments desert him at this point. The constructivist rationalists have existed for at least as long as Hayek's true liberals, the critical rationalists, but they show no sign of being sidelined by the normal evolutionary process. Should not evolution have discarded them by now?' See Gamble, *Hayek: The Iron Cage of Liberty*, p. 182.

[130] See John Varty's 'Civic or Commercial? Adam Ferguson's Concept of Civil Society', in *Democratization*, Spring 1997, Vol. 4, No. 1, pp. 29–48, for a good discussion of this question. Likewise, Gamble's following

can we deploy to sustain the legitimacy of such a society once the results of the market order are found to be unacceptable to many of its members? Hayek's social philosophy, despite its originality and sophistication, offers no convincing answers to these questions about legitimacy.

---

observation is also most pertinent in this regard: 'Hayek's greatest failure is his neglect of the problem of private power. All his efforts go into the denunciation of state power, but he has little to say about private coercion. He endorses negative liberty over positive liberty, and defines negative liberty almost wholly in terms of the liberty of property-owners. Since on his own account the majority of citizens in the market order cannot be property-owners, and since he proposes no measures to enable them to become so, he appears to accept that there can be no return to the kind of liberal order which he favours.' See Gamble, *Hayek: The Iron Cage of Liberty*, p. 190.

4

Habermas on Discursive Democracy

Communicative Reason, Law,
Private and Public Autonomy,
and the Politics of Rational
Consensus

Introduction

In his treatise on legal and political philosophy *Between Facts and Norms: Contributions to a Discourse Theory of Law and Democracy*, Jurgen Habermas describes his main theoretical task in this area as an attempt to 'show how the old promise of a self-organising community of free and equal citizens can be reconceived under the conditions of complex societies'.[1] The result of this attempt is Habermas's development of a proceduralist view of democracy and deliberative politics, in which a normative theory of democracy no longer requires some metaphysical or ethical foundation, law and morality are regarded as distinct though interpenetrated, the notion of sovereignty is interpreted as procedural rather than substantive, and individual human rights

---

[1] Jurgen Habermas, *Between Facts and Norms: Contributions to a Discourse Theory of Law and Democracy*, Cambridge: Polity Press, 1996, trans. William Rehg, p. 7. For a useful review of this work, see *Discourse & Democracy: Essays on Habermas's 'Between Facts and Norms'*, eds Rene von Schomberg and Kenneth Baynes, Albany: The State University of New York, 2002.

and political participation are inseparable and co-original, forming the twin pillars of the legitimate political order of a democratic state.

The theory proposed by Habermas is both profound and ambitious. He believes that his discourse theory of democracy is superior to its liberal and republican counterparts, a theme which will be returned to when the related theories of human rights and popular sovereignty are examined.[2] Although this theory is not free from ambiguities, what is clear is that Habermas is a rationalist, and it is his rationalism that makes him so confident in defending his discourse theory of democracy. In this theory, free and equal individuals with highly diversified interests and values can all achieve social and political solidarity under the conditions of free and non-coercive deliberation. This is only possible, however, if they adopt a particular kind of reason: communicative reason. In order to understand Habermas's political thought, his concepts of communicative action and communicative reason must therefore be examined.

Communicative Action and Communicative Rationality

A full discussion of Habermas's theory of communicative action will not be attempted since that would require a comprehensive study of his philosophy of language, which goes well beyond the scope of this study.[3] However, what will be examined is Habermas's vision of communicative reason, which he believes gives a rational and institutional justification for his discourse theory of democracy.

The starting point for Habermas's theory of communication is his belief that formal analysis of language should not

---

[2] See Habermas, 'Three Normative Models of Democracy', in *Constellations*, Vol. 1, No. 1, April 1994, pp. 1–10, for an overview on this.

[3] See his *The Theory of Communicative Action: Reason and the Rationalisation of Society, Vol. One*, and *Theory of Communicative Action: The Critique of Functionalist Reason, Vol. Two*. See also Habermas, *On the Pragmatics of Communication*, ed. Maeve Cooke, Cambridge: Polity Press, 1998. Cooke's introduction, pp. 1–19, offers a good overview to the development of Habermas's formal or universal pragmatics from the 70s to the 90s.

be restricted to semantic analysis alone. His concept of universal pragmatics has a distinctively social or intersubjective dimension which looks into the context of communication in order to make us aware that, as speakers and hearers, there are certain necessary conditions that must be presupposed for successful communication.[4] This will not be possible without mutual understanding between the speaker and the hearer, and according to Habermas, 'whoever makes use of a natural language in order to come to an understanding with an addressee about something in the world is required to take a performative attitude and commit herself to certain presuppositions'.[5] What are these presuppositions?

First of all, for mutual understanding, participants in communication must commit to whatever claims they make if they take their communication seriously. In other words, 'in seeking to reach an understanding, natural-language users must assume, among other things, that the participants pursue their illocutionary goals without reservations'.[6] If the claims one raises with one's utterances are challenged by other participants, one has the obligation to provide better reasons to defend their validity in order to persuade others to accept them. Likewise, participants have to subscribe to the same linguistic rules, such as using the same linguistic expressions, in the interaction. As a result, it is further supposed that communicating participants also tie their agreement to the intersubjective recognition of criticisable validity claims. With this intersubjectively recognised understanding, it is also to be expected that participants are ready to take on the obligations resulting from communicative consensus that will govern any relevant future interaction amongst the participants.

For communicative action freely to arrive at mutual understanding in a genuine manner, it is further supposed that the speech situation must be such that it is open to the public, inclusive rather than exclusive, free from external or

---

[4] See Cooke's introduction to *On the Pragmatics of Communication*, p. 2.
[5] Habermas, *Between Facts and Norms*, p. 4.
[6] *Ibid.*

inherent compulsion, and with equal rights enjoyed by all participants.[7] To Habermas, communicative rationality therefore 'is inscribed in the linguistic telos of mutual understanding and forms an ensemble of conditions that both enable and limit'.[8]

To understand, therefore, is to know the conditions governing the validity of a claim in communicative action, with a view to reaching agreement amongst the participants of the communication. From Habermas's perspective, linguistic interaction is primarily a matter of raising and responding to validity claims, and he has identified three kinds of validity claims that are raised by a speaker: a claim to the truth of what is said or presupposed, a claim to the normative rightness of the speech act in the given context and a claim to the truthfulness of the speaker.[9] Here, one can discern a theory of truth, a theory of justice and a theory of ethics emerging from Habermas's understanding of communicative action.

Habermas's views on the difference between law and morality will be returned to later. What must be noted at this point in relation to communicative action is that such action is participatory, cooperative and rational in nature. Communicative action is participatory not only because it requires speakers and hearers alike to take part in a speech situation; more fundamentally, mutual understanding is not possible if hearers only adopt an observer's role without directly responding to the claims made by the speakers.

Communicative action is cooperative in nature, since participants are required to enter into a cooperative relationship of commitment and responsibility by undertaking to

---

[7] See Habermas's 'Richard Rorty's Pragmatic Turn', in *On the Pragmatics of Communication*, p. 367.
[8] Habermas, *Between Facts and Norms*, p. 4.
[9] It should be noted that Habermas does allow other forms of linguistic interaction, such as strategic, figurative or symbolic interaction, but he contends that these are parasitic on communicative action. See 'Some Further Clarifications of the Concept of Communicative Rationality', in *On the Pragmatics of Communication*, pp. 307–42. For the purpose of this study, I will not go into arguments in relation to this issue, though I will discuss the relations between communicative and strategic action as and when appropriate.

behave in certain ways and to subscribe to the same linguistic rules. The success of the interaction depends on the cooperation of the parties involved. Likewise, communicative action is inherently rational in the sense that a speaker has an obligation to provide reasons for the validity claims he raises with his utterances, while the hearer is supposed to accept or reject such claims on the basis of argument.

The above-mentioned preconditions of communication and the participatory, cooperative, and rational nature of communicative action are described by Habermas as 'pragmatic presuppositions of a counterfactual sort'.[10] A reconstruction and formalisation of these unavoidable presuppositions is the work of communicative reason, which regulates both the process and the outcome of the communication.[11] The open and self-critical nature of this practice imbues communicative action with an inherent context-transcendent power, for as 'no one has direct access to uninterpreted conditions of validity, "validity" must be understood in epistemic terms as "validity proven for us"', which is always provisional and revisable by new facts, arguments or new participants in the communicative process.[12] Together with the unavoidability of the presuppositions of communicative action, it appears that Habermas has proposed a theory of communicative action that does not depend on any claim to transcendental truth, yet is in a position to avoid the pitfalls of relativism. What implications can one derive from Habermas's insights into communicative action for social integration and political order in complex societies?

---

[10] Habermas, *Between Facts and Norms*, p. 4.
[11] These presuppositions are regarded by Habermas as a set of unavoidable idealisations that forms the counterfactual basis of everyday communicative practice. See *Between Facts and Norms*. As a rule, counterfactual idealisations will only be satisfied more or less approximately in real-life practice.
[12] *Ibid.*, p. 14.

Communicative Reason and Social Integration

The telos of communicative rationality—mutual understanding—is by no means only applicable to the linguistic context; it is also applicable to the social context. As Habermas says, 'as soon as the illocutionary forces of speech acts take on an action-coordinating role, language itself supplies the primary source of social integration'. 'In such action', Habermas goes on to say, 'actors in the roles of speaker and hearer attempt to negotiate interpretations of the situation at hand and to harmonise their respective plans with one another through the unrestrained pursuit of illocutionary goals'.[13]

It is of course conceivable that social interaction as such may not necessarily lead to successful mutual understanding. In such a case, participants may try to restart the communicative process by seeking further and better reasons to negotiate a new interpreted agreement; or they may switch to strategic action, in which they treat language and other social interaction mainly as a medium for the transmission of information to help them to achieve their own goals without attempting to reach mutual agreement. Alternatively, they may just break off any communication whatsoever. Of course, if there is a general breakdown of communication, it means that social integration is impossible. It is also doubtful whether strategic action alone can give rise to a sustainable and stable social order. Further, without mutual understanding it is not clear what is meant by social. As a result, communicative action appears to be the main source of social integration when the norms governing how the participants should live together are at issue, for only under such a condition will the participants suspend the objective attitude of an observer or self-interest seeker and actively seek mutual understanding.[14] Under such circumstances

---

[13] *Ibid.*, p. 18.
[14] Obviously, there are different modes of social interaction, which are differentiated by the nature and purpose of the interaction concerned. What we are talking about here is the kind of interactions that determines how participants in communication should live together in a society. Habermas believes that normally the modes of

they should also feel obligated to respond directly and positively to the communicative offers/claims made by others, or to vindicate seriously the offers/claims made by themselves for further interaction.

The socially integrative function of communicative action becomes even more important and strained under the modern situation, in which the ties of religious authorities and the traditional bonds of ancient institutions, which previously gave rise to undisputed social consensus, have been undermined by the critical force of reason. This has made modern societies increasingly disenchanted, secularised and pluralised, and requires their normative orders to be maintained with no agreed foundations. In other words, the risk of dissension is high when modern social orders are deprived of the support of a traditional and religious consensus. As a result, to maintain social integration in cases of conflict is crucial in order to avoid the breaking off of communication. What is equally important is that social integration in such cases should not be achieved as a result of the subordination of one party to the other, for this will obviously violate all the conditions required by genuine communication. Habermas describes interactions in such cases as strategic interactions, for in the absence of mutual agreement in a particular communicative act, the features involved in the communication are transformed into facts

> communication in question are self-selective: 'To the extent that articulating and weighing policies depends on the selection of purposive-rational means or strategies (on the basis of empirical information), there must be a consensus on sufficiently clear preferences. If the preferences themselves are contested because of a clash of opposing interests, then procedurally fair compromises must be found. However if the preferences are not so much contested as they are unclear, then participants must reach an understanding in ethical discourse concerning their form of life and collective identity in order to assure themselves of shared value orientations. If there is an irreconcilable conflict of values instead of a conflict of compromisable interests, then the parties must jointly shift to the more abstract level of moral reasoning and agree upon rules for living together that are in the equal interest of all.' See 'Reply to Symposium Participants' by Habermas on p. 432 in, *Habermas on Law and Democracy: Critical Exchanges*, eds Michel Rosenfeld and Andrew Arato, Berkeley, Los Angeles and London: University of California Press, 1998.

that the participants evaluate in the light of their own preferences, rather than in the light of a mutual consensus. Naturally, in complex and diversified societies, it is not surprising to find that people, in their own self-interest or due to a lack of a mutual consensus on particular issues, resort to strategic actions in social interaction. However, in order to maintain social integration and avoid social subordination of some to the others in strategic interactions, it is imperative 'for the actors themselves *to come to some understanding* about the *normative regulation of strategic interactions*' too.[15] The 'normative regulation' Habermas has in mind is modern law, for modern law, according to him, is composed of rules that can, on the one hand, present *de facto* restrictions in strategic interactions that alter the relevant information in such a way that the strategic actor feels compelled to adapt his behaviour in the objectively required manner, yet on the other hand impose normatively valid obligations for the actors to observe.[16] How can modern law achieve this? What is the nature of law in Habermas's legal philosophy? What makes it a normatively legitimate means of regulating social interaction for free and equal individuals? It is to these questions that we must now turn.

Positive Law and Social Integration

Modern positive law, according to Habermas, consists of enacted, binding and enforceable norms to regulate the conduct of strangers who fall within its jurisdiction in a polity. In the absence of a commonly shared religious or metaphysical ethos, and with each individual having his or her own set of subjective preferences and jealously guarding his or her own autonomy, how can law be normatively accepted by social actors in a complex modern society? Habermas's answer to this question is basically Kantian in nature:

---

[15] Habermas, *Between Facts and Norms*, pp. 26–7, emphasis in the original.
[16] Habermas says, '[w]e can then also see, from a historical perspective, the core of modern law consists of private rights that mark out the legitimate scope of individual liberties and are thus tailored to the strategic pursuit of private interests'. *Ibid.*, p. 27.

the coercive law tailored for the self-interested use of individual rights can preserve its socially integrative force only insofar as the addressees of legal norm may at the same time understand themselves, taken as a whole, as the rational *authors* of those norms.[17]

In accordance with Habermas's theory of communicative action, citizens will become rational authors in the process of legislation only if, first, all those who are possibly affected by the proposed norm under consideration are allowed to participate freely as equals in its deliberation and, secondly, they can arrive at a rationally motivated agreement acceptable by all. In other words, they should only submit to the force of better argument in arriving at a rationally motivated agreement.

Habermas believes allowing addressees of coercive law to participate as rational authors in the making of such law provides the key to preserving the socially integrative function of the law in modern complex societies. This is so because, on the one hand, the state's guarantee to enforce enacted law offers a functional equivalent for the stabilisation of behavioural expectations, actions which were formerly carried out by traditional authorities and, on the other hand, the communicative process involved in the legislative process allows all participants to examine critically the validity or acceptability of the legal norms concerned, because in theory this process can expose all legal norms and values to critical testing, thereby arriving at a commonly accepted rational resolution at the end of the legislative process.[18]

It should be noted that in order to participate as a *free and equal* author in this process, citizens must have many of their negative rights, such as freedom of speech, the right to protection by the due process and the right to access to all relevant information, protected. Equally important is the fact that to be a genuine *rational author* in the process, citizens must exercise their political rights at the same time, making reasonable contributions to the communicative

---

[17] *Ibid.*, p. 33, emphasis in the original.
[18] *Ibid.*, pp. 37–8.

process in order to arrive at a rationally motivated consensus. As a result, Habermas claims that in his theory of law and democracy, the co-originality of the individual's private rights and public autonomy is presupposed. Furthermore, given the unstructured or free-floating nature of ordinary political communication, the legislative process for the achievement of rationally motivated agreements among citizens should also be legally institutionalised as part of the legal system and be regulated by law itself. In Habermas's own words:

> The normative intuition behind a self-organising legal community can be restated as follows: a legal order *is* legitimate to the extent that it equally secures the co-original private and political autonomy of its citizens; at the same time, however, it *owes* its legitimacy to the forms of communication in which civic autonomy alone can express and prove itself. This is the key to a proceduralist understanding of the law.[19]

How attractive is this proceduralist understanding of law and what is its relation to morality, politics and civil society?

Law and Morality

From the quotation cited at the end of the last section, it is clear that for Habermas, law owes its legitimacy not to morality, but to the institutionalised legal procedure that ensures undistorted public forms of communication among the citizens. In other words, Habermas proposes a kind of procedural justice of law and believes that communicatively produced legal results, no matter what they are, are legitimate so long as they are produced in accordance with the proper legal procedure.[20] The need to adopt such a

---

[19] See Habermas, 'Paradigms of Law', in *Habermas on Law and Democracy*, p. 19, emphasis in the original.

[20] As Habermas says, 'the legal code gives a socially binding character to procedurally correct results ... Legal institutionalisation thus has the sense of grafting a quasi-pure procedural justice, as Rawls puts it, onto discourses and their imperfect procedural rationality.' See *Between Facts and Norms*, p. 179. According to Rawls, 'pure procedural justice obtains when there is no independent criterion for

proceduralist approach in law for social integration should by now be clear, for in post-traditional societies there are no foundational or comprehensive norms creating legitimate law for social integration; as such, modern law must, unlike classical natural law, be self-sustaining and self-regulating. As a result, legitimacy must emerge from legality, and morality cannot be relied on as a kind of higher law to justify the legitimacy of law. How can a proceduralist understanding of law produce its own normativity to justify law's validity claims? What is the relationship between law and morality, given the fact that both are there to regulate interpersonal relations from a normative perspective? This section will deal with the latter question first, while the next section looks at the thesis of co-originality of private and public autonomy, which constitutes what Habermas regards as the normative background condition for a legitimate proceduralist paradigm of law.

To Habermas, the relationship between law and morality is both close and complex. He believes that a legal order should not contradict basic moral principles. The two, in fact, stand in a complementary relationship. While moral and legal questions refer to the same problems of legitimating interpersonal relationships, of coordinating interpersonal actions through justified norms and of resolving conflicts by using recognised normative principles and rules, Habermas points out that there are qualitative as well as functional differences between law and morality and that their relationship is in the main coeval rather than hierarchical.[21]

To start with, while post-traditional morality represents only a form of cultural knowledge in which moral principle functions as a rule of argumentation for deciding moral questions rationally, law is not only a symbolic system, but

---

the right result: instead there is a correct or fair procedure such that the outcome is likewise correct or fair, whatever it is, provided that the procedure has been properly followed'. See John Rawls, *A Theory of Justice*, Oxford, Melbourne and Cape Town: Oxford University Press, 1972, p. 86. Rawls believes that gambling is an example of pure procedural justice.

[21] Habermas, *Between Facts and Norms*, pp. 106–7. Also chapter 3.

also an action system with institutionalised binding forces as well.[22] In other words, while moral discourse, which aims at the impartial evaluation of action conflicts and hopes to win the respect of all rational beings, is essentially cognitive, critical, and, in theory, open-ended in nature, law, in adjudicating disputed cases, must be able to make a definitive and binding conclusion to the evaluative discourse on action conflicts at some point, and must obligate the parties involved to follow its conclusion through a systematic and institutionalised procedure. For in post-traditional societies, with the collapse of a shared and unquestioned ethical life and the advent of pluralism, rational morality views all normative claims 'through the powerful but narrow lens of universalisability' in order to form an impartial judgement of morally relevant action.[23] As such, according to Habermas, post-traditional morality's main concern is 'correct judgement', which 'facilitates a knowledge that is meant to orient one's action', but 'does not thereby *dispose* one to act rightly'.[24] As a result, 'the constitution of the legal form became necessary to offset deficits arising with the collapse of traditional ethical life', for law can supplement post-traditional morality in a manner effective for action by virtue of a binding character deriving from its institutionalised and authoritative procedure, in which legal norms are agreed, enacted, interpreted and implemented, action disputes are resolved in accordance with manifested and accepted criteria and mechanism, and legal rights and duties are determined by, reflected on and amended by all affected legal consociates.[25]

In addition, while the universalistic orientation of the modern moral consciousness observes no limit in the boundary of its application, it also disregards the discrepancies between uncontested moral demands and organisational or physical constraints. In this respect, law is reflexive in its own jurisdictional power since it contains secondary

---

[22] *Ibid.*, pp. 106–7, 110.
[23] *Ibid.*, p. 113.
[24] *Ibid.*, emphasis in the original.
[25] *Ibid.*, p. 13.

rules that serve the production of primary rules for guiding behaviour.[26] 'In contrast to naturally emergent rules, whose validity can be judged solely from the moral point of view, legal norms have an artificial character', Habermas contends, 'they constitute an intentionally produced layer of action norms that are reflexive in the sense of being applicable to themselves'.[27]

While post-traditional morality is universalistic in orientation because it provides a critical and impartial perspective to evaluate morally relevant action, 'law does not regulate interaction contexts *in general* but serves as a medium for the self-organisation of legal communities that maintain themselves in their social environment under particular historical conditions'.[28] As a result, any society that wants to regulate its common life by means of law cannot fully separate the question concerning normative regulation of behavioural expectations from questions concerning collective goal setting. This is another major difference between law and morality, and leads to an expansion of the type of considerations relevant for legal and political law-making, because both ethical and pragmatic reasons, in addition to moral ones, have to be considered.[29]

One way to demonstrate this difference is to look at the question of equality before the law. While both moral and legal rules are general in the sense of equally and fairly applicable to all people involved, moral norms are directed to every person, but legal statutes only address the members of the particular legal community concerned. As Habermas says,

> *The material or substantive equality in law* — which accords equal treatment to equal cases — is not wholly a question of justice ... Legal material touches on collective goals and goods in a way that allows questions bearing on the concrete form of life to arise, if not questions of shared identity as well ... [T]he participants must not only clarify what is equally good for every citizen but also determine who they

---

[26] *Ibid.*, pp. 114–18.
[27] *Ibid.*, p. 111.
[28] *Ibid.*, pp. 151–2, emphasis in the original.
[29] *Ibid.*, p. 152.

are as members of a political community and how they would like to live. Moreover, the goals they choose in the light of strong evaluations confront them with the question of how they can best achieve these goals. The sphere of justice questions thus expands to take in problems of achieving self-understanding and questions of the rational choice of means — and naturally problems of balancing interests that cannot be generalised but call instead for fair compromises.[30]

In justifying legal norms, therefore, moral, ethical (in the sense of coming to a self-understanding about a particular conception of the good) and pragmatic (in the sense of seeking suitable means for realising given goals and preferences) justifications will all be used, thus making it clear that the question of the validity of legal norms cannot be directly derived from morality, though they should be compatible with our moral consciousness.[31] Furthermore, the Kantian requirement in Habermas's conception of law — that coercive law can maintain its legitimate and socially integrative function only if the addressees of the law are at the same time the rational authors of it — together with his emphasis on mutual understanding among social participants in communicative action also brings home the fact that we cannot equate legal self-legislation to moral self-legislation; for apart from the fact that the procedural and communicative perspective of Habermas's theory requires a participant dimension to determine the actual outcome in legal and political self-legislation,

> it is not just the legal form alone that distinguishes political from moral self-legislation, but the contingency of the form of life, of the goals and interest positions establishing the identity of the self-determining political will in advance.[32]

With these differences in mind, it is now clear that while the moral principle acts as a rule of argumentation to ensure that 'equal consideration is given to the interests of all those who are possibly involved', the principle of democratic legal self-legislation

---

[30] *Ibid.*, pp. 154–5, emphasis in the original.
[31] *Ibid.*, pp. 158–62.
[32] *Ibid.*, p. 157.

explains the performative meaning of the practice of self-determination [through an institutionalised legal process] on the part of legal consociates who recognise one another as free and equal members of an association they have joined voluntarily.[33]

The existence of contingent elements in particularistic forms of life and collective goals in concrete legal and political communities points to the fact that important issues arise from Habermas's legal and political theory which relate to his idea of constitutional patriotism and the question of nationalism. A closer examination of these issues reveals that there are problems and tensions in the relation between the universalistic orientation and the contingent and particularistic elements in Habermas's legal and political theory, and especially in its application to his idea of constitutional patriotism. The idea of constitutional patriotism will be discussed later in this chapter, and in the concluding one, in the context of civil order and globalisation, but the fact that this idea is ultimately derived from Habermas's thesis of the co-originality of private and public autonomy in a discursive democracy makes us to first examine this theoretically more fundamental question in the next section.[34]

---

[33] This is what Habermas calls the 'discourse principle', which is neutral to morality and law. See *ibid.*, pp. 108, 110.
[34] For some of Habermas's most relevant works on nationalism or patriotism, see his 'Citizenship and National Identity', in *Between Facts and Norms*, Appendix II; 'Historical Consciousness and Post-Traditional Identity: The Federal Republic's Orientation to the West' in *The New Conservatism: Cultural Criticism and the Historians' Debate*, ed. and trans. Shierry Weber Nicholsen, Cambridge: Polity, 1989, chapter 10; 'Overcoming the Past' in *New Left Review*, No. 203, Jan./Feb. 1994, pp. 3–16; 'The European Nation-State: On the Past and Future of Sovereignty and Citizenship', in *The Inclusion of the Other: Studies in Political Theory*, eds Ciaran Cronin and Pablo De Greiff, Cambridge, Massachusetts: The MIT Press, 1998, chapter 8; and 'What is a People?' and 'The Postnational Constellation and the Future of Democracy', both in *The Postnational Constellation: Political Essays*, chapters 1 and 4 respectively. For a good criticism of Habermas's constitutional patriotism, see Margaret Canovan, 'Patriotism is Not Enough', in *British Journal of Political Science*, No. 30, 2000, pp. 413–32. Also see Canovan's *Nationhood and Political Theory*, Cheltenham: Edward Edgar, 1996.

The Co-originality of Private and Public Autonomy

The coeval relationship between law and morality, according to Habermas, forecloses the possibility of justifying legal validity by means of morality, but the self-justifying nature of Habermas's modern law is not legal positivism; for law, to Habermas, is not the result of the habitual obedience to the commands of the sovereign by the subject. Instead, the legally institutionalised procedure is self-justifying and self-regulating mainly because it must embody the conditions both for the protection of legal consociates' negative liberties and for their positive rights to participation in legislation, and it is this, not the form of law as such, that makes law legitimate.

On the face of it, in the light of the discursive nature of the theory of communicative action, it appears natural that Habermas will put the positive rights of political participation first; for without such participation, it is difficult to envisage how addressees of law can at the same time become the authors of law through a rational and discursive law-making process. However, this one-sided formulation is rejected by Habermas, who insists that while 'the scope of citizen's public autonomy is not restricted by natural or moral rights just waiting to be put into effect', it does not follow that the 'individual's private autonomy [is] merely instrumentalised for the purpose of popular sovereignty'.[35] This has to be the case, for the rights to political participation must be guaranteed 'in such a way that provides each person with equal chances to exercise the communicative freedom to take a position on criticisable validity claims'.[36] These private rights of equal freedoms and protection are 'enabling conditions' to facilitate an individual's public autonomy and as such are presupposed by the discursive political process and 'cannot *restrict* the legislator's sovereignty, even though they are not at her disposition'.[37]

The co-original and interactive nature of private and public autonomy comes out perhaps most clearly when

---
[35] *Between Facts and Norms*, p. 127.
[36] *Ibid.*
[37] *Ibid.*, p. 128, emphasis in the original.

Habermas discusses the different paradigms of law and models of democracy. The Lockean or liberal model that gives priority to the protection of subjective individual rights encounters, according to Habermas, both theoretical and empirical problems. Theoretically, liberal subjective rights are pre-political rights presumed to exist before the individual engages in the legal and political process. Such an understanding not only fails to appreciate the post-metaphysical nature of modern society, it has also arbitrarily removed individual subjective rights from the political process, thus impoverishing the integrative and communicative nature of the political.

Empirically, the right of each person to do as he or she pleases within the limits of general laws is legitimate only under the condition that these laws in practice really guarantee equal treatment of the individuals concerned. However, the formal and abstract nature of the laws under the liberal paradigm fails to take account of the actual social condition in which material inequalities are everywhere to be seen, and the market process cannot on its own bring about a social equilibrium to satisfy genuinely equal treatment for all. As a result, Habermas rejects the one-sided emphasis on private autonomy.

To reject the one-sided emphasis on private autonomy does not mean to undermine the importance of such autonomy. Habermas criticises the social welfare paradigm of law, in which the government uses legal means to interfere with the social and political process in order to ensure material equality among the citizens, as a kind of moral paternalism undermining individual autonomy.[38] Similarly, the one-sided emphasis on public autonomy is

[38] As Habermas says in his 'Paradigms of Law', 'The welfare-state provides services and apportions life opportunities by guaranteeing social security, health care, housing, income provisions; education, leisure, and the natural bases of life, it grants each person the material basis for a humanly dignified existence. A welfare state with such overwhelming provisions, however, almost inevitably tends to impose supposedly 'normal' patterns of behaviour on its clients. This normalising pressure obviously runs the risk of impairing individual autonomy, precisely the autonomy it is supposed to promote by providing the factual preconditions for the equal opportunity to

equally untenable. Against the communitarian reading of the republican model of democracy, Habermas argues that political participation by the citizens as such is not enough, for if such participation is premised on 'an *ethical constriction of political discourse*' in which political questions are being restricted to the type of ethical questions in which citizens ask themselves who they are and who they would like to be, it depends too much on the virtue of the citizens' devotion to the public weal, and fails to appreciate the diversity and complexity of modern society.[39] In the end, such an ethical reading will not only instrumentalise the private autonomy of the citizens for the so-called 'common good', it will also ignore the need to accommodate different conceptions of the good favoured by different sectors of the community by an open and rational deliberative political process, thus replacing the political by the ethical.

Habermas's co-originality thesis is nothing if not controversial. As Simone Chambers observes, many critics have difficulties in accepting this thesis and insist that Habermas should come down either on the side of human rights or political participation, though there appears to be an even split about which side he should choose.[40] To republican-communitarian theorists like Frank I. Michelman, by refusing to grant primacy to the right to political participation to those whose search for a normative political order ultimately depends on a shared substantive ethical life, Habermas is 'a closet rights fundamentalist'.[41] To Michelman, Habermas's contention is untenable because the concrete content and shape of the private rights of those so-called 'free and equal individuals' do not exist *a priori*, for only by participation in a shared form of life can they validly decide what constitutes, in a constitutional state gov-

---

exercise negative freedoms.' See *Habermas on Law and Democracy*, p. 17.
[39] See Habermas, 'Three Normative Models of Democracy', pp. 3–6.
[40] See Simone Chambers, 'Can Procedural Democracy be Radical?', in *The Political*, ed. David Ingram, Oxford: Blackwell, 2002, p. 188.
[41] *Ibid.*, p. 188.

erned by the rule of law, these subjective freedoms of the individual.[42]

For liberals like Charles Larmore, however, in the contest between individual rights and popular sovereignty, 'at bottom Habermas unmistakably privileges the second of these values', for as 'enabling conditions', individual rights are ultimately only a set of necessary means for the realisation of the autonomous wills of the individuals in democratic self-rule who 'can regard themselves as legitimately bound by the rules of political association only to the extent that these rules spring from no higher source than the citizens themselves'.[43]

As a principle for democratic self-rule (rather than as a moral principle), it can be argued that Habermas is right to insist that individual rights and political participation are co-original, in the sense that each of them presupposes the other so as to fulfil the democratic requirement of enabling the addressees of legal and political rules to be at the same time authors of those rules. In other words, both individual rights and political participation require each other as constitutive conditions for the procedure of deliberative

[42] *Ibid.*, p. 181. See also Frank I. Michelman's 'Family Quarrel', in *Habermas on Law and Democracy*, in which (on pp. 321-2) Michelman argues, '[c]onstitutionalism requires enactment *at the originary level* of what are called *laws*, because constitutionalism *means* a rule of law, a government of laws. "Laws" correspondingly mean resolutions that can *rule*, which is to say the laws can effectively govern the actions of secondary appliers. Required, in other words, are originary resolutions that not only are nondiscrimatorily general but also *already carry significations sufficiently concrete to bind and constrain their addressees* ... What a constitutionalist originary justificational discourse must justify, then, is always a resolution already concrete enough to constrain, decisively enough to satisfy that hard-won prudence of separated powers, a *post*-originary legal discourse of application. For resolutions of that character, republicanism maintains, persuasive justification is inconceivable without reference to an ethical context', (emphasis in the original). That is why to Michelman, Habermas's insistence on the context-independent and universalistic character of the subjective rights of the individuals is inconceivable.

[43] See Charles Larmore's, 'The Foundations of Modern Democracy: Reflections of Jurgen Habermas', in Larmore, *The Morals of Modernity*, Cambridge: Cambridge University Press, 1996, pp. 217-18.

democracy: neither one of them can just use the other as a means (i.e. as a dispensable or derivative condition) to achieve its own aims. This defence notwithstanding, it will be argued in the concluding sections of this chapter that a closer examination of Habermas's concept of public autonomy shows that the relationship between his ideas of communicative power and the political public sphere in the constitutional state is very ambiguous, casting doubt on whether his theory of deliberative democracy can ultimately and adequately fulfil his ambitious claim to support a pluralistic political order with socially integrative and legitimate laws agreed by all rational and legal consociates.

The Co-originality Thesis: Political, Not Moral

The fundamental point to start with in Habermas's co-originality thesis is that it is a *political* principle for democratic self-rule; in other words, it is meant to bring with it the legal institutionalisation of a decision-making process for democratic social integration. This should be distinguished from the moral principle of discourse, which, unlike the political-democratic principle, is not (according to Habermas) an action system, but a knowledge-based symbolic system.[44] Some of the criticisms of the co-originality thesis are misguided precisely because the critics appear to forget that Habermas is talking about the decision-making procedure in a democracy rather than about moral discourse as such.

As discussed in the section 'Law and morality' in this chapter, the democratic self-rule discourse, as a political process, occurs in the context of a concrete legal-political community with some kind of shared ethical identity and collective goals. As such, when it comes to the question of justifying the legal and political norms in such a community, the kinds of validity claims involved will not be lim-

---

[44] 'Postmetaphysical morality represents only a form of cultural *knowledge*, whereas law has, in addition to this, a binding character at the institutional level. Law is not only a symbolic system but an action system as well.' See *Between Facts and Norms*, p. 107, emphasis in the original.

ited to questions of justice or abstract impartiality only, but will also relate to concrete ethical questions about the collective identity of the community and to pragmatic questions of efficiency and fair compromise. What Habermas insists upon, in the question of individual rights in a legal-political community, is not that there should be one *a priori* pre-political form of rights applicable to all communities irrespective of their historical and social contexts;[45] rather, he is saying that no matter what concrete forms these rights adopted in a community through a democratic discursive procedure take, they must satisfy the constitutive presupposition that individuals are legally protected as free and equal citizens in that particular community, to enable them to participate in undistorted political discourses for self-legislation and determination.[46] The accusation, therefore, by republican or communitarian critics that Habermas' co-originality thesis ignores the ethical context of a community is unjustified, and to characterise Habermas as 'a closet rights fundamentalist' is certainly an exaggeration, if not bizarre, for the individual legal rights required by the co-originality thesis are not only sensitive to the context of the concrete community concerned, they are presupposed (but not instrumentalised) by the democratic discursive process of a political community, in so far as that community wants to ensure an undistorted political procedure of self-determination for its citizens.

Liberals like Larmore, on the other hand, are unhappy with the fact that in Habermas's political theory individual rights are not there mainly to protect individuals against possible encroachments by state power or the collective will of the community. They believe that this is so because ultimately Habermas wants to see popular sovereignty as the sole normative foundation of the modern democratic state,

---

[45] For a discussion of why human rights, as legal-political rights, should not be confused with moral rights, see Habermas, 'Kant's Idea of Perpetual Peace', in *The Inclusion of the Other*, chapter 7.
[46] See Habermas's reply to Michelman, in *Habermas on Law and Democracy*, pp. 389–90.

making the collective will of the citizens the only source of the norms that bind them.[47]

On the face of it, the legal institutionalisation of individual rights in Habermas's deliberative democratic theory is there to protect individuals from any illegal or illegitimate encroachments by the state or other entities, for those rights are there to protect the individual right-bearer's freedoms. In fact, Habermas goes even further when he says that individual rights are there to allow right-bearers to decide individually, without any concern about whether so doing is acceptable to others. 'This is why', Habermas contends,

> we can understand the private autonomy of a legal subject essentially as the negative freedom to withdraw from the public space of illocutionary obligations to a position of mutual observation and influence. Private autonomy extends as far as the legal subject does *not* have to give others an account or give publicly acceptable reasons for her action plans. Legally granted liberties entitle one to *drop out of* communicative action, to refuse illocutionary obligations; they ground a privacy freed from the burden of reciprocally acknowledged and mutually expected communicative freedoms.[48]

In other words, individual rights are not there serving merely as instruments of political participation; their value as a protection of the negative freedom of individuals is quite distinct.[49]

But as a democratic principle, even though it must presuppose the validity of the private autonomy of the citizens, the political context is such that it is required to regulate interpersonal conduct in such a way that addressees of coercive law must at the same time be the authors of such law. As a result, any genuinely political principle that takes the value of democracy seriously must go beyond the protection of private autonomy and presuppose the validity of free and equal political participation by the citizens as

---

[47] See Larmore, *The Morals of Modernity*, p. 218.
[48] Habermas, *Between Facts and Norms*, p. 120, emphasis in the original.
[49] See William Rehg's clear-headed analysis in this regard in his 'Against Subordination: Morality, Discourse, and Decision in the Legal Theory of Jurgen Habermas', in *Habermas on Law and Democracy*, chapter 12.

a whole. Thus the discursive-deliberative model of Habermas's democracy must not be satisfied with the liberal claim of the primacy of individual rights; instead, it must argue for the mutual presupposition of private and public autonomy. In this respect, although it is reasonable to follow the liberals to argue that while the legal-institutional protection of individual rights in a democracy must be regarded as absolute, in order to ensure that the citizens concerned genuinely are free and equal individuals in the polity, and in order for them to be the authors (not just addressees) of the rules governing their common spheres, supporters of deliberative democracy must go a step further to insist that individuals must also have the rights to political participation *at the same time* to shape the development of legal and political institutions. Only the mutual presupposition of these two aspects of their rights will ensure that the participatory process of the democracy concerned is undistorted, thus satisfying the communicative rationality presupposed in Habermas's social and political theory. Larmore is therefore unconvincing when he argues that Habermas's idea of democratic self-rule 'depends on an unacknowledged premise expressing an antecedent moral commitment and affirming indeed the existence of a fundamental individual right'.[50]

Viewed from this perspective, it is clear that Habermas's co-originality thesis of private and public autonomy presupposes a conception of the individual whose self must be respected as an end in itself yet at the same time must be allowed to be the co-author of all legitimate rules governing the political process in the society. This will be further considered in the section 'The individual as an end and the need for mutual respect', where we will be seeking to understand the kind of autonomous individuals implied by Habermas's social and political theory.

---

[50] Larmore, *The Morals of Modernity*, p. 219. Likewise, Ulrich K. Preuss's concern, that Habermas's theory may bring about the dire consequence of forcing the individuals to communicate, is equally one-sided. See Preuss, 'Communicative Power and the Concept of Law', in *Habermas on Law and Democracy*, p. 335.

Equally important, however, is that the discursive and deliberative model of law required by the co-originality thesis points to a kind of state constitutionalism in which human rights and political participation are regarded as the common political bond for all legal consociates within the polity. At the same time cultural diversity within this political community will be respected as long as it is compatible with the common political bond of the community. Habermas believes that properly understood, this kind of constitutionalism, or what he also calls 'constitutional patriotism', can be developed into a kind of normative resource to anchor the people's political loyalty to the constitutional state, as well as to a public identity that goes beyond the nation-state, for the ability of the nation-state to continue to inspire political loyalty is increasingly called into question by problems created by multiculturalism and globalisation. A closer look at Habermas's idea of constitutional patriotism will follow in the next section.

Constitutional Patriotism as the Political Bond in the Age of Post-traditional Society[51]

Habermas's co-originality thesis has elevated human rights and political participation to the status of being the two main pillars of constitutionalism. Both these pillars (or the private and public autonomy of the citizens concerned) are individualistic in nature, for the former ensures a private domain for every individual free from all illegitimate interferences, while the latter creates conditions for every citizen to be the co-author of all legitimate rules of conduct for the society. Although Habermas rightly points out that '[a] con-

[51] This section will concentrate mainly on the theoretical problems related to Habermas's idea of constitutional patriotism. The historically specific context which leads Habermas to develop this idea will not be touched upon due to the scope of this study. For a good study of this context, see Jan-Werner Muller, *Another Country: German Intellectuals, Unification and National Identity*, New Haven and London: Yale University Press, 2000. Noel O'Sullivan also provides us with a succinct and interesting historical and theoretical background of the debate of constitutional patriotism in post-1945 Germany in chapter 4 of his *European Political Thought Since 1945*, Hampshire and New York: Palgrave MacMillan, 2004.

stitution can be thought of as a historical project that each generation of citizens continues to pursue',[52] he is also keenly aware of the fact that from a normative point of view, 'the social boundaries of an association of free and equal consociates under law are perfectly contingent', for in the real world 'who gains the power to define the boundaries of a political community is settled by historical chance and the actual course of events—normally, by the arbitrary outcomes of wars or civil wars'.[53]

In other words, while it is clear what constitute the indispensable normative principles regulating all free and equal legal consociates in a constitutional state, the co-originality thesis by itself does not directly settle the question of who in fact constitute the citizens of the state concerned, since both the elements of choice and chance are inevitably present here. Nor does it explain whether and why these citizens are willing to stick with the constitutional state through thick and thin, even to the extent of risking their lives to protect it.

At one time, particularly since the French Revolution in the history of Europe, the nation-state appeared to provide a convincing answer to the question of what constitutes a people, while at the same time maintaining the political solidarity of the community. For, on the one hand, the nation, understood in the pre-political sense of an ethnic community integrated geographically and/or culturally by a common language, customs and traditions, seems to be able to provide a natural source of social integration, whilst, on the other hand, the struggle for more civil rights by the common people against the nobility provides the source of democratic legitimation for political integration, thus turning the so-called 'naturally formed ethnic people' into democratic citizens. In short, nationalism and democracy may join hands under certain happy circumstances to solve these two problems (i.e. what is a people, and the bond of political solidarity) at once by providing a homogeneous cul-

---

[52] See Habermas, 'Struggles for Recognition in the Democratic Constitutional State', in *The Inclusion of the Other*, p. 203.
[53] See Habermas, 'The European Nation-State: On the Past and Future of Sovereignty and Citizenship', in *The Inclusion of the Other*, p. 116.

tural/national background for democratic participation.[54] However, owing to a number of conceptual as well as empirical considerations, Habermas does not believe that the nation-state is necessarily sustainable in the post-traditional world.

The fundamental problem in this connection is that the universalistic conception of an egalitarian and participatory legal community (as required by the co-originality thesis) and the particularistic presupposition of a community united by pre-political and naturalistic bonds are being uneasily joined together to form the concept of the national state. While this tension 'remains harmless as long as a cosmopolitan understanding of the nation of citizens is accorded priority over an ethnocentric interpretation of the nation' in the constitutional state,[55] it is not difficult to detect that the cosmopolitan understanding required by the co-originality thesis is implicitly denied and endangered when 'the integrative force of the nation of citizens is traced back to the prepolitical fact of quasi-natural people, that is, to something independent of and prior to the political opinion-and will-formation of the citizens themselves'.[56]

The tension between the cosmopolitan and the ethnocentric understanding of the nation of citizens is not just about universalism and particularism. More fundamentally, the cosmopolitan understanding presupposes the necessity and possibility of shared rules and procedures, in accordance with which the participants can try to iron out their differences and arrive at a commonly accepted conclusion through communicative action and political participation, with the process of participation and communication regarded as constitutive of the resultant consensus of the political community. The ethnocentric understanding, however, assumes that the pre-political entity of the nation is a natural fact whose integrative power is pre-given or

[54] *Ibid.*, p. 111. Gellner offers a not dissimilar analysis of the same question in his discussion of nationalism. See the section 'Civil or National Society?' in chapter 2 of this book.
[55] Habermas, 'The European Nation-State: On the Past and Future of Sovereignty and Citizenship, p. 115.
[56] *Ibid.*

pre-destined and that the main political task is simply to identify this entity and ensure that it is free to establish itself as a state.

One manifestation of this tension and its potential danger, as suggested by Habermas, is how differently the question of 'the freedom of the nation' will be construed by these two different understandings. When adopting the universalistic and egalitarian approach, the nation of citizens

> may indeed be patriots who understand and uphold their constitution as an achievement in the context of the history of their country. But they construe the freedom of the nation—following Kant—in cosmopolitan terms, namely, as the authorization and obligation to enter into cooperative agreements or to establish a balance of interests with other nations within the framework of a peaceful federation (*Volkerbund*).

In contrast, however, if the ethnocentric approach is being adopted,

> [t]he naturalistic conception of the nation as a prepolitical entity ... suggests a different interpretation, according to which the freedom of the nation consists essentially in its ability to assert its independence by military means if necessary. Like private persons in the market, peoples pursue their respective interests in the free-for-all of international power politics. The traditional image of external sovereignty is dressed up in national colors and in this guise awakens new energies.[57]

Habermas, however, like Gellner, does not believe that national consciousness is something naturally endowed or given, for 'collective identities are made, not found', and the so-called 'unity of the cultural nation' is the result of the propaganda and imagination of many of the writers, historians, scholars and intellectuals of the people concerned in the course of nation building in the history of the nineteenth and twentieth centuries.[58] Unfortunately, the history of European imperialism and nationalism of the past two centuries appears to point to the fact that

---

[57] *Ibid.*, p. 114.
[58] Habermas, 'What is a People?', in *The Postnational Constellation*, p. 19.

the idea of the nation did not so much reinforce the loyalty of the population to the constitutional state but more often served as an instrument to mobilize the masses for political goals that can scarcely be reconciled with republican principles.[59]

As a result, again in agreement with Gellner, Habermas thinks that the relationship between nationalism and democracy is at most 'merely a transitional, historical constellation', and 'nationalism is not a necessary or permanent precondition of a democratic process'.[60] It follows that the tension inherent in this artefact — that is the national state — if left unchecked, may challenge Habermas's idea of a constitutional state based upon the co-originality of human rights and political participation, and theoretically speaking, 'only a nonnaturalistic concept of the nation can be combined seamlessly with the universalistic self-understanding of the democratic constitutional state'.[61]

As a result, when it comes to the question of political solidarity in democracy, Habermas's proposed discursive and proceduralist model of constitutionalism must learn to stand on its own feet. The political will-formation and public communication process, in other words, must somehow embed the legally institutionalised role of the citizens in a political culture imbued with the concept of freedom — a culture which pervades social integration and structures it in a way that is not incompatible with the universalistic principles of constitutional democracy.[62] This, in short, is the theoretical reason that drives Habermas to develop his idea of constitutional patriotism.

Critics of constitutional patriotism are quick to point out that the universalistic democratic principles presupposed

---

[59] Habermas, 'The European Nation-State: On the Past and Future of Sovereignty and Citizenship', pp. 105 and 116.
[60] See Habermas, 'On the Relation between the Nation, the Rule of Law, and Democracy', in *The Inclusion of the Other*, p. 132.
[61] Habermas, 'The European Nation-State: On the Past and Future of Sovereignty and Citizenship', p. 115.
[62] Also see Habermas, 'Citizenship and National Identity: Some Reflections on the Future of Europe', in *Theorizing Citizenship*, ed. Ronald Beiner, Albany: State University of New York Press, 1995, pp. 256–64.

by it are too thin a bond to sustain citizens' political solidarity in a political community, for, as Margaret Canovan points out,

> the claim that an impartial state can form a benign umbrella soaring above rival national or ethnic identities and attracting patriotic loyalty ignores the most crucial political question. Where is the state to draw its power from? What holds up the umbrella?[63]

To these queries Habermas might well reply that he finds no reason to support the claim that while it was possible for the idea of ethnic nation as an artefact in the ninteenth and twentieth centuries to create a mode of solidarity between persons who were initially strangers, it is inherently impossible for a postnational political identity to create a political bond among democratic citizens in an age of cultural diversity and plurality.[64] The existence of the United States of America as a multicultural society united by a common political culture and the possibility being considered by the European Union of admitting an Islamic country like Turkey are evidence that Habermas's aspiration to develop his idea of constitutional patriotism into a supranational political bond for democratic citizens is not doomed from the start.[65]

Other common criticisms of constitutional patriotism are also inconclusive. For instance, the claim that a state endorsing constitutional patriotism must necessarily be turned into 'a kind of confessional state', in the sense that a serious attempt must be made to inculcate the constitutional principles into the citizens concerned, fails to appreciate the need for the citizens to be the co-authors of these principles in the first place, as required by Habermas's co-originality thesis.[66] Also, the fact that these principles must be the outcome of a fair and open political procedure (in which power and bargaining are involved) participated in by all should also

---

[63] See Canovan, 'Patriotism is Not Enough', p. 423.
[64] Habermas, 'What is a People?', pp. 14–19.
[65] See *The Economist*, 'Turkey and the European Union: The Coming Crescent', 9 October 2004, p. 13.
[66] See Canovan, 'Patriotism is Not Enough', p. 420.

help to clear up the misunderstanding that constitutional patriotism presupposes the absence of conflict, and hence of politics, by its reliance on communicative reason and action.[67] This will become clear if we look into Habermas's conception of communicative power, which will be discussed in a later section of this chapter.

In any event, Habermas believes that the challenges posed by multiculturalism (created by increasing international exchanges and large-scale immigration over the years) and by globalisation in this post-traditional world have created problems that can no longer be solved within the framework of nation-states, for a culturally pluralistic society cannot rely on a homogeneous national/pre-political culture for social integration, and the progressive undermining of nation-states' ability to deal with the power of international capital and environmental problems (such as acid rain and global warming) has called for theoretical as well as political responses on the supranational level. On both counts, Habermas thinks that his procedural approach to human rights and equal political participation makes his idea of discursive democracy better equipped than other political forms to handle problems of this kind. The question of globalisation and constitutional patriotism will be discussed in the concluding chapter of this book. This section will take a closer look at the case of multicultural societies and constitutional patriotism.

Thanks to its procedural properties, Habermas contends that the democratic process has rendered a previous background consensus constructed on the basis of cultural homogeneity superfluous, for the public, discursively structured process of opinion- and will-formation may not only make a reasonable political understanding possible even among strangers, but also, if necessary, fill any gap that opens in social integration and generate a common political culture to serve as the political bond that binds the

---

[67] See O'Sullivan, *European Political Thought Since 1945*, pp. 115–16.

culturally heterogeneous population together in the larger political community.[68]

Habermas, however, is quick to add that multicultural societies can be held together by a political culture

> only if democratic citizenship pays off not only in terms of liberal individual rights and rights of political participation, but also in the enjoyment of social and cultural rights ... [for] democratic citizenship can only realize its integrative potential—that is, it can only found solidarity between strangers—if it proves itself as a mechanism that actually realizes the material conditions of preferred forms of life.[69]

In other words, multicultural societies require a politics of recognition

> because the identity of each individual citizen is woven together with collective identities, and must be stabilized in a network of mutual recognition. The individual's existential dependence on intersubjectively shared traditions and identity-forming communities explains why the integrity of the legal person cannot be secured without equal cultural rights in culturally differentiated societies.[70]

In short, while the solidarity of the citizens in multicultural societies could possibly be shifted onto the more abstract foundation of constitutional patriotism, this common political culture has to respect, recognise and provide reasonable material conditions for the right of each and every citizen of the political community to pursue his or her own individual, sub-cultural identity, provided that the sub-cultures do not override or contradict the need to maintain the more abstract, egalitarian and universalistic political culture shared by all. In return, the common political culture must remain neutral and decoupled from any of the sub-cultures identified by different groups of citizens within the political community. If this is deemed possible, then political solidarity no longer depends upon cultural or

---

[68] See Habermas, 'The Postnational Constellation and the Future of Democracy', pp. 73–4.
[69] Habermas, 'The European Nation-State: On the Past and Future of Sovereignty and Citizenship', pp. 118–19.
[70] Habermas, 'The Postnational Constellation and the Future of Democracy', p. 74.

national solidarity, and democratic citizens can maintain two identities simultaneously — namely to be both a fellow political participant in the political process and a stranger culturally to those who do not share his or her non-political collective identity.

The Individual as an End and the Need for Mutual Respect

The conditions constituting mutual understanding as required in communicative action and the co-originality of private and public autonomy presuppose that there is no such thing as an isolated, abstract individual in Habermas's conception of the human person. Instead, 'it takes entrance in the public sphere of a linguistic community for a natural creature to develop into both an individual and a person endowed with reason'.[71] The mutual understanding requirement in communicative action already implies that one must treat the individual as an end in himself or herself, for unlike strategic action, communicative rationality can only be achieved in an intersubjective manner, for if one treats another person only as a means or an instrument for the satisfaction of his or her own ends, the latter person in effect is regarded by the first person more or less as an object only, not as a second person whose intention is to be understood and whose agreement is to be sought in order to arrive at mutual understanding. As Habermas says,

> [e]ven in cases of conflict, the persons involved are to go on interacting in an attitude of communicative action. They are to attune themselves, from the participant perspective

---

[71] See Habermas, *The Future of Human Nature*, Cambridge: Polity Press, 2003, p. 35. This latest work by Habermas contains some very illuminating discussion of the possible moral problems of genetic engineering from a Kantian perspective, and sheds a lot of light on Habermas's conception of the individual as presupposed by his social and political theory. However, I have no intention of examining Habermas's extremely interesting contribution to the debate about how the further development of genetic engineering may affect the ethical self-understanding of the human individual, as this would go beyond the scope of my study here. See also Habermas, 'An Argument Against Human Cloning: Three Replies', in *The Postnational Constellation: Political Essays*, chapter 8.

of a first person, to the other as a second person, with the intention of reaching an understanding with him instead of reifying and instrumentalizing him, in the observer perspective of a third person, for their own ends.[72]

Further still, the intersubjective and participatory nature of communicative action, apart from presupposing that every person should be treated as an end and never simply as a means by the others, implies that becoming a human person is inevitably also a socialising process:

> Individuation, as a part of life history, is an outcome of socialization. For the organism to become, with birth, a person in the full sense of this term, an act of social individuation is required, that is, integration in the *public* context of interaction of an intersubjectively shared lifeworld.[73]

As an end in itself, the human individual must not be instrumentalised; the human self should be inviolable as such. However, the capacity to become human is to be achieved 'through the socializing medium of thick linguistic communication' in the intersubjectively shared lifeworld.[74] The unique and social aspects of the individual are therefore interconnected in Habermas's individual, and to treat such an individual as an end in itself implies that an individual is fully respected by others only if his or her private autonomy, sub-cultural identity, and personal preferences are sufficiently protected from intrusion by others so long as they do not contradict others' private and public autonomy, and their co-authorship and participation in any communicative act of mutual understanding or agreement are facilitated adequately. To treat every person as an end in itself therefore means to respect his or her individual self and to respect others in their intersubjective and communi-

---

[72] Habermas, *The Future of Human Nature*, p. 55.
[73] *Ibid.*, p. 34, emphasis in the original. For a fuller discussion of the relation between individuation and socialisation, see Habermas, 'Individuation through Socialization: On George Herbert Mead's Theory of Subjectivity', in Habermas, *Postmetaphysical Thinking: Philosophical Essays*, Cambridge, Massachusetts and London: The MIT Press, 1992, trans. William Mark Hohengarten, chapter 7.
[74] Habermas, *The Future of Human Nature*, p. 54.

cative dealings in the world. Individual autonomy and mutual respect are therefore inseparable:

> On the one hand, there is the nature of the person 'being an end in itself' who as an inexchangeable individual is supposed to be capable of leading a life of his own; on the other hand, there is the equal respect which everybody in his quality as a person is entitled to. Therefore, the universality of moral norms ensuring equal treatment for all cannot be an abstracted one; it has to be sensitive to the individual situations and life-projects of every single person.[75]

In the social and legal context, to be sensitive to the individual situations and life-projects of every single person requires us to observe private and public autonomy of the legal consociates at the same time, and the participation and agreement of all the individuals concerned are required if we want to arrive at legitimate arrangements for regulating the interpersonal dealings in the society without undermining individual autonomy and mutual respect for all.

Political Participation, Rational Consensus and Majority Rule

Properly understood, Habermas's proceduralist paradigm of law and democracy is derived from his understanding of communicative action and communicative rationality, and is meant to be applicable to pluralistic and post-traditional society in order to facilitate social and political integration by legally institutionalising the private and public autonomy of the citizens in open, fair and undistorted discourses for the determination and resolution of public issues, the results of which are translated into legitimate laws and binding regulations. The persuasive force of Habermas's position is partly derived from the discursive intuition that since there is no privileged position for the comprehensive validation of religious and ethical beliefs which could regulate interpersonal relationship in post-metaphysical condi-

---

[75] *Ibid.*, p. 56. Likewise, in 'Struggles for Recognition in the Democratic State', Habermas says, '[a] correctly understood theory of rights requires a politics of recognition that protects the integrity of the individual in the life contexts in which his or her identity is formed.' See Habermas, *The Inclusion of the Other*, p. 208.

tions, action norms will be regarded as valid only if all those who are possibly affected can agree as participants in rational discourses.[76] The performative requirement of translating this discursive principle or intuition into socially integrative institutions for free and equal individuals cannot rely on morality alone; instead, the political procedure of democratic self-rule and the legislative procedure of institutionalising regulative norms in binding decisions and laws are required. But is it realistic, given the pluralism of modern society, to require that legally and politically binding decisions should be the result of a rational consensus of all involved?

The simple answer to this question is a clear no, for in the real world, rational unanimity is rarely observed in political, even democratic, decision-making. But this does not refute Habermas's theory, for he can argue that the failure to achieve rational unanimity is not due to any inherent defect of his discourse theory, but is normally the result of circumstantial and contingent limitations (e.g. time constraints in a decision-making situation or imperfect knowledge at a particular point in time) that are difficult to avoid in practice. Overall, it is fair to say that Habermas appreciates the practical difficulties involved in this respect and does not insist on rational unanimity as a democratic decision-making yardstick in practice. He is satisfied with majority rule provided that the preconditions for a rational and open political procedure are satisfied. One can see this quite clearly in his discussion of the nineteenth-century German democrat Julius Frobel's views on the relationship between consensus and majority rule.[77]

The crucial link connecting the requirement of rational consensus (namely that the addressee of binding rules should at the same time be the author of them) and majority rule in Frobel's formulation is, according to Habermas, that the latter must have the presumption of the former on its

---

[76] Habermas, *Between Facts and Norms*, p. 107.
[77] See Habermas, 'Popular Sovereignty as Procedure', in *Between Facts and Norms*, particularly pp. 474–7. A similar discussion can be found on pp. 304–6.

side by satisfying the rational procedural requirements of will-formation as far as possible:

> Consensus and majority rule are compatible only if the latter has an internal relation to the search for truth: public discourse must mediate between reason and will, between the opinion-formation of all and the majoritarian will-formation of the representatives.

A majority decision may come about only in such a way that its content is regarded as the rationally motivated but *fallible* result of an attempt to determine what is right through a discussion that has been brought to a *provisional* close under the pressure to decide.[78]

In other words, majority rule as a decision-making principle is acceptable only if it observes the same presupposed conditions of communicative action and rationality, even though circumstantial limitations like 'the pressure to decide' in an actual political situation mean that the communicative action has to be cut short in its pursuit of a mutual agreement among all the participants, and has to be satisfied instead with a provisional and fallible agreement of the majority. Habermas believes that while such a majority will is not identical with reason, it has the presumption of reason on its side. However, as this is only a provisional and fallible agreement, the minority is not required to resign its will or declare its opinion incorrect, though it will have to abide by the majority decision in the political sphere until it is able to persuade the majority to revise that provisional decision.[79]

But is the majority rule principle really compatible with rational unanimity? One obvious difference between the two is that for the latter the participants will submit only to the force of better argument in seeking rational agreement in the process of democratic self-rule, whereas for majority rule participants agree to subscribe to such a procedure *not* because of the force of better argument, but because of, among other things, the practical limitations imposed by the need to decide. As such, the minority is allowed to retain

---

[78] *Ibid.*, p. 475, emphasis in the original.
[79] *Ibid.*

its judgement irrespective of the fact that the majority conviction will prevail and the minority is required to observe the decisions passed by the majority until such decisions are revised by another majority decision.

If Habermas really takes his discourse theory seriously, why should he allow the intrusion of majority rule in the decision-making process, the justification for which does not, strictly speaking, depend on the force of better argument, but on the practical considerations that we must somehow have an acceptable mechanism to resolve differences in a timely manner, even when we fail to arrive at rational unanimity about political decisions and actions?

One possible defence Habermas could offer is that because of the complexity of modern politics, legal and political decision-making not only has to deal with practical constraints like time pressure, but also with issues involving non-generalisable interests that require compromises among the participants. In these respects, it is obvious that practical constraints and non-generalisable interests will render the achievement of rational unanimity improbable, if not impossible. As a result, the requirement of rational unanimity can only apply to these areas indirectly, in the sense that citizens could agree, through a meta-discourse, on a mechanism that they all think acceptable to deal with these kinds of decisions, and regard the results produced by this mechanism as binding. The mechanism of majority rule, designed in line with the requirement of equal and free participation for all citizens concerned, may therefore be found acceptable in that meta-discourse as a fair decision-making mechanism for the resolution of differences of this kind in a democracy.

This meta-discourse argument, however, does not quite do the trick. For one thing, contrary to what Habermas believes, majority rule as a decision-making process does not have an internal relation to the search for truth, for the outcomes of this rule may have more to do with practical considerations than with the force of better argument. In other words, the authority of majority rule rests less with rational unanimity than with the necessity to resolve unavoidable differences in real political matters. If consensus is compatible with majority rule only because of the latter's internal relation with rationality, this plainly is not the case.

The need to rely on mechanisms like majority rule to resolve political differences appears to point to the fact that in legal and political matters in a post-metaphysical society it is necessary to accept that people more often than not have to agree to disagree in order to maintain a stable social and political order. As such, what is important is not to strive for rational unanimity in decision-making; rather, there must be a common and accepted legal procedure that is sensitive to the unavoidable differences among the participants, yet is authoritative enough to command respect, and therefore encourage adherence to the outcomes produced by that procedure. In this regard, William E. Connolly criticises Habermas's aspiration to perfect consensus in legal-political matters on the ground that it 'understates the extent to which our limited resources of reason and evidence unavoidably generate a plurality of reasonable answers to perplexing practical questions'. Connolly goes on to argue that Habermas's theory

> fails to appreciate the creative role for politics in those persisting situations where public action must be taken and the resources of knowledge are insufficient to generate a single result. As an ideal, it aspires to take the heat out of the cauldron of contested interpretations and orientations to action. It is in this sense closer to a collectivisation of administration than to the democratisation of politics.[80]

Connolly is right to criticise Habermas's over-reliance on the resources of reason to settle legal and political disagreements, but it is not fair to say that Habermas fails to appreciate the creative role which it is possible for democratic politics to play. The problem with Habermas's discourse

---

[80] William E. Connolly, 'The Dilemma of Legitimacy', in his *Politics and Ambiguity*, Wisconsin: The University of Wisconsin Press, 1987, p. 88. See also Noel O'Sullivan, 'Power, Authority and Legitimacy: A Critique of Postmodern Political Thought', in *Political Theory in Transition*, ed. O'Sullivan, London and New York: Routledge, 2000, chapter 7.

theory of democracy lies rather in his ambition to square the circle of the Kantian moral ideal of rational unanimity with the political requirement of authoritative decision-making in legal and political matters.

Communicative Power, Legitimate Law and Administrative Power

In Habermas's discourse theory of democracy, law is the medium for ensuring social integration in the post-metaphysical world by the creation of a political order in which individuals are regarded as free and equal. Modern law can fulfil this normative task because it serves as an institutionalisation process in which the subjective rights of individuals and their political rights to participate are equally protected at the very beginning by the law, for the former is there to make sure that individuals are free and are able to participate in undistorted discourse and the latter is there to allow citizens to be the authors of the binding rules applicable to all. Law is legitimate to the extent that it embodies both private and public autonomy of the individuals.

From the perspective of public or political autonomy, citizens cannot just be the passive recipients of the legal arrangements decided by some authority above, for this amounts to some kind of paternalism not acceptable to the discourse theory of democracy; instead, as Habermas says, 'the production of legitimate law requires that the communicative freedom of citizens be mobilised'.[81] The mobilisation of the communicative freedom of citizens will, according to Habermas, give rise to a kind of power called 'communicative power', which is a discursively produced and inter-subjectively shared motivating force for the generation of legitimate law. A closer look at Habermas's concept of communicative power will show that he is, contrary to Connolly's criticism, very mindful of the creative force in the political system and in civil society and believes that legitimate law-making cannot do without such a creative

---

[81] Habermas, *Between Facts and Norms*, pp. 146–7.

power, though in the end his general political theory fails to explain the problematic relations between authority and power. But first, a fuller explanation of Habermas's concept of communicative power is in order.

Habermas's concept of communicative power is very much influenced by Hannah Arendt, whose view of power is different from Max Weber's classical formulation. 'In contrast to Weber, who sees the fundamental phenomenon of power as the probability that in a social relationship one can assert one's own will against opposition', says Habermas, 'Arendt views power as the potential of a *common will* formed in noncoercive communication.'[82] Indeed, in her little classic *On Violence*, Arendt defines power as 'the human ability not just to act but to act in concert'. For her, 'power is never the property of an individual; it belongs to a group and remains in existence only so long as the group keeps together'.[83] Power, according to Arendt and endorsed by Habermas, is a 'consensus-achieving force', and is opposed to violence, which is the physical strength of the individual or a group of individuals used for the instrumentalisation of another's will for one's own purpose.[84]

Having endorsed Arendt's concept of power, Habermas thinks that it is necessary to differentiate between the concept of political power as consensus-achieving communicative power on the one hand, and the effective implementation of collective binding decisions by administrative power on the other. It is clear that only the former is capable of generating legitimate law, for 'a communicative power of this kind can develop only in undeformed public spheres; it can issue only from structures of undamaged intersubjectivity found in nondistorted communication'.[85]

---

[82] *Ibid.*, p. 147, emphasis in the original.
[83] Hannah Arendt, *On Violence*, San Diego, New York and London: A Harvard/HBJ Book, 1969, p. 44.
[84] See 'Hannah Arendt: On the Concept of Power', by Habermas in his *Philosophical-Political Profiles*, trans. Frederick G. Lawrence, London: Heinemann, 1983, pp. 171–87, for a more thorough discussion of Arendt's concept of power by Habermas. Also *Between Facts and Norms*, p. 148, and *On Violence*, p. 46.
[85] Habermas, *Between Facts and Norms*, p. 148.

In other words, Habermas has incorporated Arendt's concept of power into his concept of communicative rationality (in which the quest for mutual understanding and rational unanimity is what is presupposed) and come up with the concept of communicative power, which is conceived as 'an *authorising* force' for the creation of legitimate law and for the founding of political institutions.[86]

A constitutional state, however, cannot be established by communicative power alone. The discursive formation of a common will to found legitimate rules and institutions is one thing, the implementation of collective binding decisions is quite another. So, according to Habermas, 'the concept of the political in its full sense *also* includes the use of administrative power within the political system, as well as the competition for access to that system. The constitution of a power code implies that an administrative system is steered through authorisations for rendering collectively binding decisions.' Legitimate law is therefore viewed by Habermas 'as the medium through which communicative power is translated into administrative power', and the idea of the constitutional state is interpreted 'as the requirement that the administrative system, which is steered through the power code, be tied to the lawmaking communicative power and kept free of illegitimate interventions of social power [such as market power and bureaucratic power]'.[87]

It is therefore clear that in Habermas's constitutional state there is a tripartite relationship between communicative

---

[86] *Ibid.*, emphasis in the original. For Arendt, according to Habermas, such power emerges in its purest form in those moments when revolutionaries seize the power scattered through the streets, when a population committed to passive resistance opposes foreign tanks with their bare hands, when convinced minorities dispute the legitimacy of existing laws and engage in civil disobedience and so on. However, as pointed out by O'Sullivan, one should note that Arendt's conception of the political is, in the end, largely elitist, and 'her willingness to disenfranchise members of the electorate who do not share her enthusiasm for the pursuit of immortality through action' makes her concept of power as a democratic force for the creation of legitimate law highly problematic. See Noel O'Sullivan, 'Difference and the Concept of the Political in Contemporary Political Philosophy', *Political Studies*, Vol. 45, 1997, pp. 746-7.

[87] Habermas, *Between Facts and Norms*, p. 150.

power, the law and the administrative system. Communicative power, as the consensus-achieving process among the citizens or legal consociates, is the very process that renders any collectively binding decision legitimate. In other words, the law-making process of the constitutional state must be guided by communicative power if its law is to be accepted as legitimate. The law itself is the very medium which puts the collective consensus of the people into legal language and the legal system is there to institutionalise the process of law-making to facilitate social integration. The administrative system is there to implement the provisions of the law, which are the collectively binding decisions of the legal and political system reflecting the spirit and direction of the consensus achieved when citizens are exercising their communicative power; and in the process of implementation, the administrative system may need to use administrative power, which must be freed from other social power, to ensure that decisions are enforced and obeyed, and to deter delinquencies or disobedience.

Communicative Power and Authority

It is important to note that communicative power, as the guiding force for the creation of legitimate law, is not to be found in the formal legislative or political decision-making process only. In fact as a social phenomenon and as a special manifestation of the exercise of communicative freedom of the citizens, it is mainly to be found in the public sphere[88]

---

[88] In *Between Facts and Norms*, Habermas describes the public sphere 'as a network for communicating information and points of view (i.e. opinions expressing affirmative or negative attitudes); the streams of communication are, in the process, filtered and synthesised in such a way that they coalesce into bundles of topically specified *public* opinions. Like the lifeworld as a whole, so, too, the public sphere is reproduced through communicative action, for which mastery of a natural language suffices; it is tailored to the *general comprehensibility* of everyday communicative practice.' See p. 360, emphasis in the original. Habermas's earliest treatment of the concept of the public sphere can be found in his *The Structural Transformation of the Public Sphere*, trans. Thomas Burger with the assistance of Frederick Lawrence, Cambridge, MA: The MIT Press, 1989. For subsequent developments, see Habermas, 'Further Reflections on the Public

and civil society.[89] This influential political opinion- and will-formation power not only, according to Habermas, confers legitimacy on law under normal circumstances, but also acts as an institutional founding force at times of political upheaval like revolutions or major social movements. As a political force, it is both creative and egalitarian, for it is the result of the people acting in concert for the creation of a common political will that constitutes such a power. It seems unfair, therefore, to accuse Habermas of neglecting the creative capacity of the political, as suggested by Connolly. The same argument can be used to defend Habermas's idea of constitutional patriotism from similar criticisms.

However, like the problem with the quest for rational unanimity, there is no guarantee that in our post-traditional world, general consensus is readily available on controversial political and legal issues; even if we look at the extraordinary times when communicative power does appear to succeed in producing a massive consensus-achieving force, such as at a time of popular revolution, it is mostly the case that the people agree about what they do not want, yet are as diverse as ever about what they positively want to replace the existing state of affairs.[90] As a result, communi-

---

Sphere', in *Habermas and the Public Sphere*, ed. Craig Calhoun, Cambridge, MA and London: The MIT Press, 1999, chapter 17.

[89] To Habermas, 'What is meant by "civil society" today ... comprises those nongovernmental and noneconomic connections and voluntary associations that anchor the communication structures of the public sphere in the society component of the lifeworld. Civil society is composed of those more or less spontaneously emergent associations, organisations and movements that, attuned to how societal problems resonate in the private life spheres, distil and transmit such reactions in amplified form to the public sphere. The core of civil society comprises a network of associations that institutionalises problem-solving discourses on questions of general interest inside the framework of organised public spheres.' *Between Facts and Norms*, pp. 366–7.

[90] For example, when commenting on the '1989 Revolution in Europe', Ralf Dahrendorf says, '... but the honeymoon did not last. It could not last. Once the common enemy had disappeared, more normal divisions within the hitherto united opposition emerged, like industrial and rural Solidarity, and other groups of Christian-democratic and nationalist persuasion, or the political

cative power alone does not appear to be able to perform the function of an authoritative decision-making mechanism. If Habermas is prepared to settle for anything less than rational unanimity, he will face the same problems as in the question of majority rule; namely he not only has to compromise his Kantian ideal of allowing all addressees of binding rules to be the authors of these rules simultaneously, but also has to accept that people abide by the authoritative decision-making procedure for reasons other than the pursuit of rational unanimity. In fact, it seems that Habermas is at least aware of this problem, for he admits that the process of the generation of communicative power is not only creative but also 'wild', 'anarchic' and 'unrestricted'.[91]

However, the problem does not stop there. The ambiguity of Habermas's position is further illustrated by his claim that 'the public opinion that is worked up via democratic procedures into communicative power cannot "rule" of itself but can only point the use of administrative power in specific directions'. This is so because 'only the political system can "act"' and it is the political system that is

> specialised for collectively binding decisions, whereas the communicative structures of the public sphere constitute a far-flung network of sensors that react to the pressure of society-wide problems and stimulate influential opinions.[92]

If communicative power does not rule and only the political system is there for collectively binding decision making, this is very different from his earlier claim that communicative power is the 'authorising force' for the 'creation of legitimate law', for such a force should be in a position to issue

---

parties which took the place of the Civic Forum in Czechoslovakia and the New Forum in East Germany.' See Ralf Dahrendorf, *Reflections on the Revolution in Europe: In a Letter Intended to Have Been Sent to a Gentleman in Warsaw, 1990*, London: Chatto & Windus, 1990, p. 8.

[91] See Kenneth Baynes's 'Democracy and the *Rechtsstaat*: Habermas's *Faktizitat und Geltung*', in *The Cambridge Companion to Habermas*, ed. Stephen K. White, Cambridge: Cambridge University Press, 1995, p. 218.

[92] Habermas, *Between Facts and Norms*, p. 300.

collectively binding decisions and rules.[93] If communicative power does not rule, why does Habermas argue that popular sovereignty, which in effect is the political opinion- and will-formation process of the people through the mobilisation of communicative freedom, is procedural in nature?[94] Furthermore, if communicative power does not rule, what does Habermas mean when he says that law is the very medium to transform communicative power into administrative power, as he has argued in the tripartite relationship in the constitutional state? In such a case, there is no guarantee that law will necessarily transform communicative power, which are merely influential opinions pointing to a desirable direction for the use of administrative power, into authoritative and binding decisions to guide the exercise of administrative power.

It is instructive to note that there is very little discussion of the concept of political authority in Habermas's voluminous political writings. It is also instructive to note that while Habermas adopts Arendt's concept of power in his consensus and legitimacy generating communicative power, Arendt in fact has distinguished the concept of power from the concept of authority, and argues that with the disappearance of the latter the former appears.[95] The ambiguities found in Habermas' idea of communicative power are perhaps best explained by the fact that his theory of deliberative democracy lacks a coherent conception of authority to help describe his tripartite relationship in the constitutional state. At times, his communicative power has been doubling up as an authorising force to determine legitimate law; at other times, the same idea becomes just an influential opinion pointing to a desirable way for imple-

---

[93] *Ibid*, p. 150.
[94] See his 'Popular Sovereignty as Procedure', in *Between Facts and Norms*, Appendix I.
[95] *On Violence*, p. 45. Arendt says that the hallmark of authority is the 'unquestioning recognition by those who are asked to obey'. She has also famously commented that during the campus student revolt at Berkeley in the 1960s, 'when authority leaves, power enters'. For Arendt's view on authority, see her 'What is Authority?', in Hannah Arendt, *Between Past and Future*, New York: Penguin, 1977, reissued 1993, pp. 91–141.

menting administrative power. In the case of the former, authority has been reduced to power, threatening the stability of the political order and reducing all post-traditional political relations ultimately to power relations.[96] In the case of the latter, Habermas is perhaps unconsciously admitting that what is politically desirable after all is not necessarily authoritative,[97] thus inviting criticisms from the left that he is whitewashing the political status quo by exaggerating the influence of communicative power in the generation of legitimate law in a structurally unequal capitalist society.[98]

Proceduralist Democracy: Between Radicalism and Resignation?

The ambiguities in Habermas's treatment of the tripartite relationship between communicative power, law and administrative power lead to two interpretations of his proceduralist theory of democracy, as convincingly shown by William E. Scheuerman in his article 'Between Radicalism and Resignation: Democratic Theory in Habermas's *Between Facts and Norms*'.[99] On the one hand, building on the work of socialist-feminist theorist Nancy Fraser, Habermas develops a two-track model of representative democracy, in which an organised, strong public, consisting of legislative bodies and other formal political

---

[96] See Noel O'Sullivan, 'Power, Authority, and Legitimacy: A Critique of Postmodern Political Thought'.

[97] 'The members of an association may be much or little engaged in considering the desirability of the terms in which they are associated but this cannot itself be the terms of their association.' See Michael Oakeshott, 'The Vocabulary of a Modern European State (Concluded)', in *Political Studies*, Vol. XXIII, No. 4, 1975, p. 410. Oakeshott further says, '"political" utterances, concerned with the conditions of association in respect of their desirability, postulate the recognition of the authority of the conditions whose desirability they may question, even where what is questioned is the desirability of the shape of an office of authority or the credibility of the beliefs in which it is recognised to have authority'. *Ibid.*

[98] See William E. Scheuerman's 'Between Radicalism and Resignation: Democratic Theory in Habermas's *Between Facts and Norms*', in *Habermas: A Critical Reader*, ed. Peter Dews, Oxford: Blackwell, 1999, pp. 153–77.

[99] *Ibid.*

institutions, functions alongside an unorganised, weak public within a broader civil society, in which citizens rely on devices like political associations and the mass media to take part in free wheeling political debate in order to generate communicative power which will influence the direction of the political system.[100] On the other hand, Habermas also relies on the study of the German sociologist Bernhard Peters's 'realist-inspired model of democratic decision making'.[101] Peters believes that given the structural asymmetry in terms of social and economic power relations in capitalist societies, the political centre (comprising parliament, the judiciary and the administrative system) has far greater influence over collective decision-making than the political periphery (comprising a host of associations and organisations.)

According to Scheuerman, Habermas's two-track theory of deliberative democracy oscillates hesitantly between critical radicalism and realist resignation, for he at times stresses that the primacy of deliberatively derived law assures that communicative power effectively determines the direction of the political system and asserts itself against administrative and market mechanisms, thus believing that the weak public or the periphery is where the real political force lies in shaping and determining collectively binding decisions.[102] Yet at other times, when considering the complexity of modern social life, Habermas appears to argue that the deliberative periphery inevitably plays a minor role in determining the policy-making process, at least in time of normal politics, thus lessening civil society's influence on decision-making. According to this interpretation, only in exceptional situations like mass social movements or movements of civil disobedience does the communicative power

---

[100] See Nancy Fraser, 'Rethinking the Public Sphere: A Contribution to the Critique of Actually Existing Democracy', in *Habermas and the Public Sphere*, chapter 5.
[101] *Habermas: A Critical Reader*, p. 164.
[102] *Ibid.*, p. 159.

generated within civil society and the public sphere seem to take on a renewed significance for decision-making.[103]

Scheuerman is therefore justified in criticising these fundamental ambiguities in Habermas's political theory. When compared with the young Habermas of the 1960s, at the time when he was still very much influenced by the tradition of the critical theory of the Frankfurt School and published his *The Structural Transformation of the Public Sphere*, Scheuerman laments the loss of radicalism in the works of the mature Habermas, as exemplified in his definitive study in politics and law *Between Facts and Norms*.[104] In this study, however, the concern is less about radicalism than about the coherence of Habermas's political theory. In the final analysis, perhaps Habermas is too ambitious in his attempt to introduce a democratic theory to the post-traditional world. He is too ambitious because he places too much faith in reason and communicative rationality, thus setting a criterion of rational unanimity for authoritative decision-making that is almost impossible to achieve. His over-reliance on rationality might bring some kind of utopian-like moralism into the realm of politics, undermining the legitimacy of political authority but offering nothing to replace it in maintaining political order.

Habermas's theory is also inadequate, however, because in spite of his democratic theory, the central political question of authority is nowhere to be seen, which is the main reason why Habermas fails to identify the proper relationship between communicative power, law and administration. This lack of a coherent theory of authority in Habermas's philosophy indicates that no political theory can adequately tackle the central political questions of post-traditional societies without achieving much greater clarity on this crucial topic.

---

[103] *Ibid.*, p. 165.
[104] See n. 88 above. In the Preface to *Between Facts and Norms*, Habermas says, 'If I scarcely mention the name of Hegel and rely more on the Kantian theory of law, this also expresses my desire to avoid a model that set unattainable standards for us.' See p. xix.

5

Oakeshott on Civil Association

Moral Agency, Law and Politics

Introduction:
Philosophical Understanding and Civil Association

Perhaps the most important contribution made by Oakeshott to modern political theory is his attempt to understand how autonomous individuals can possibly be related to each other in a comprehensive and compulsory association (i.e. a state), in which the individuals concerned are obligated to subscribe to the authority of the rules of the association, yet at the same time can preserve their freedom. This attempt can be found in his theory of civil association. If one weakness in Habermas's discourse theory of democracy is its lack of a coherent concept of authority, an attraction of Oakeshott's political theory as seen in its mature formulation in his *magnum opus*, *On Human Conduct*,[1] lies precisely in his understanding that authority, obligation

[1] Michael Oakeshott, *On Human Conduct*, Oxford: Clarendon Press, 1991. *On Human Conduct* was first published in 1975 by Oxford University Press. A very interesting controversy about the philosophy of Oakeshott is whether there is a break in his earlier more idealist approach (as exemplified in Oakeshott's first book *Experience and Its Modes*, Cambridge: Cambridge University Press, 1933), and his later more sceptical approach. Paul Franco, in *The Political Philosophy of Michael Oakeshott*, New Haven and London: Yale University Press, 1990, argues that there are some subtle changes of emphasis but there is no break in the development of

and autonomous human agents are among the central postulates of the idea of civil association, in which social and political diversity and the authority of civil association are not antithetical, but are required by each other.[2]

Oakeshott is primarily a philosopher, and a very disciplined and uncompromising one. This was the point Terry Nardin made when he wrote, 'even if we accept the view that Oakeshott's most valuable and enduring contribution is as a theorist of politics, we cannot fully understand this contribution unless we read his work in the context of a wider range of ideas'.[3] To understand his theory of civil association, one must therefore start with his views on some general philosophical ideas.

To Oakeshott, philosophical reflection is an attempt to understand in other terms what one already understands, in which the understanding sought is a disclosure of the conditions of the understanding enjoyed.[4] In other words,

---

Oakeshott's conception of philosophy and political theory. Steven Anthony Gerencser, in *The Skeptic's Oakeshott*, New York: St. Martin's Press, 2000, however, contends that starting from 'The Voice of Poetry in the Conversation of Mankind', in *Rationalism in Politics and Other Essays*, London and New York: Methuen, 1962, rpt. 1981, pp. 197–247, Oakeshott's later philosophy has abandoned some fundamental idealist assumptions of his earlier philosophy. For the purpose of this study, I am not going to enter into such a debate, for I believe that my focus here does not require me to tackle issues of this kind.

[2] Oakeshott prefers to use this more old-fashioned description to refer to what we normally call a 'modern state', for he believes that the latter, like many modern political vocabularies, is highly ambiguous theoretically. See his 'On the Character of a Modern European State', in *On Human Conduct*.

[3] See Terry Nardin's recent book *The Philosophy of Michael Oakeshott*, Pennsylvania: The Pennsylvania State University, 2001, pp. 1–2. Nardin's is perhaps the best book so far on Oakeshott's ideas from a general philosophical perspective. Patrick Riley is essentially making a similar point when he says, '[s]urely it was that intimation of eternity that led Oakeshott to cast his definitive thoughts, in On Human Conduct, in the grave vocabulary of Roman jurisprudence: the language of lex, cives, civitas, respublica, societas, universitas; it was not his (nonexistent) relation to "Mrs Thatcher's policies" that mattered to him, but his hoped-for relation to Aristotle, Cicero, Hobbes and Hegel'. See Riley, 'Michael Oakeshott: Philosopher of Individuality', in Review of Politics, Fall 1992, Vol. 52, Issue 4, p. 651.

[4] Oakeshott, *On Human Conduct*, p. vii.

philosophical reflection presupposes the possibility of understanding; and for us as human beings, understanding is an unsought condition: 'To be human and to be aware is to encounter only what is in some manner understood.'[5] Understanding, as an engagement, always begins in an already understood: a verdict, or a fact, whose conditional sufficiency is accepted in the first place. However, for a theorist, this initial verdict, like all understanding, is also an invitation to further critical inquiry, an inquiry to look at the conditions presupposed or required by the verdict. The undertaking to understand the world we inhabit in a theoretical manner is thus 'a continuous, self-moving, critical enterprise of theorizing', and a philosopher is one who is determined to inhabit an ever more intelligible and less mysterious world.[6] Temporary platforms of conditional understanding are always being reached, and one is free to enjoy them without looking further to their presupposed conditions, 'but each is an arrival, an enlightenment, and a point of departure'.[7] While the engagement of understanding thus understood implies an infinite journey of conditional understanding, it does not require the notion of an unconditional or definitive understanding,[8] for 'what constitutes its unconditionality is the continuous recognition of the conditionality of the conditions'.[9]

To understand is to notice, to distinguish, to remember, to recognise and to identify likeness and unlikeness in what is going on. 'The language of noticing, recognizing and remembering resemblances and differences is a language of characteristics.'[10] When the invitation to inquire about the conditions presupposed by these initially understood characteristics is accepted, these characteristics are detached

---

[5] *Ibid.*, p. 1.
[6] *Ibid.*, p. 2.
[7] *Ibid.*, pp. 2–3.
[8] *Ibid.*, p. 3.
[9] *Ibid.*, p. 11. This apparently is a revision of Oakeshott's position in *Experience and its Modes*, in which he argues that philosophy aims at experience without reservation or arrest, without presupposition or postulate, without limit or category.
[10] Oakeshott, *On Human Conduct*, p. 3.

from their contingent circumstances and are combined to compose the features of ideal characters. Such ideal characters emerge, says Oakeshott,

> from a selection, combination, and arrangement of characteristics in which recollection has superseded remembering, in which observation is directed by anticipatory guesses, and in which the characteristics upon which attention is focused cease to be recognized merely in terms of resemblances and differences and merely as indications of one another and are understood as the lines or marks which together delineate a conceptual identity.[11]

Such a conceptual identity may be a crude or a sophisticated construction; it is both an achievement in conditional understanding and an instrument for exploring understanding. To recognise what constitutes the ideal character of play, for example, is an achievement in conditional understanding on its own, but it can also assist one in identifying a particular going-on as in the performance of William Shakespeare's *King Lear*. 'To identify ... is to specify a *this* in terms of an ideal character composed of characteristics; it is to understand a "going-on" as a unity of particularity and genericity.'[12]

At this level of understanding, one may take the ideal character achieved as unproblematic and investigate its relationships with other such identities to form a conceptual map or theorem which explains their relationships, or one may seek to understand the identity in terms of its conditions or postulates, thus resuming the journey of understanding at a higher level in earnest. A particular going-on can be understood in terms of its characteristics as 'cycling'. This conceptual identity of course can be related to other similar identities like 'punting' or 'canoeing' and be understood as a certain kind of sport for individuals; however, to theorise them in terms of postulates is to explore a platform of understanding composed of theorems such as mechanics in relation to which any one of these goings-on is no more than one contingent happening from which an identity

---

[11] *Ibid.*, p. 4.
[12] *Ibid.*, p. 5, emphasis in the original.

capable of being understood in the terms of mechanics may be abstracted.[13]

While the theoretical quest for understanding is 'perpetually *en voyage*', Oakeshott also believes that it 'may be arrested without being denied'. For 'the unconditional engagement of understanding must be arrested and inquiry must remain focused upon a *this* if any identity is to become intelligible in terms of its postulates'.[14] The appropriate level to make such arrests in understanding may vary, depending upon the purpose of the inquiry; but any such conditional platform of understanding must be 'an autonomous adventure in theorizing, insular, inextinguishable, resistant to "reduction", having its own conditional "truth", and capable of its own conditional perfection'. The starting-place for such a conditional platform is an identity understood and not yet understood, and its conclusion is this identity transformed by being understood in terms of its postulates.[15]

The focus of this chapter is on Oakeshott's theory of civil association. As a form of human association, civil association is concerned with human beings and their activities,

---

[13] *Ibid.*, p. 10.
[14] *Ibid.*, p. 11, emphasis in the original.
[15] *Ibid.* In *Experience and Its Modes*, Oakeshott distinguishes in detail three such arrests: practical experience, history and science. Each of these presupposes an autonomous and irreducible conditional understanding of its own. The world of practice, for example, postulates human needs and desires. It presupposes that facts are alterable, and accepts what works as true. The world of history presupposes a historical past wholly unrelated to the present, as well as that historical change cannot be explained by general and unchanging laws. In addition, it also assumes that what is historically true is what can be made intelligible by relating a historical event to other significant and related events. The world of science, in contrast, is concerned with what is constant and capable of being quantified. It aims to understand the world in terms of mathematically expressible laws and statistical generalisations, and develops its truth criteria in terms of these generalisations. In *Rationalism in politics*, Oakeshott adds another arrest in his essay 'The Voice of Poetry in the Conversation of Mankind'. Likewise, both his study of Hobbes' political theory and his own theory of civil association have demonstrated that what we commonly called 'political activities' have postulates which form another autonomous platform of conditional understanding.

utterances and relationships. Therefore, the goings-on to be identified in civil association, unlike the goings-on identified in planetary movement, must be themselves exhibitions of intelligence. A human action, such as a wink, is necessarily an expression of reflective intelligence, the result of human intent, want or desire; whereas a blink, a physical movement, is caused by the reflex action of a certain muscle of the human eye, and is unrelated to human want or desire. Likewise, a neighbourly relationship within a human community is not determined by geographical proximity but is the result of the mutual subscription to a social practice by the individuals concerned, and such a practice can only be subscribed to if the participants concerned have learnt how to do so.[16] By contrast, the proximity of the earth and the moon in the solar system has nothing to do with reflective intelligence, and there is nothing to be learnt by the objects themselves before a relationship can be established in terms of the physical laws of gravitational force. Although this relationship can be understood by human beings, it does not in itself exhibit self-understanding.

Goings-on exhibiting reflective intelligence and goings-on not exhibiting such intelligence are, therefore, categorically distinct. They belong to two different categories of identities in two different orders of inquiry, neither of which can be reduced to the other. Oakeshott calls the former a 'procedure' and the latter a 'process', and identifies human and civil associations as goings-on of the former kind, since they exhibit reflective intelligence.[17] Within each order of inquiry, however, there are also different idioms of inquiry. The Gettysburg address by Abraham Lincoln in 1863, for example, can be studied as a piece of material for political persuasion, in which people can try to figure out what persuasive tactics were used in the speech and how successful they were in rallying the morale of the troops of the Union. It can also be used as a piece of historical evidence to try to make sense of some of the important episodes of the Ameri-

[16] Oakeshott, *On Human Conduct*, p. 57
[17] *Ibid.*, pp. 12–15.

can Civil War. Alternatively, it can be studied as an attempt to try to elucidate the conditions and nature of democracy. Each of these idioms (the art of persuasion, history and political theory) of inquiry is distinctive, leading to very different problems and understandings; none of them, however, can replace the others without creating irrelevancy.[18] 'Each such idiom is an unambiguous system of theorems which has acquired (or which aspires to) the condition of a distinguishable "science"', argues Oakeshott, and 'each is autonomous in being constituted in terms of theorems exclusively its own, and each is capable of its own conditional perfection.'[19]

Oakeshott's theory of civil association is a study of intelligent and compulsory human relationships of a certain kind. While an understanding of such a theory may lead some to aspire to the conditions presupposed by civil association, his aim is not the practical undertaking of persuading others to accept or create such an association; it is mainly a theoretical attempt to spell out the ideal character of civil association, in which the postulates and conditions required by such an association and by the human relationships constituting it are articulated or made explicit in as coherent a manner as possible. Such an ideal mode of understanding, if coherently articulated, may be used as a theoretical instrument for the understanding or even assessment of actual or historical modes of human association.[20] It does not, however, follow that it is deficient if such an ideal character is not to be found in the empirical world,

---

[18] As Oakeshott says, 'to become the subject of an inquiry designed to make it intelligible in terms of its postulates, an identity must be recognized not only to be "problematic", but to be a specific problem; that is, it must be recognized to be unambiguous not only in predicating what I have called an exclusive "order" of inquiry but also in prescribing what I shall now call a particular "idiom" of inquiry. For a categorially unambiguous identity may still have contingent ambiguities which must be resolved before it can become the subject of an inquiry.' See *ibid.*, p. 16.

[19] *Ibid.*, p. 17.

[20] While the second essay of *On Human Conduct* develops the ideal mode of the civil association, the third uses it to help to understand the history of the emergence of modern European states and their ambiguous character, which involves both civil and enterprise

for all ideal characters, as identifications and abstractions of the characteristics of the particular goings-on concerned, must be detached from the contingent circumstances involved in those goings-on. So, what are the main postulates to be identified in the ideal character of civil association? How are they related to each other? What specific human relationships are required in such an ideal mode? It is these questions which must now be considered.

Free Agents and Civil Association

Civil association, as a kind of human association, is constituted by more or less durable human relationships.[21] Human relationships, according to Oakeshott, are recognised to be themselves expressions of intelligence that may be enjoyed only if they have been learned and understood by the participants and in virtue of acknowledgement of the authority of their conditions or the recognition of their utility.[22]

For human beings to be able to learn about, and to continue to enjoy such relationships, presupposes that, on the one hand, there are certain formal conditions or practices that are thought to be proper or useful to be observed while doing so; it also presupposes that, on the other hand, the participants concerned have the ability to make intelligent choices to do or to say this rather than that for the fulfilment of some imagined and wished-for outcomes.[23] These

---

association. So far as using the ideal mode to assess actual or historical human association is concerned, it is true that Oakeshott does not think that the former can be used as a practical guide for the development or improvement of the latter. Nevertheless he has no hesitation in condemning the urge to impose upon a state the character of an enterprise association as profoundly shameful. See *ibid.*, p. 321.

[21] *Ibid.*, p. 111.
[22] *Ibid.*, pp. 23-4.
[23] Oakeshott describes a practice as 'a set of considerations, manners, uses, observance, customs, standards, canons, maxims, principles, rules and offices specifying useful procedures or denoting obligations or duties which relate to human actions and utterances. It is a prudential or moral adverbial qualification of choices and

choices, as expressions of reflective intelligence, are not determined by the genetic make-up of the individuals concerned; rather, they reflect their acquired wants and desires, the results of their deliberation, and their beliefs that through actions, utterances and performances of some sort to be carried out separately or jointly with other similarly related participants, they would be able to seek satisfaction by pursuing some imagined future outcomes of their choices. In other words, durable human relationships presuppose the ability to choose substantive performance and to subscribe to some formal relationships in doing so at the same time. As Oakeshott says,

> an action ... is an identity in which substantive performance and procedural consideration may be distinguished but are inseparably joined, and in which the character of agent and that of practitioner are merged in a single self-recognition.[24]

Civil association, as human association, thus postulates conduct *inter homines* and free (i.e. intelligent) human agency.[25]

Oakeshott believes that human agents are 'inherently' free. By this, he does not mean that all human individuals are 'substantially self-directed' in their actions; rather, he means that the contingent situation facing the individual, his chosen response (i.e. doing) in relation to that situation and the wished-for outcome of the doing are made intelligible as a result of the individual's own understanding.[26] In other words, an agent 'is what he understands himself to be, his contingent situations are what he understands them to be, and the actions and utterances in which he responds to them are self-disclosure and self-enactment'.[27] As an intelligent, self-reflective being, a human agent has a 'history', not

---

performance, more or less complicated, in which conduct is understood in terms of procedure.' See *ibid.*, p. 55.
[24] *Ibid.*, p. 57.
[25] *Ibid.*, pp. 23–41 and 111–12.
[26] *Ibid.*, pp. 36–7.
[27] *Ibid.*, p. 41.

a 'nature'. 'He is what in conduct he becomes.'[28] Therefore, one is free 'not because his situation is alterable by an act of unconstrained "will" but because it is an understood situation and because doing is an intelligent engagement'.[29] After all, 'what is called "the will" is nothing but intelligence in doing'.[30] There is, therefore, a built-in requirement of human intelligence in Oakeshott's theory of association, in which the individual's autonomous decision to do this rather than that is respected.

While civil association is human association postulating free agency, it is not human association of just any kind. It is therefore necessary to specify further the kind of human relationships required in civil association and to discern what distinguishes such an association from other modes of human association. The three most significant features distinguishing civil relationship from other human relationships are that the former is non-instrumental in practice, that it is constituted by a system of rules and that it is a relationship in terms of a recognition of rules as rules.[31] In order to spell out these observations it is necessary to distinguish the civil relationship from other equally important but categorically distinct human relationships, particularly enterprise relationships and moral relationships. Only after this is done can the strength of Oakeshott's political theory be appreciated, and the major contribution he made to providing a way to accommodate the authority of the state with respect for human autonomy be assessed.

Transactional Association and Enterprise Association

To start with, Oakeshott looks at what he calls 'the most rudimentary mode of human relationships' — transactional association — and attempts to identify the features that char-

---

[28] *Ibid.*
[29] *Ibid.*, p. 37.
[30] *Ibid.*, p. 39. See also 'A Place of Learning', in Michael Oakeshott's *The Voice of Liberal Learning*, ed. Timothy Fuller, New Haven and London: Yale University Press, 1989, pp. 17–42, in which Oakeshott says, '[a] human being is "free", not because he has "free will", but because he is *in* himself what he is *for* himself.' See p. 19, emphasis in the original.
[31] Oakeshott, *On Human Conduct*, pp. 122, 111, 148.

acterise the nature of such an association.[32] Transactional association is 'intermittent' and a 'reciprocal' relationship, in which two or more agents seek the satisfaction of their different current wants.[33] This association is intermittent because it is intrinsically terminable, since the sole purpose of such a relationship is to help each so related to achieve their different but specified wished-for outcome, the satisfaction of which may dissolve the relationship, and the frustration of which may destroy it. Oakeshott describes such a mode as 'relationship in terms of power',[34] for the agents concerned are related as 'bargainers for the satisfaction of wants', each trying to make the effective use of his or her power via his or her performance to solicit the hoped-for response from other participant(s) engaged in the same relationship in order to procure an imagined and wished-for outcome.[35]

As an intermittent relationship, transactional association is an unlikely candidate for civil association, for the latter is about durable human relationships, not constituted for the satisfaction of evanescent wants. Agents related in transactional association will certainly also be related to each other by some mutually acknowledged rules or practices to facilitate the procurement of their wished-for outcome, but these are only prudential considerations facilitating the transactional relationship, they do not constitute the substantive transactions concerned.[36] The completion of the transaction will not only bring an end to the relationship concerned, it will at the same time make those prudential practices irrelevant.

However, not all purposive associations are evanescent, for many human wants are either long-lasting or may take some time before they can be satisfied in full, and it may also

---

[32] See Oakeshott, 'The Rule of Law', in *On History and Other Essays*, Oxford: Basil Blackwell, 1983, p. 121.
[33] *Ibid.*, p. 112- 13.
[34] *Ibid.*, pp. 121–2.
[35] Oakeshott, *On Human Conduct*, p. 113.
[36] Agents such as a punter and a bookmaker are related to one another in terms of certain gambling practices designed to promote their gambling transaction. *See ibid*.

require the joint efforts of those who share the same purpose to procure the wished-for outcome. A political party, for example, may have to spend years before being able to achieve its purpose of becoming the ruling party, and once it has become the ruling party it would like to maintain such a status for as long as possible. Needless to say, such a party requires agents who share the same purpose to join together in an association for the pursuit of their wished-for outcome, and such an association could be very long lasting indeed. Oakeshott calls associations of this kind 'enterprise associations'. It should be pointed out that the common purpose that underpins enterprise association could be as diverse and different as the form that embodies it. As Oakeshott says,

> [a]gents thus related may be believers in a common faith and concerned or not concerned to propagate it, or they may be partners in a productive undertaking (a bassoon factory); they may be comrades or allies in the promotion of a 'cause', colleagues, expeditionaries, accomplices, or conspirators; they may be joined in belonging to the same profession or in having the same trade; they may enjoy a 'common life' or they may be united merely in having common enemies; they may comprise an army, a 'village community', a sect, a fellowship, a party, a fraternity, a sodality, a *collegium*, or a guild. The ties of this association may be close like those of a corporation; or they may be the looser ties of partnership or alliance. The relationship may be long lasting or soon dissolved. The common purpose may be simple or complex, clearly defined or vaguely imagined; its achievement may be a near or a distant prospect, or no prospect at all, but an interminable engagement in the continuous promotion or protection of an enduring interest. The response sought may be that of others not thus associated, or it may be an enjoyment of the associates themselves.[37]

Agents in an enterprise association are, therefore, related first and foremost in terms of the common substantive purpose that they all share. But since pursuing or promoting a common purpose is 'nothing other than responding to continuously emergent situations by deciding to do *this* rather

---

[37] See *ibid.*, p. 114.

than *that* in the hope or the expectation of procuring an imagined and wished-for outcome connected with that purpose' by the associates, enterprise association must also be related in terms of what Oakeshott calls the 'management of the pursuit of the common purpose'.[38] In other words,

> an enterprise is a 'policy', and enterprise association is a 'managerial' engagement; it is agents related to one another in the substantive activity of choosing performances contingently connected with a common purpose or interest, or in their acknowledgement of such choices and performances as their own.[39]

Enterprise association, therefore, is 'a many in one', where the singleness lies in the subscription to the common substantive purpose by the associates and in the recognition of the managerial decisions taken by the association in the pursuit of the common purpose.[40] As an enduring relationship, it is likely that an enterprise association may also have certain rule-like arrangements governing its transaction of business, such as an article of association or rules regulating admission or resignation of membership and so on. However, these arrangements neither define the common purpose of the association, nor belong to any part of its managerial decisions. It is not possible to identify an enterprise association by virtue of recognition of these rules alone, and 'even a denial of the authority of these rules would not itself be an act of disassociation', for they are there only to facilitate the operation of enterprise association, not to define it.[41]

Oakeshott goes on to suggest that 'there is virtually no limit to the capacity of an agent to be related to others in this [i.e. the enterprising] manner'.[42] As free and autonomous agents, human beings in theory should be capable of relat-

---

[38] *Ibid.*, p. 115, emphasis in the original.
[39] *Ibid.* 'Whether this "management" is performed by all the associates in unanimous or majority decisions', says Oakeshott, 'or by a directorate, or by one deputed to manage the affairs of the association ... does not affect its character.'
[40] *Ibid.*, p. 117.
[41] *Ibid.*
[42] *Ibid.*

ing to others for the joint pursuit of their commonly imagined and wished-for outcome in as many ways as they wish, and the only internal limit is their own imagination and aspiration, unless they are coerced not to do so. For enterprise associations with conflicting purposes (such as a vegetarian association and a beef-eating association), to co-exist in a society should not pose any problems, so long as they do not force people who do not share their purposes to join them, or overtly threaten the existence of other enterprise associations. Even if there is an agent who would like to join the vegetarian and the beef-eating associations at the same time, the problem is primarily his, not of the associations concerned.

A compulsory enterprise association, according to Oakeshott, is 'a self-contradiction', for it is a denial of free agency.[43] If human relationships really postulate free agency, in which individuals are regarded as intelligent beings who are capable of making choices, having beliefs and engaging in performances in the pursuit of their respective wished-for outcome, it would be a denial of their autonomy and humanity if they are not allowed to extricate themselves from any association the purpose of which they no longer believe in. If the state, as a compulsory association, is constituted in the manner of an enterprise association, it appears that the state not only does not protect the freedom of the individual, but also creates an enduringly coercive relationship for those who do not share the purpose of the state concerned, unless we assume that all human beings happily believe in one and the same purpose. As Oakeshott's theory of civil association is to theorise an association in which state authority and individual freedom are compatible with each other, compulsory enterprise associations are certainly not what he is looking for, so the precise character of civil association is yet to be sought in other possible human relationships.

---

[43] *Ibid.*, p. 119.

Practice and Purpose in Human Conduct

An enterprise association is a relationship in the first place in terms of a common purpose (or a series of common purposes the priority of which is determined by the system). It is also a relationship in terms of the managerial decisions made in response to the continuously changing contingent situations which the association has encountered for the procurement of wished-for outcomes related to the common purpose. Such a relationship is a substantive one because what ultimately links the associates concerned is the concrete course of action that has been taken, and the respective roles played by the associates in the chosen course of action for the procurement of their commonly wished-for outcome. The meaning of the concrete course of action taken must be understood in the context of the associates' common purpose, and the contents of the action concerned are decided by the managerial decisions of the association. For instance, the common purpose for the members of a green party is, say, environmental protection, for the promotion of which the party leadership may decide that active participation in the forthcoming general election with a pro-environment platform is most effective. As a result, members of the green party, at this moment, are related in terms of the course of action taken (i.e. participation in the general election), the meaning of which (i.e. electoral campaign for environmental protection) is understood in the context of its common purpose, and the substantive performances of the decided course of action itself (placing candidates for the elections and arguing for environmental protection policy in public forums during the election campaign, etc.) are what concretely connect the associates together. In making managerial decisions and executing their substantive performances, the party may observe certain prudential practices (such as the art of effective political campaigning) to facilitate the procurement of their wished-for outcome, but these practices on their own do not define the relationship of the enterprise association. It is a substantive relationship not only because the associates share the same purpose, but also because they are related in terms of the continuous subscription to the managerial decisions of the association via participation in the concrete courses of action derived from such decisions for the achievement of its common purpose. The common beliefs or wants of the associates are translated into concrete courses of action, the management of which is meant to be instrumental to the fulfilment or satisfaction of the beliefs or wants shared by the concerned associates.

However, apart from the substantive aspect, human relationships also have another dimension: the formal aspect, or the conditional context for substantive human action.[44] This aspect qualifies but does not determine performance.[45] In other words, while the formal aspect cannot issue managerial instructions for action for the procurement of a wished-for outcome, it shapes the quality of the course of action taken by the agents of an association by establishing conditions or considerations to be subscribed to while acting. Oakeshott calls formal conditions and considerations 'practices', for a practice is there 'to specify procedural conditions to be taken into account [by agents] when choosing and acting', and each practice constitutes a specific formal relationship between the participants who are related to each other in the proper *personae* (e.g. teacher-learner, ruler-subject, friends) reflecting the relationship in question.[46] A practice can be either prudential or non-instrumental. A prudential practice (like the art of cookery or the art of effective political campaigning) is useful for procuring a certain sort of substantive satisfaction, the conditions of which will be considered or subscribed to by only those who are engaging in the pursuit of that particular sort of substantive satisfaction. A non-instrumental practice is not related to procuring any substantive satisfaction and thus has no extrinsic purpose, and if the set of conditions prescribed in such a practice is 'to be subscribed to in all or any of an agent's actions or utterances', then such a practice

---

[44] *Ibid.*, p. 54.
[45] *Ibid.*, p. 120.
[46] *Ibid.*, pp. 56–9.

is, for Oakeshott, a practice of morality.[47] Oakeshott calls moral practice 'the practice of all practices', for 'no agent, whatever the circumstances of his conduct, is outside its jurisdiction', and it is, along with a common tongue, one of the two most important practices we have in the human world.[48] But is such a comprehensive moral relationship synonymous with civil association, in which not only free agency but also state authority are presupposed?

Morality and Civility

Moral relationship, as a formal relationship, is not a prudential art concerned with the success or failure of substantive performances. As Oakeshott says, 'it is not instrumental to the achievement of any substantive purpose or to the satisfaction of any substantive want ... A moral practice ... does not stand condemned if no [prudential] advantages were to accrue.'[49] In a non-instrumental relationship, moral agents are not related in terms of the utility of the conditions prescribed in the relationship, for such a relationship cannot issue any managerial instructions for substantive performances and is indifferent to any benefits derived from the satisfaction of any substantive want. Agents are related to one another, rather, in the acknowledgement of the authority of the conditions so prescribed.

Being a non-instrumental relationship whose members do not need to share a common substantive purpose and are related in terms of their common observation of the formal conditions prescribed in the relationship, a moral association is an association related in terms of a non-prudential practice. As stated earlier, the one key feature in Oakeshott's idea of civil association is that it is an association related in terms of a non-instrumental practice. In this sense, moral associations and civil associations belong to the same cate-

---

[47] *Ibid.*, p. 122.
[48] *Ibid.*, pp. 60- 1. To Oakeshott, '[a man] comes to consciousness in a world illuminated by a moral practice and as a relatively helpless subject of it. The nurture of children is everywhere performance governed by a moral practice.' *Ibid.*, p. 63.
[49] *Ibid.*, p. 60.

gory; and indeed, civil association is characterised by Oakeshott as 'association in terms of moral considerations', though he at the same time qualifies this by saying that this 'does not mean that there is no moral relationship which is not civil relationship; it means only that the conditions of civil association are moral conditions in not being instrumental to the satisfaction of substantive wants'.[50] So what distinguishes morality from civility?

The imagery of language is invoked by Oakeshott to describe moral as well as civil practice. He calls morality 'a vernacular language of colloquial intercourse' and civility 'a vernacular language of civil understanding and intercourse';[51] however, he further specifies this: 'the language of civil intercourse is a language of rules', for the civil condition (or *civitas*, as Oakeshott sometimes prefers to say) is 'composed entirely of rules' and 'is rule-articulated association'.[52]

As a vernacular language, both morality and civility are historical achievements of human beings; but unlike civil practice, 'no moral practice can be reduced to the rules, the duties, or the "ideals" it obtrudes, and *rightness* is never more than an aspect of moral response'.[53] In other words, as a language, moral practice is both 'an instrument of self-disclosure used by agents in diagnosing their situations and in choosing their responses' and 'a language of self-enactment which permits those who can use it to understand themselves and one another, to disclose to one another their complex individualities'.[54] This means that the former concerns the conditions governing rightful interpersonal relationship, the latter the quality and character of the moral agents in doing. According to Oakeshott, the conditions

---

[50] *Ibid.*, p. 122. Similarly, Oakeshott also says, 'law and morals normally have the same centre but not the same circumference'. See Michael Oakeshott, *Morality and Politics in Modern Europe: The Harvard Lectures*, New Haven and London: Yale University Press, 1993, ed. Shirley Robin Letwin, p. 16.
[51] Oakeshott, *On Human Conduct*, pp. 63, 122.
[52] *Ibid.*, p. 124.
[53] *Ibid.*, p. 68, emphasis in the original.
[54] *Ibid.*, p. 63.

imposed by the rules in civil association upon conduct 'cannot concern the supreme moral consideration which related to the sentiments or motives in which actions are performed', since although civil practice is also non-instrumental in nature, its focus is narrower and does not concern itself with everything that concerns moral practice.[55]

When moral conduct is understood in its self-disclosure aspect, our moral language is addressing itself to the conditions to which human agents subscribe in choosing their action and pursuing their separate satisfaction in response to one another. The conditions governing the relationships among agents in their pursuit of wished-for outcomes are interpersonal, and good conduct in this regard is choosing and doing while subscribing to these conditions. Failure to subscribe to these conditions is regarded as wrongdoing.[56] When moral conduct is understood, however, in its self-enactment aspect, our moral language is then addressing itself to the motives in which an action is performed; as such, it relates to an agent choosing motives which he approves of, and 'is related to his understanding and respect for himself, to the integrity of his character'.[57] Conduct that notably fails to observe these requirements is regarded as losing one's integrity and is therefore shameful.[58]

While concrete moral action must necessarily involve both aspects of morality, they are nevertheless distinguishable, and a moral practice may give more weight to one and less to the other.[59] As civil association is concerned with enduring human relationships in interpersonal intercourse, it is not surprising that the conditions prescribed in the rules of civil association are concerned with the disclosure aspect rather than the enactment aspect of morality. '[O]ur concern with the sentiment in which the action of another is performed', Oakeshott adds,

---

[55] Oakeshott, 'The Rule of Law', p. 141.
[56] Oakeshott, *On Human Conduct*, p. 74.
[57] *Ibid.*, p. 75.
[58] *Ibid.*, p. 77.
[59] *Ibid.*, p. 71.

is limited by a recognition of our hardly avoidable ignorance and by the conviction that in ordinary human intercourse a man's choices of what to do and the compunctions they exhibit matter more than the sentiment in which he makes them.[60]

Apart from the consideration of moral motives and sentiments, there is another major difference between morality and civility: this is their relationship to rules. *Civitas*, as Oakeshott says, is composed entirely of rules. But in a moral practice, moral rules or rule-like principles are merely 'abridgements'.[61] This is so because as a historical achievement, the conditions constituting a moral practice are not 'theorems or precepts about human conduct', and the 'abstract nouns (right and wrong, proper and improper, obligation, dueness, fairness, respect, justice, etc.)' are nothing but 'faded metaphors' whose meanings can only be properly understood in the context of the moral practice concerned, not *vice versa*.[62] Moral ideals are not, in the first place, the products of reflective thought, the verbal expressions of unrealised ideas, which are then translated into human behaviour; they are the products of human behaviour, of human practical activity, to which reflective thought gives subsequent, partial and abstract expression in words.[63] While it is possible to abstract from moral practice a set of moral rules which try to convert certain practices into more precise obligations or exact duties, the rules 'are not commands to be obeyed but relatively precise considerations to be subscribed to'.[64] As a result, while the civil condition is composed entirely of rules, rules in a moral

---

[60] See *ibid.*, p. 77.
[61] *Ibid.*, p. 66.
[62] *Ibid.*, p. 63.
[63] See Oakeshott, 'The Tower of Babel', in *Rationalism in Politics and Other Essays*, 1962, rpt. 1981, pp. 72–3. Michael Walzer gives a very good account of this approach to morality in his *Interpretation and Social Criticism*, Cambridge, MA and London, England: Harvard University Press, 1987, in which he says, '[t]he experience of moral argument is best understood in the interpretative mode. What we do when we argue is to give an account of the actually existing morality. That morality is authoritative for us because it is only by virtue of its existence that we exist as the moral beings we are.' See p. 21.
[64] Oakeshott, *On Human Conduct*, p. 68.

practice are at best merely derivative if morality is properly understood.

Furthermore, another major consideration that separates morality from civility is that it is difficult to distinguish the rightness of the conditions prescribed by a moral rule from the authenticity or validity of the rule, for as morality concerns itself with the rights and wrongs of human conduct, it is reasonable to expect that the conditions asserted by a moral rule are only valid if they are being regarded as right or just. [65] However, in the case of *civitas*, as a system entirely composed of rules, it is also related in terms of the recognition of rules as rules. In other words, unlike other moral associations, a main feature of civil association is that the validity of its rules is derived solely from their authority (i.e. recognition of rules as rules), not from their prescribed conditions being regarded as right or just.[66] In order better to understand this, we must now give a fuller account of some additional major features of civil association, particularly the nature and character of the rules in such an association.

Civil Rules as Non-Instrumental and Authoritative Assertions

If the civil condition is composed entirely of a system of rules, then it is important to know what a rule is and what kind of rule is constitutive of the civil condition. By now, it should be clear that since civil association is a non-instrumental association, the rules that constitute it must also be non-instrumental. In other words, rules in civil association in the first place are not advices, warnings or pleas, for these are persuasive utterances tied to particular occasions instrumental to the satisfaction of substantive wants. Likewise, being non-instrumental, civil rules, unlike prudential practices/rules (such as 'honesty is the best policy in

---

[65] Oakeshott, 'The Rule of Law', p. 135. Oakeshott also says on the same page, 'it would be difficult to find a moralist, who, if he understood moral relationship as association in terms of rules, was not disposed to abandon authenticity [i.e. authority] in favour of "rightness" as the ground of moral obligation'.

[66] *Ibid.*, pp.128–129

maintaining good, long term, interpersonal relationships'), have no direct use for the agents of the association while pursuing their individual wants or interests. As prudential considerations, the validity of the recommendations made in the advices, warnings or pleas, and the usefulness of the prudential practices adopted by the associates is intimately tied up with their utility in procuring wished-for outcomes. The validity and authority of the non-instrumental rules in civil association, on the other hand, is categorically different, since, being non-instrumental, they are indifferent to the satisfaction of substantive wants. As Oakeshott says,

> the word 'authority' denotes a formal consideration, independent of all others, in which an utterance or an action is identified, understood and responded to, not in terms of what it prescribes or of the personal qualities of an agent or the confidence he inspires, *but in relation to an office, a practice or a procedure, or a rule recognized as such*.[67]

Furthermore, although orders and commands, being imperative, may be derived from rules, they are only *ad hoc* specific utterances calling for obedience or compliance from assignable agents in particular situations, and are used up on those occasions. By contrast, a rule which stipulates adverbial conditions for subscription by those who fall under its jurisdiction in the performance of all or any actions 'subsists and is known in advance of the hypothetical situations to which it may subsequently be found to relate and is not used up in being invoked or subscribed to'.[68] In addition, Oakeshott further contends that adverbial conditions can only be subscribed to adequately or inadequately, not be obeyed or disobeyed. In other words, unlike following an instruction, following a non-instrumental rule does not require one to follow any substantive or specific action; instead, in choosing and acting, one is required to do so in a certain manner or in accordance with a certain formal

---

[67] See Oakeshott, 'The Vocabulary of a Modern European State', in *Political Studies*, Vol. XXIII, July 1975, pp. pp.199–200, emphasis added.
[68] Oakeshott, 'The Rule of Law', p. 129.

condition that has no direct bearing on the satisfaction or achievement of substantive wants.

Since a rule does not prescribe any substantive action, it is not an utterance but an authoritative assertion.[69] As authoritative assertions, rules prescribe norms of conduct.[70] These prescriptions

> may be imperative or they may be authorizations, they may specify forbearances or confer powers, and they may identify offences, but what they enjoin, authorize, or identify are not substantive actions but considerations to be acknowledged and taken account of in acting.[71]

In a very important sense, *civitas* can be composed entirely of rules only if, first, its rules are purely non-instrumental and, secondly, it is recognised as an ideal condition in which the validity or authority of rules are acknowledged in terms of rules only (i.e. recognition of rules as rules), not in terms of any other things. Instrumental rules alone cannot constitute an association without a substantive and extrinsic purpose; for in the absence of such a purpose, there is nothing for these rules to relate to in the association. But if *civitas* is a condition with a substantive purpose, it cannot be composed entirely of rules; instead, it must be related in terms of a purpose that is extrinsic to the rules found in the association. To be related entirely in terms of rules therefore means that the rules concerned must, in addition to being composed of formal adverbial conditions to be subscribed to by the participating agents, be non-instrumental in nature.

Furthermore, as authoritative assertions, the validity of the rules in *civitas* is itself a matter to be decided by reference to the rules of the civil condition, since to be willing to participate in a rule-governed practice presupposes that there is a recognised right (i.e. complying with the conditions as prescribed by the rules) and wrong (i.e. failure to comply

---

[69] Oakeshott, *On Human Conduct*, p. 125. Oakeshott also argues that habits or regularities of behaviour are not rules of conduct, for they are obviously not authoritative. See *ibid*.
[70] *Ibid*., p. 126.
[71] *Ibid*.

with the conditions proscribed by the rules) way of doing things in practice. The deliberation as to what is right and what is wrong in a given case is certainly a matter of reasoning, but the reasons adduced must be derived from the prescriptions stipulated in the relevant rules governing the case, rather than from a balance of interests, benefits or conflicting moral intuitions external to the rules. Similarly, the reasons adduced must also not be derived from deductions from any so-called 'first-order moral or political principles or values' independent of the rules; otherwise what is authoritative is those first-order moral or political principles, not the system of rules of the civil condition, and the civil condition cannot therefore be composed entirely of rules. The participants falling within the jurisdiction of these rules have an obligation to follow them in order to follow the right way (i.e. the prescribed conditions as correctly understood) of doing things; otherwise, they are either not complying with the rules of the practice as required, or the practice concerned is not composed entirely of rules.[72] As a

---

[72] Peter Winch also proposes a similar argument in his article 'Authority' in Anthony Quinton's *Political Philosophy*, Oxford: Oxford University Press, 1967, rpt. 1985, in which he says, 'the acceptance of authority is not just something which, as a matter of fact, you cannot get along without if you want to participate in rule-governed activities; rather, to participate in rule-governed activities *is*, in a certain way, to accept authority. For to participate in such an activity is to accept that there is *a right and a wrong way of doing things*, and the decision as to what is right and wrong in a given case can never depend *completely* on one's own caprice (Cf. Wittgenstein: *Philosophical Investigations*, I, 258).' See also *Political Philosophy*, p. 99, emphasis in the original. Peter Winch's 'Rules: Wittgenstein's Analysis' in his *The Idea of a Social Science and its Relation to Philosophy*, London, Melbourne and Henley: Routledge & Kegan Paul and New Jersey: Humanities Press, 1958, rpt. 1984, pp. 24–33, is also highly relevant here. Likewise, David Mapel's discussion of the idea of specifying a moral or legal rule is also highly relevant: 'In "specifying" a rule, we neither "apply" it deductively nor "balance" it intuitively, nor do we use some combination of these methods, as philosophers such as W. D. Ross and H. L. A. Hart have suggested. Rather, we tailor our norms to cases by making them more specific. As Henry Richardson argues, however, in specifying a norm we must be *refining* that norm, not just *replacing* it with another; otherwise, "specification" is as *ad hoc* as "balancing."' See 'Purpose and Politics: Can There Be a Non-Instrumental Civil Association?', in

result, to recognise the authority and validity of the rules in *civitas* has 'nothing whatever to do with approval or disapproval of the conditions prescribed [by those rules], with having consented or not consented to these conditions, or with the outcome in human conduct of their being observed or not observed'.[73] All it requires is that in *civitas*, the agents so related must recognise rules as rules, for it is a practice composed entirely of a system of non-instrumental rules.

Civil Association and Its Institutions

So, the ideal character of civil association postulates free agents who are related to each other in an intelligent and durable human association in terms of a system of non-instrumental (i.e. moral) rules, in which the agents all recognise the formal conditions (which qualify but do not determine substantive actions) asserted by the rules as authoritative. Agents are required to subscribe to them in their self-chosen substantive performances in the separate or joint pursuit of their imagined and wished-for outcomes.

As autonomous agents, they are free to form any enterprise associations for the pursuit of their common purpose and engage in whatever transactional intercourses they like for the satisfaction of their different wants, as long as they are adequately observing the conditions prescribed by the rules of civil association. As such, the civil condition is highly compatible with social diversity, for

> there is no end to the number and variety of the minorities of interest into which they [i.e. the free agents in the civil association] may circumstantially compose themselves or the collocations (sex, family, race, profession, hobby and so on) in terms of which they may from time to time recognize themselves.[74]

Being an ideal condition composed entirely of rules, the validity of which is also to be decided by the rules them-

---

The Political Science Reviewer, Vol. 21, Spring, 1992, p. 76, emphasis in the original. Also see Oakeshott, 'The Vocabulary of a Modern European State', p. 203.
[73] Oakeshott, *On Human Conduct*, p. 127.
[74] Oakeshott, 'The Rule of Law', p. 137.

selves, *civitas* is a self-contained condition with a self-determined jurisdiction. As the formal conditions prescribed by the rules of the association are equally applicable to all agents who are related in terms of these rules, this ideal character also postulates a formal relationship of equality among its agents.[75] Unlike the rules of a game, which are both simple and somewhat arbitrary, the rules in *civitas* are far more complex and systematic. Their scope is as wide as their focus is sharp:

> they relate to the miscellaneous, unforeseeable choices and transactions of agents each concerned to live the life of 'a man like me', who are joined in no common purpose or engagement, who may be strangers to one another, the objects of whose loves are as various as themselves, and who may lack any but this moral allegiance to one another.[76]

Rules like these are rules of a certain kind, and Oakeshott calls them 'law' or *lex*.[77]

So far, an impressive theory of the abstract conditions of civility has been formulated by Oakeshott, in which free agents are related in terms of a system of non-instrumental rules that creates conditions allowing freedom of choice and free association of individuals. However, as 'general abstract considerations cannot themselves be the terms of any association, what has to be understood in these considerations is their relation to contingent situations'.[78] In order to ensure continual and general subscription to the system of laws as postulated in *civitas*, and in order to allow the agents (or *cives*)[79] to know the conditions prescribed by the law, civil association postulates three more institutional procedures for these purposes. The first is a procedure of adjudication (i.e. a court of law) for resolution of legal uncertainties arising from disputes about the adequacy of

[75] Oakeshott, *On Human Conduct*, p. 125.
[76] *Ibid.*, p. 129.
[77] *Ibid.* Again, Oakeshott prefers to use the word *lex* to stress the non-instrumental character of law, for the latter has already become somewhat corrupted in the common usage of political discourse.
[78] *Ibid.*, p. 130.
[79] Again, another archaic term rescued by Oakeshott to avoid the corruption of modern political vocabulary. See *ibid.*, pp. 108-9.

circumstantial response by agents to the rules of conduct as prescribed by the law, in which authoritative interpretations of the meaning of the prescribed conditions, together with authoritative rulings, are provided for in relation to the disputed situations to bring the disputes concerned to a close.[80]

Secondly, civil association postulates an authoritative procedure of legislation for the deliberation, enactment, amendment and repeal of individual pieces of *lex*. This is required for the endurance of civil association, for even though it is likely that legislative innovations are less often required than adjudicative rulings to keep civil association going,[81] it cannot rule out that there may be 'notable changes of belief or sentiment about the desirable conditions of civil conduct' that require deliberation on the alteration of and amendment to some of the conditions prescribed by the law in civil association.[82] The fact that *lex* or formal conditions of civil conduct can be deliberated upon for alterations or amendments points to the important political dimension of civil association, in which the desirability, *not* authority, of any particular rules of civil association is subject to critical evaluation. In fact, even the constitutional shape of the legislative office in civil association can be deliberated upon in the light of the beliefs and sentiments of the *cives*, for 'the rule of law does not itself specify any particular constitution or procedure in respect of this legislative office'.[83]

While the procedure of adjudication in civil association is to ascertain the meaning of *lex* to resolve legal disputes, and the procedure for legislation is to make changes to *lex* in accordance with changes in circumstantial situations, civil association also requires a procedure or office for the engagement of what Oakeshott calls 'ruling', which is the

[80] *Ibid.*, p. 131.
[81] 'Whereas enterprise association depends upon continuous "managerial" decisions about how its purpose shall be pursued, civil association depends not upon continuous legislative innovation but upon continuous adjudicative conclusion.' See *ibid.*, p. 138, n. 1.
[82] *Ibid.*
[83] Oakeshott, 'The Rule of Law', p. 138.

exercise of authority (as prescribed by *lex*) over civil association and the administration of *lex* in cases of injustice or wrongdoings, leading to penalties determined by the courts.[84] Oakeshott describes the engagement of ruling as a power relationship; for while the officers who are authorised to do the policing and administering are just executing court orders or are the custodians of the smooth operation of conditions as prescribed by *lex*, they are nevertheless trying to seek imagined and wished-for satisfactions in the responses of others, who are compelled to pay damages or to rectify their wrongdoings in accordance with the provisions of the law.[85]

Civil Association as the Rule of Law

With these three institutional postulates of civil association in place, the full character of civil association as a distinctive mode of human association has become more or less clear. Oakeshott uses the term *societas* to describe a modern state understood in terms of the postulates identified in civil association, and the term *universitas* for the enterprising state. Both terms are derived from Roman private law.[86] Oakeshott also thinks it appropriate to describe civil association as embodying the rule of law, for such an expression

> denotes a self-sustained, notionally self-consistent, mode of human association in terms of the recognition of the authority or authenticity of enacted laws and the obligations they prescribe in which the considerations in terms of which the authenticity of a law may be confirmed or rebutted are themselves enacted law; in which the jurisdiction of the law is itself a matter of law and in which the necessary condition that the associates be aware of the obligations the law imposes is subsumed under the principle that ignorance of the law is no defence against the imputation of having failed to observe its prescription.[87]

Civil association, in the main, is constituted by a system of non-instrumental rules institutionally enacted and

---

[84] *Ibid.*, pp. 141-4.
[85] Oakeshott, *On Human Conduct*, pp. 144, 148.
[86] *Ibid.*, p. 199.
[87] Oakeshott, 'The Rule of Law', p. 139.

known as law or *lex*, in which all authoritative offices, and the rights and obligations of the officials and *cives* concerned, are a matter for the law to decide.[88] Since agents related in terms of civil association can subscribe to the law only if the conditions prescribed by law are known and understood by them, there is also an inherent requirement in the rule of law that laws must not be secret and retrospective; also, as law is the only medium that can make authoritative pronouncements concerning the rights and obligations applying to all *cives* of the association, it is imperative that there shall be 'no obligations save those imposed by law, all associates equally and without exception subject to the obligations imposed by law, no outlawry, and so on'.[89]

In addition, when it comes to relating *lex* to contingent situations in order to ascertain whether there is any inadequate subscription to the prescribed conditions of law, the law court has a duty to uphold the integrity of the system of law in order to allow the rule of law to prevail. In other words, when considering actual performances in a legal dispute, the judge must deliberate the case strictly in respect of its legality only. The questions about the desirability of the prescribed conditions involved in the dispute and about whether the legal conclusion of the dispute may undermine the interests of certain parties involved in the dispute are all

---

[88] Many scholars have pointed out that Oakeshott's idea of an institutionalised system of law as the rule of law resembles H.L.A Hart's definition of law as a union of primary rules of obligation and secondary rules of recognition. See Hart's *The Concept of Law*, Oxford: Oxford University Press, 1961. In a previously unpublished manuscript entitled 'Law', Oakeshott also uses the term 'constitutional rules of recognition' to describe those rules that would belong to Hart's idea of secondary rules of recognition. See Luke O'Sullivan's compilation of the latest posthumously published works of Michael Oakeshott, *What is History and other essays*, Exeter: Imprint Academic, 2004, p. 423. But as Terry Nardin rightly points out, 'the distinction between instrumental and non-instrumental rules, which is crucial both to any non-consequentialist view of morality and to Oakeshott's theory of law as institutionalised morality, is absent from Hart's discussion, which rests on utilitarian premises'. See his *The Philosophy of Michael Oakeshott*, p. 195, n. 9.

[89] Oakeshott, 'The Rule of Law', p. 140.

174   *The Quest for Civil Order*

irrelevant, for they are either political questions or questions that belong to substantive, not legal and non-instrumental, considerations.[90] But what is meant by deliberation strictly in accordance with legality?

As a general rule, no piece of legislation can anticipate the occurrence of all possible contingent situations; for that matter, how an actual contingent situation is related to the legislation concerned can never be exhaustively provided for in the legislation itself. In other words, in order to ascertain the meaning of the law in a legal dispute, the job of the judge is 'to declare a conclusion which is not, and could never be given in *lex*; namely, how a prescribed norm of conduct stands in relation to a contingent situation'.[91] The judicial conclusion, therefore, is there to connect *lex* with a contingent situation by putting forward an authoritative pronouncement on the meaning of the law in that particular situation, in order to resolve some legal uncertainties, but the judge should only amplify the meaning of *lex* in a procedure that is recognised by the law itself.[92] This amplified meaning of *lex* has, in a sense, extended the meaning of the law concerned, for such a judicial conclusion cannot be given by *lex* in the first place. However, the amplification must be done 'justifiably' (i.e. the authority of the amplification must be its relation to *lex*), 'appropriately' (i.e. there is a legal need to settle a contingent dispute about the meaning of *lex*) and 'durably' (i.e. the judicial conclusion must be capable of entering into the existing legal system without significantly upsetting its equilibrium).[93] Oakeshott admits

---

[90] In this context, Oakeshott criticises Ronald Dworkin's idea of adjudication as allowing judge to usurp the office of the legislator. See *ibid.*, pp. 144–5, n. 6.
[91] Oakeshott, *On Human Conduct*, p. 133.
[92] *Ibid.*, p. 136.
[93] *Ibid.*, pp. 133–6. David Mapel suggests that Oakeshott has something like the notion of specification of rules in mind when he discusses such a procedure of adjudication in civil association. However, Mapel's understanding of the notion of specification of rules may not be consistent with Oakeshott's idea of adjudication, for while Oakeshott is clearly thinking of specifying the meaning of a rule in a legal dispute as amplifying the meaning of *lex* in its application to a not foreseeable contingent situation in accordance with the

that like all casuistical undertaking, judicial deliberation is a 'devious engagement', and there is no guarantee that there is only one correct answer to a specific legal dispute; but again, it is up to the judicial procedure to come up with a final authoritative conclusion for its resolution.[94] In other words, in *societas* (a state related in terms of the rule of law), not only public offices and governmental procedures should be governed and recognised by law, but the law and its deliberation must also possess certain relevant attributes (sometimes called the 'inner morality of law') in order to maintain its non-instrumental character as well as to protect the integrity of the system itself.[95]

---

authorised procedure, what Mapel has in mind in the reflection of the meaning of a rule is to specify it in terms of some more or less general principle that somehow can be derived from the rule under deliberation. In the case of Oakeshott, the need to specify the rule in dispute is to settle the meaning of the rule concerned in the context of the unforeseeable contingent situation and make it consistent with the rest of the legal system, yet in the case of Mapel it is not at all clear why it is necessary to specify the rule concerned or what the focus is of such a deliberation. See Mapel's otherwise highly interesting article, 'Purpose and Politics: Can There Be a Non-Instrumental Civil Association?', pp. 75–8.

[94] Oakeshott, 'The Rule of Law', p. 145.
[95] Perhaps that is why Martin Loughlin says, 'Oakeshott's political theory may in fact be viewed as an ambitious attempt to provide a framework in which H.L.A. Hart's normative version of legal positivism may be synthesized with Lon Fuller's analysis of the internal morality of law.' See his *Public Law and Political Theory*, Oxford: Clarendon, 1992, p. 80. See also Mapel's discussion of why Oakeshott does not need to take sides in the debate between Hart and Fuller on the definition of law and whether legal positivism or natural law theory provides a better understanding of the nature of law in 'Purpose and Politics: Can There Be a Non-Instrumental Civil Association?', pp. 67–70. Loughlin, however, misunderstands Oakeshott's theory of law when he says that the authority of law is provided by what Oakeshott called the *jus* of *lex*, for, contra Loughlin, the quality of *jus* of *lex* concerns the rightness or desirability of law, not its authority. See *Public Law and Political Theory*, p. 81. For more reliable guides in this respect, see Richard B. Friedman's 'Oakeshott on the Authority of Law', in *Ratio Juris*, Vol. 2, No. 1, March 1989, pp. 27–40, and Shirley Robin Letwin's 'Morality and Law', in *Ratio Juris*, Vol. 2, No. 1, March 1989, pp. 55–65. In addition, Friedman's recent article 'Michael Oakeshott and the Elusive Identity of the Rule of Law', in *The Intellectual Legacy of Michael Oakeshott*, eds Corey Abel and Timothy Fuller, Exeter:

Civil Association: Conservatism vs Radicalism

So how coherent is Oakeshott's idea of *societas* as an account of civil association as a relationship in which autonomous individuals can enjoy social and political diversity yet at the same time acknowledge the compelling authority of the state in the pursuit of their different and separate wished-for outcomes?

One obvious and immediate query, coming particularly from those with a more radical disposition, is that by emphasising the authority of the rules of *societas* and by placing what appears to be overriding emphasis on the need to maintain the integrity and consistency of the system of existing laws in any changes and interpretations of them, Oakeshott's theory of civil association appears to have an in-built conservative tendency, which prefers the *status quo* to the freedom of the individual. It is unlikely, this objection maintains, that such a theory would accommodate genuine diversity, not to say constructive radicalism, if the *status quo* contains a lot of injustice in the first place. Even a sympathetic critic like Bhikhu Parekh says,

> As Oakeshott is deeply concerned with moral autonomy and integrity, it is strange that he should expect *cives* neither to evaluate the laws nor to disobey them even when they seem to them to be morally dubious. A theory of civil association whose authority is based on a suspension of critical moral reflection and active dissent clearly leaves much to be desired.[96]

Indeed, after being greeted as 'the greatest living British philosopher of conservative disposition' by *National Review* when *On Human Conduct* was published in 1975,[97] Oakeshott may find it unsurprising if people presume that there are assumptions of a conservative kind in his works.[98]

Imprint Academic, 2005, pp. 160–80, is among the best articles on Oakeshott's idea of the rule of law.

[96] See his 'Oakeshott's Theory of Civil Association', *Ethics*, Vol. 106, October 1995, p. 177.

[97] See back cover of *On Human Conduct* published by Clarendon Paperbacks.

[98] There are, of course, notable exceptions. See for examples, Wendell John Coats, Jr., 'Michael Oakeshott as a liberal theorist', in *Canadian*

At times, some of his utterances lend support to this suspicion. For example, in 'On Being Conservative', Oakeshott says,

> government ... as the conservative in this matter understands it, does not begin with a vision of another, different and better world ... [and] the intimations of government are to be found in ritual, not in religion or philosophy; in the enjoyment of orderly and peaceable behaviour, not in the search for truth or perfection.[99]

But this presumption proves to be illusive on closer examination.

To start with, let us not forget that the prescribed conditions of law in *societas* are formal and non-instrumental; they do not demand substantive performances. Agents in *societas* are free to enjoy as much social diversity as they please by engaging in many enterprise undertakings. As a result, 'it is not at all inconsistent', says Oakeshott, 'to be conservative in respect of government and radical in respect of almost every other activity'.[100]

Further, one must not misrepresent Oakeshott's political conservatism as a doctrine for the maintenance of the political *status quo*. The discussion on Oakeshott's idea of morality and civility as a vernacular language should have already made it clear that what he is against is ideological rationalism in politics and morality rather than necessary innovations and improvements. As a vernacular language or a practice, abstract moral or political principles are only abridgements of the practice, not its foundation or criteria by which all our moral and political activities must be judged. According to Oakeshott, a practice, when properly

---

Journal of Political Science, Vol. XVIII, 4, December 1985, pp. 773–87; John Gray, 'Oakeshott as a liberal', in *Post-Liberalism: Studies in Political Thought*, New York and London: Routledge, 1993, chapter 4; and Paul Franco, *The Political Philosophy of Michael Oakeshott*. We must also not forget that as a philosopher, Oakeshott regards philosophy as a 'radically subversive' undertaking. See his 'Political Philosophy', in *Religion, Politics, and the Moral Life*, ed. Timothy Fuller, New Haven and London: Yale University Press, 1993, p. 140.
[99] Oakeshott, *Rationalism in Politics and Other Essays*, rpt. 1981, p. 188.
[100] *Ibid.*, p. 195.

understood, 'is never immune from innovation and it may be said to be continuously reconstituted in being used'.[101]

Parekh is mistaken in stating that Oakeshott does not expect *cives* to evaluate the laws, and that authority in civil association is based on suspension of critical moral reflection of *lex*. What Oakeshott insists upon is that such evaluations of *lex* must conceptually presuppose the authority of the conditions prescribed by the *lex* of *societas*; for 'it is inherently impossible to be associated merely in terms of the consideration of the desirability of the conditions of that association'.[102] Provided that this condition is met, Oakeshott even goes so far as to say that *cives* 'may be associated [in a voluntarily formed enterprise association] for the express purpose of considering, in respect of their desirability, the terms in which they are otherwise associated [in a civil association]'.[103] Such is the scope of political and social diversity allowed in Oakeshott's civil association.

In this respect, it is interesting to discover that an advocate of radical democracy and feminism, Chantal Mouffe, is perceptive enough to see the potentially creative force of Oakeshott's theory of civil association. Mouffe does not think it plausible to follow the communitarian's vain search for a substantive common good for the political community in this age of radical difference. She also finds problems in Kantian liberalism's attempt to privatise the good by giving absolute priority to rights in a liberal state, thus hollowing out the moral and ethical contents of the political community.[104] In her search for a radical mode of political associa-

---

[101] Oakeshott, *On Human Conduct*, p. 120.
[102] See Oakeshott, 'The Vocabulary of Modern European State (Concluded)', p. 410.
[103] *Ibid*. Similarly, I think Peter Winch is right to say this: 'The very notion of a human will, capable of deliberating and making decisions, presupposes the notion of authority.' See 'Authority', p. 98.
[104] See Chantal Mouffe 'Citizenship and the Political Community', in *The Return of the Political*, London, NY: Verso, 1993, pp. 63–6. Oakeshott also agrees that the moral ideal of liberal democracy is the weakest part of that doctrine. See his *The Social and Political Doctrines of Contemporary Europe*, New York: Cambridge University Press, 1950, p. xxi.

tion which respects individual freedom, does not depend on the existence of a substantive common good, yet at the same time can maintain a common moral–political bond that creates a linkage among the participants in the association, she finds that 'Oakeshott's idea of civil association as *societas* is adequate to define political association under modern democratic conditions', for within Oakeshott's rule-articulated civil association those rules prescribe norms of conduct to be subscribed to in seeking self-chosen satisfactions and in performing self-chosen actions. The identification with those rules of civil intercourse creates a common political identity among persons otherwise engaged in many different enterprises. This modern form of political community is held together not by a substantive idea of the common good but by a common bond, a public concern. It is therefore a community without a definite shape or a definite identity and in continuous re-enactment.[105]

Although Mouffe does not substantiate her claim, she also takes it for granted that Oakeshott is a conservative who fails to exploit the radical potential of his theory of civil association.[106] For Mouffe, however, the fact that civil association does not require a definite shape in the form of a common substantive good, and is continuously subject to enactment, is a great advantage not only as a guarantee of individual liberty, but also by making it possible to change the moral and political contents of the association by introducing principles of liberty and equality that are sensitive to different social relations and subject positions (e.g. gender, class, race, ethnicity, sexual orientation), so as to

---

[105] Mouffe, 'Citizenship and the Political Community', p. 67.
[106] *Ibid.*, p. 68.

shape and re-enact civil association in the image of radical democracy.[107]

While Mouffe may be correct in thinking that Oakeshott's theory of civil association does possess the potential for creative and even radical changes within *societas*, there is no reason to see Oakeshott's ideas about civil association as necessarily conservative in the sense of favouring small changes or the *status quo*. There is the danger that Mouffe's attempt to introduce her more radical ideas to *societas*, if carried out in an unqualified manner, will easily turn her feminist and radical principles into foundational yardsticks of the rationalistic kind, which will abruptly impose a preconceived vision on, instead of continuously intimating necessary changes to, the development of civil association. In a non-instrumental society, abstract principles are not unconditional considerations for change and development. Any attempt to turn them into that not only undermines the nature of *societas*, but also shows a fundamental misunderstanding of Oakeshott's theory of civil association. In this regard, Noel O'Sullivan may be right to point out that Mouffe's radical endeavour risks 'collapsing the civil model into a form of utopia — the utopia of the rainbow coalition.'[108]

Politics and Civil Association

Perhaps a closer look at how we should evaluate the desirability of the rules of conduct in *societas* (i.e. the political

---

[107] *Ibid.*, pp. 65 and 71–3. Naturally, since *lex* in *societas* includes rules of recognition as well as rules of conduct, the re-enactment of civil association may include the debate on re-shaping the constitution as well as on other aspects of civil association. There is no reason to think that Oakeshott's theory of civil association would not allow debates on and alterations to the manner in which *societas* is governed. In this regard, Gerencser is probably mistaken when he seems to suggest that Oakeshott's theory only allows political criticisms of the primary rules of *respublica*, but requires unqualified consensus regarding the constitutional and secondary rules. See the last two chapters of his *The Skeptic's Oakeshott*.

[108] See Noel O'Sullivan, 'Difference and the Concept of the Political in Contemporary Political Philosophy', in *Political Studies*, Vol. 45, 1997, p. 751.

engagement of the *cives*) will help us to better understand the scope of political freedom and creativity allowed in civil association. Oakeshott regards such an engagement as 'at once acquiescent and critical'.[109] It is necessarily acquiescent because, as has been shown, without assent to the authority of *respublica* (i.e. the public concern or consideration of *cives*), there cannot be a non-instrumental, rule-following, practice to create conditions for political deliberation.[110] On the other hand, it is necessarily critical because, as alterations to the conditions prescribed by *lex* are unavoidable, questions 'concerned with approval or disapproval and with desirabilities [of the prescribed norms of *societas*]' are bound to arise.[111]

Since political deliberation about the desirability of *lex* is concerned with its moral and legal conditions instead of its instrumental values in facilitating 'managerial' decisions for the procurement of substantive and extrinsic interests and outcomes, the criteria to determine what is desirable are not to be sought extrinsically or in any means–end type considerations. Furthermore, as an enduring human relationship, the conditions prescribed by *lex* in *societas* are the results of intelligent human choices, not the consequences of any physical process. Consequently, the desirability of these conditions 'cannot be deduced from the so-called dictates of Reason' or demonstrated to be correct as such; instead, their desirability is the result of the considered judgement or misjudgement of the free agents whose deliberations are made in the context of *respublica*.[112] In other words, any political opinion on a legislative proposal in *societas* is bound to be 'contentious'; this is so not because such a proposal might involve some substantive interests that pull in different directions, with different parties or sectors clamouring for different advantages, but because it is

---

[109] Oakeshott, *On Human Conduct*, p. 163. 'The best institutions', says Oakeshott, 'are those whose constitution is both firm and self-critical.' See 'The Political Economy of Freedom', in *Rationalism in Politics and Other Essays*, 1962, rpt. 1981, pp. 41–2.
[110] Oakeshott, *On Human Conduct*, pp. 147 and 164.
[111] *Ibid.*, p. 164.
[112] *Ibid.*, p. 139.

the result of 'the necessary absence of a ready and indisputable criterion for determining the desirability of a legislative proposal'.[113]

So, matters concerning the desirability of the prescribed conditions of *lex* are necessarily contentious, and since it is possible to consider the alterability of these conditions and there are prescribed procedures (essentially legislative in nature within *societas*) for doing so, citizens in Oakeshott's civil association enjoy political freedom. They may engage in political arguments and may approve or disapprove of proposed norms of conduct or other conditions prescribed by *lex*. But they can only do so as long as they fully understand that they are deliberating about non-instrumental rules and their subscription to these rules (which relate them as *cives*) is presupposed in the first place. In this respect, David Mapel is correct to point out that this feature of civil association 'opens up the maximum amount of space for criticism'.[114] In the light of the essentially contentious character of political deliberations in civil association, it is therefore incorrect for Mouffe to say, 'what is completely missing in Oakeshott is division and antagonism'.[115]

Nevertheless, since there cannot be extrinsic criteria to determine the desirability of *lex*, political criticisms are necessarily immanent criticisms. Therefore, it is inherently impossible for *cives* to launch a total critique of the desirability of the whole system of *lex*, for immanent criticisms, though critical of certain existing prescribed or proposed conditions, can only make sense (i.e. as desirable or not in the light of other accepted conditions) within the system itself, and any innovations proposed must be capable of being accommodated by the system itself. As such, 'every

---

[113] *Ibid.*, p. 140. See also Oakeshott's 'Political discourse', in *Rationalism in Politics and Other Essays*, 1991, pp. 70–95.
[114] See David Mapel, 'Civil Association and the Idea of Contingency', *Political Theory*, Vol. 18, August 1990, p. 405, quoted from Gerencser, *The Skeptic's Oakeshott*, p. 136.
[115] See 'Citizenship and the Political Community', pp. 68–9. To Oakeshott, however, war and belligerence are enemies of civil association. See *On Human Conduct*, p. 273. More on this will be discussed below.

proposal for deliberate innovation in the conditions of conduct specified in a *respublica*', says Oakeshott, 'is both an appeal to current achievements in civility and an exploration of the intimations of these achievements; and there is no mistake-proof manner of doing this'.[116]

Oakeshott describes the requirement that proposed innovations in the prescribed conditions of a *respublica* must be capable of being accommodated by the system of *lex* as a 'substantive' consideration.[117] This is so because they obviously aim to achieve a purpose, namely that the continuity and coherence of the system of *lex* must be maintained before any political innovations can be turned into authoritative utterances of civil association. In addition to this consideration, there are two other 'aids to reflection' in political deliberation on the question of desirability. The first is whether the proposed prescription is incapable of enforcement, and the second is whether subscription to civil conditions should be required of performances only in respect of their capacity to harm other agents.[118]

According to Oakeshott, the main consideration about enforcement is not so much a worry about an inherently unenforceable law as about the undesirable extension of the apparatus of detection to a degree that is not likely to be tol-

---

[116] *Ibid.*, p. 180. In this regard, Glenn Worthington is rather confusing when he writes that, 'In questioning the desirability of a civil rule, politics must forego questioning the desirability of the whole civil association. The act of questioning the whole of civil association, which is the authority of the civil rules rather than the desirability of particular rules, is not an act of politics but an act of either (self) exile or subversion.' See his 'Oakeshott's Claims of Politics', *Political Studies*, Vol. 45, 1997, p. 733, quoted from Gerencser, *The Skeptic's Oakeshott*, p. 200, n. 51. Since questions of desirability logically can only arise as a result of the acknowledgement of the authority of *respublica*, it is misleading to suggest that political criticism can question the desirability of the whole of civil association. I am also not sure if the act of questioning the whole of civil association is an act of self-exile. As Michael Walzer argues, an exile, like John Locke when he took refuge in Holland in the 1680s, is still offering social and political criticisms against his home country rather than clamouring for the conquest or total conversion of his native association. See chapter 2 of his *Interpretation and Social Criticism*.
[117] Oakeshott, *On Human Conduct*, p. 179.
[118] *Ibid.*, p. 178.

erated by the *respublica*. While Oakeshott is always cautious in reminding us not to elevate considerations like this into an unconditional principle, as 'criteria of approval or disapproval untouched by contingency are necessarily absent',[119] it is clear that this consideration has a built-in bias against concentrations of power, even for detection of delinquencies for the protection of civil association by the government, not to say against concentrations of power by other organisations.[120] In this respect, Oakeshott is prepared to use legal intervention to promote effective competition against monopolies of all sorts, for 'effective competition is not something that springs up of its own accord ... both it and any alternative to it are creatures of law'.[121] Further, Oakeshott has no hesitation in endorsing the Chicago economist Henry C. Simons' policy of 'making competition effective wherever effective competition is not demonstrably impossible',[122] and does not think that policies of this kind will compromise the rule of law.[123] He calls Simons' proposals 'more radical than the projects of the collectivists'.[124] We fail to appreciate the creative and radical potential of Oakeshott's theory of civil association if we fail to notice its implications in this respect.

However, this creative and radical potential notwithstanding, political criticisms in civil association in the end are all unavoidably immanent criticisms, and the exploration of innovations is essentially the pursuit of intimations that are implied but not yet fully apparent in the system of civility itself. Whether such intimations are small or large,

---

[119] *Ibid.*
[120] 'Strength we think to be a virtue in government, but we do not find our defence against disintegration either in arbitrary or in very great power. Indeed, we are inclined to see in both these the symptoms of an already advanced decay', says Oakeshott in 'The Political Economy of Freedom', p. 42.
[121] *Ibid.*, p. 47.
[122] *Ibid.*, p. 55. Simons' proposals included, amongst other things, prohibiting most big corporations from holding stock in other corporations in order to preserve more economic freedom and equality. See *ibid.*, pp. 56-7.
[123] Oakeshott, 'The Rule of Law', pp. 162-3.
[124] Oakeshott, 'The Political Economy of Freedom', p. 55.

cautious or bold, conservative or radical is for the political participants to decide, to judge and to accept or to reject in the light of their circumstantial considerations, so long as they do not mistake such considerations for unconditional criteria for change. Indeed, the reason given by Oakeshott in his example about the enfranchisement of women in his inaugural lecture 'Political Education' — that is, women in all or most other important respects had already been enfranchised — may also be used, with suitable adaptations, in the present time to support gay marriage in the political debate about the legal recognition and legal protection of the rights and duties of gay couples in most Western liberal societies;[125] questions about whether this is a conservative or radical matter or whether it should be accepted are, as always, contentious and subject to different opinions and judgements in different civil associations.[126]

Freedom, Diversity and Autonomy

The state understood in the mode of civil association, in which citizens are related by their common subscription to the authority of the rule of law, thus postulates free agents and social diversity. Since their subscription to the authority of non-instrumental rules known as *lex* only qualifies but does not determine citizens' self-chosen substantive performances, it only provides the conditional context for their several or joint pursuits of imagined and wished-for satisfaction. It is in this sense that *lex* serves as a common bond and common concern for all.

Robert Grant calls the freedom inherent in human agency 'elementary',[127] for the potential for the development of human agency depends very much on the individual's decisions to cultivate his individuality. A free agent, therefore,

---

[125] See also Oakeshott, *Rationalism in Politics and Other Essays*, 1962, rpt. 1981, p. 124.

[126] *The Economist*, normally regarded as a conservative defender of the market economy, wrote in a leader of its 28 February 2004 edition (p. 11) in support of gay marriage, which arguably is a highly socially radical proposal. This is but one telling example to show that the line between conservatism and radicalism is never easy to draw.

[127] Robert Grant, *Oakeshott*, London: The Claridge Press, 1990, p. 96.

does not have a nature, only a history, and 'he is what in conduct he becomes'.[128] What needs to be cultivated, as Grant suggests, 'is how to turn this "unsought freedom of conduct" into a satisfaction in its own right',[129] so that the individual agent is recognised

> as a substantive personality, the outcome of an education, whose resources are collected in a self-understanding; and conduct is recognized as the adventure in which this cultivated self deploys its resources, discloses and enacts itself in response to its contingent situations, and both acquires and confirms its autonomy.[130]

As a cultivated historical achievement, 'human individuality has neither the amorphous quality of a "bundle of perceptions"', says Shirley Robin Letwin in her study of the moral character of an English gentleman, 'nor the fixity of a "core of personality "'. To Letwin (and to Oakeshott as well), 'It is a personal identity which is more or less stable and fixed only at death. This changing but steady distinctness is most accurately described as a "character"'. In other words, the character of the individual is what constitutes the individuality of free agency. This is the result of how the individual chooses to understand, respond to or enjoy what he or she encounters in life, and is indeed 'the essence of [his or her] humanity'.[131] This character of the individual, however, is to be accomplished by learning, not in the sense of copying established patterns or reciting substantive utterances, but in the sense of 'mastering a language of one sort or another, and knowing a language does not dictate what should be said'.[132] The cultivation of individuality is therefore an undertaking that is inevitably both personal and social at the same time: personal in the sense that each is allowed to develop his or her personal style, no matter how

---

[128] See Oakeshott, *On Human Conduct*, p. 41.
[129] Grant, *Oakeshott*, p. 96.
[130] Oakeshott, *On Human Conduct*, pp. 236–7. Oakeshott's insights in this respect are also spelt out in his works on learning and education. See his *The Voice of Liberal Learning*.
[131] See Shirley Robin Letwin's extremely interesting *The Gentleman in Trollope: Individuality and Moral Conduct*, London and Basingstoke: MacMillan, 1982, p. 60.
[132] *Ibid.*, p. 62.

idiosyncratic it is; social in the sense that such a cultivation is possible only if the individual concerned is capable of making use of the resources of our civilisation, particularly those resources, such as a common language and a common morality, that help him or her to make sense of the world and give meaning to interpersonal relationships.

Individual autonomy, cultivated by the individual in his or her unique style and acquired in his or her self-understanding, is thus regarded by Oakeshott as a 'virtue'.[133] Though there is no predetermined destination or collective goal for such a virtue, its continuous cultivation and exploration, using the tools of civility and morality, appears to be a necessary condition for keeping human civilisations healthy, and this may well mean that as a moral being, the individual has an implied duty to enrich his personal autonomy as best he can by also nurturing the conditions in favour of the development of civility and morality, though the ways of doing so should be as diverse as each individual's imagination permits.[134] Given the non-instrumental nature of civil association whose prescribed conditions for interpersonal intercourses only qualify but do not determine substantive performances, free agents thus have maximum scope to develop their own distinct individuality as much as they like, and Oakeshott describes the recogni-

---

[133] Oakeshott, *On Human Conduct*, p. 239. Patrick Riley calls Oakeshott a philosopher of individuality. See his 'Michael Oakeshott: Philosopher of Individuality', pp. 649-64. Likewise, Wendell John Coats, Jr, regards Oakeshott as 'one of the pre-eminent political theorists of modern European individualism'. See Coats, Jr, 'Michael Oakeshott as Liberal Theorist', p. 773. By contrast, I suspect that what leads John Liddington to suggest that the freedom intrinsic to agency is the absence of causation, no more and no less, is his failure to appreciate this aspect of free agency. See his 'Oakeshott: Freedom in a Modern European State', in *Conceptions of Liberty in Political Philosophy*, eds Zbigniew Pelczynski and John Gray, New York: St. Martin's Press, 1984, p. 299.

[134] Richard E. Flathman characterises Oakeshott as 'a theorist of high citizenship'. See his 'Citizenship and Authority: A Chastened View of Citizenship', in *Theorizing Citizenship*, ed. Ronald Beiner, Albany: State University of New York Press, 1995, pp. 105-51, particularly on pp. 131-7.

tion given in civil association to moral agency as 'civil freedom'.[135]

A distinct but equally important freedom for free agents is the right to join any enterprise association of their choice for the pursuit of jointly agreed satisfactions. This is important since only substantive actions can develop individuality, and these may involve joining with like-minded associates in the pursuit of agreed goals. Since civil association does not have any common substantive purpose of its own, it does not prescribe any enterprise associations of its own except the executive office of the government for administering and policing the rule of law, and citizens are free to exercise choices of their own not only to form and join any enterprise associations, but also to extricate themselves from any of them if they subsequently find that the associations concerned no longer suit their individual purposes.[136] Civil association therefore not only recognises civil freedom, but also creates conditions favourable to the development of social diversity and freedoms of association and transaction.

However, if enterprise associations are compulsory, or if a state is understood as an enterprise association in the mode of *universitas*, agents so related will be unable to extricate themselves from the association even if they no longer agree with the substantive purposes advocated by those in control of the state. Such a situation would, according to Oakeshott, 'have severed the link between belief and conduct which constitutes moral agency'.[137] In other words, civil freedom is undermined. This, however, is sometimes denied.

In a thought-provoking article entitled 'Oakeshott: Freedom in a Modern European State', John Liddington has articulated a profound challenge to this, querying whether it is possible to distinguish the formal from the substantive aspect of human conduct and suggesting that all laws, Oakeshott's *lex* included, are there to secure the satisfaction

---

[135] Oakeshott, *On Human Conduct*, p. 157.
[136] *Ibid.*, p. 143.
[137] *Ibid.*, p. 158.

of people's wants and to restrict individual freedom by determining their performances.[138] So, when it comes to the evaluation and justification of law, it is always a matter of balance, according to Liddington.

A major attack on Oakeshott's distinction is provided by Liddington's queries about the nature of criminal law. In his article, Liddington refers to a footnote in Oakeshott's *On Human Conduct* in which Oakeshott tries to use two examples in the criminal law to explain why a rule in fact can never tell a performer what choice he or she should make and what action he or she should take, but only announces conditions to be subscribed to in making choices by the performer. In that note, Oakeshott says: 'a criminal law, which may be thought to come nearest to forbidding actions, does not forbid killing or lighting a fire, it forbids killing "murderously" or lighting a fire "arsonically"'.[139] Liddington finds such examples wanting and asks,

> but if a law prohibiting murder can be a procedural [i.e. formal] law, what would not count as a procedural law? If a law prohibiting fire-raising may be said to qualify rather than determine the performance of fire-lighting, why may not a law prohibiting (say) 'bourgeois' education be said to qualify rather than determine the performance of learning and teaching? And if, as Oakeshott's view would seem to imply, a law prohibiting larceny does not necessarily restrict substantive freedom [i.e. an individual's choice of substantive performance], why should we suppose that a law prohibiting private property necessarily restricts it? If the one may be said merely to qualify the acquisition of property, why not the other?[140]

To Liddington, in a nutshell, the problem is, 'what exactly is the difference between the form and the substance of conduct?'[141] And, if, as presumed by Liddington, such a distinction cannot be sustained, then laws in civil association will also determine, not just qualify, substantive performances.

---

[138] Liddington, 'Oakeshott: Freedom in a Modern European State', p. 308.
[139] Oakeshott, *On Human Conduct*, p. 58, n. 1.
[140] Liddington, 'Oakeshott: Freedom in a Modern European State', p. 313.
[141] *Ibid.*, p. 314.

As a result, the state even understood in the mode of civil association cannot guarantee civil freedom, for it will compel, through its laws, its citizens to perform actions and to make choices that they do not necessarily believe in.

But Oakeshott never says that to qualify a substantive performance by law in no way affects one's choice of action or how that action is performed; otherwise, what is the point of having the law and its prescribed conditions? In the footnote referred to by Liddington, Oakeshott says, '[practices and rules] exclude (forbid) or enjoin them [i.e. actions] in terms of prescribed conditions'.[142] In other words, rules do not determine actions and choices directly because they cannot; for rules and practices on their own cannot themselves be performed. Only individuals capable of making intelligent choices can determine their substantive performances, though in doing so they would have to take into account the prescribed conditions of the law which may affect how the individuals concerned should perform their actions.[143]

What Liddington seems to dispute is the distinction between forbidding or determining substantive performances and prescribing conditions that must be observed in choosing and acting. When Liddington says: 'but if a law prohibiting murder can be a procedural law, what would not count as a procedural law?',[144] he is denying the possibility of the above-mentioned distinction, for murder — the premeditated killing of a person without legal authorisation — is regarded by him as a substantive performance, and prohibition of it as a curtailment of individual freedom, though

---

[142] Oakeshott, *On Human Conduct*, p. 58, n. 1.
[143] 'A practice cannot itself be "performed". Purely regularian conduct is impossible: to make a grammatically faultless utterance is always to say *something*, to use an implement "properly" is always to make *something*, to follow a routine is always to do *something*, and to act "dutifully" is always to perform some substantive action whose "meaning" for the agent lies not in the conditional duty, but in its imagined and wished-for response.' *Ibid.*, p. 58, emphasis in the original.
[144] Liddington, 'Oakeshott: Freedom in a Modern European State', p. 313.

whether this is morally a good thing or not is another matter.[145]

But is the alleged formal condition of 'no premeditated killing of a person without legal authorisation' in acting and choosing in a civil association really a determination of substantive performance? It is of course true to say that to commit the offence of murder in law must involve the substantive performance of killing somebody; just as speaking something ungrammatically must involve the substantive act of speaking something. But does it follow that to *qualify* a substantive performance by legal conditions which make this killing 'murder' is the same as to *determine* a substantive performance? Acting unlawfully certainly presupposes the existence of a substantive performance; just as speaking ungrammatically involves certain substantive utterances. But like the grammatical rules that are there to discourage ungrammatical mistakes without determining what a speaker says, the non-instrumental rules of *lex* forbid substantive performances to be performed in a certain manner, but do not determine what act to choose. The legal prohibition 'no speeding' may rule out the substantive act of driving over 70 miles per hour on a highway, but it does not determine where the driver should go, or which route he or she should take. The condition of 'no premeditated killing of a person without legal authorisation' does not determine what an agent shall choose to believe and what concrete course of action he or she will take, but only the rightful manner in which the chosen substantive performance should be executed. In addition, it is important to point out that the adverbial conditions defined by law must be, according to Oakeshott, 'narrowly specified in terms of the evidence required to substantiate or to rebut the considerations alleged'.[146] This is necessary because being non-instrumental, the rules concerned should be framed in

---

[145] For an illuminating analysis of the elements constituting the idea of murder, see G.E.M. Anscombe's 'Murder and the Morality of Euthanasia', in *Human Life: Action and Ethics: Essays by G. E. M. Anscombe*, eds May Geach and Luke Gormally, Exeter: Imprint Academic, 2005, pp. 261–77.

[146] Oakeshott, *On Human Conduct*, p. 58, n. 1.

a manner that will not easily be interpreted too broadly, to include other non-legal or instrumental/purposeful considerations. It is therefore not at all clear what conditions Liddington intends to specify when he refers to what he ambiguously called 'bourgeois' education in his challenge; as a result, it is impossible to say whether prohibition of such an education will determine or qualify the performance of learning.

If Oakeshott's contention is tenable, human conduct necessarily displays two aspects: one formal and one substantive, with the former prescribing conditions to be subscribed to by actors in doing, and the latter embodying the substantive choices and performances made by the individuals concerned. Unlike command, which enjoins substantive performances directly, the law against murder or arson cannot determine actions on its own; their prescribed conditions, which exclude or enjoin actions *in a certain manner*, will only come into play if some one has already decided on a certain action, though the existence of these conditions may often deter him or her from choosing actions *in a way* that might contravene them.

The philosophical question of whether it is ultimately possible to maintain the distinction between form and substance in law is difficult, but what seems clear is that a law prohibiting murder, like other rules and practices, is still formal in the sense of only prescribing conditions to be observed in acting without determining substantive performances directly. In addition, it is erroneous to think (as implied by Liddington's criticisms) that when a prescription is in an adverbial format, it is necessarily a rule, since any substantive choices can be, in theory, recast as adverbial considerations.[147] As Peter Winch, following Wittgenstein, has demonstrated, to establish the notion of a rule of conduct depends not only on the outward appearance of some formula-like pattern, but on other related concepts, such as the notion of making a mistake and the possibility of the meaning of the rule being grasped and understood by

---

[147] Gerencser, *The Skeptic's Oakeshott*, p. 133.

others.[148] Simply to recast any considerations in adverbial form then does not make it part of civil association. One must not forget that laws in civil association are not only formal (as all practices are) and adverbial; they must also be non-instrumental. Being non-instrumental, the laws in civil association do not create any prescribed conditions aiming at the satisfaction of substantive wants or outcomes chosen by individuals. Even in the prescribed adverbial conditions (which must be narrowly constructed), it appears that normally they should come into play only when performances may have the capacity to harm others, for Oakeshott clearly thinks that it is only in respect of cases where possible harm might be done to other agents that 'subscription to civil conditions should be required of performances'.[149] Whether the prescribed conditions are approved by individuals does not affect the authority of the laws, for it is in their nature to determine what is right and wrong conduct on the part of individuals, not the other way round. Furthermore, even if a legislative proposal in civil association 'may begin in a want, a wish for a benefit, or a plea for the removal of a disadvantage [it] must lose this character', argues Oakeshott, 'and acquire another (a political character) in being understood, advanced and considered as a proposal for the amendment of the *respublica* of civil association'.[150]

Conclusion

Oakeshott's theory of civil association is remarkable for its scope and coherence. However, as Oakeshott himself acknowledges, 'the engagement of caring for the conditions

---

[148] *The Idea of a Social Science and its Relation to Philosophy*, pp. 24–33. 'The notion of following a rule', says Winch, 'is logically inseparable from the notion of *making a mistake*. If it is possible to say of someone that he is following a rule that means that one can ask whether he is doing what he does correctly or not. Otherwise there is no foothold in his behaviour in which the notion of a rule can take a grip; there is then no *sense* in describing his behaviour in that way, since everything he does is as good as anything else he might do, whereas the point of the concept of a rule is that it should enable us to *evaluate* what is being done.' See p. 32, with emphasis in the original.
[149] Oakeshott, *On Human Conduct*, p. 178.
[150] *Ibid.*, p. 170.

of a civil association ... calls for so exact a focus of attention and so uncommon a self-restraint that one is not astonished to find this mode of human relationship to be as rare as it is excellent'.[151] Historical circumstances and human dispositions are such that no state except perhaps Andorra has found it possible to achieve this condition without qualification or interruption.[152] As a result, the character of a modern European state, according to Oakeshott, is best understood as an unresolved tension between the irreconcilable conditions of *societas* and *universitas*.[153]

The most obvious circumstantial factor that compromises the character of civil association is war. The extent to which war and military preparation may impose the character of an enterprise association upon a civil association is 'in proportion to the magnitude of the claims it makes upon the attention, the energies, and the resources of subjects; and the wars of modern times have been progressively more demanding in this respect'.[154] In this connection, one may readily add that states in pursuit of their respective foreign relations easily succumb to the lure of enterprise association, for, out of self-protection or self-interest, it is very tempting for them to put their national *interests* ahead of other considerations in the implementation of their foreign policy.[155] Furthermore, the ability of modern governments to wield great power with the advancement of technology and the need for public authorities to deal with issues like poverty, mass immigration or great natural calamities are all circumstances that tempt political leaders to develop policies that of necessity aim at the satisfaction of wants and interests in their statecraft.[156] Finally, there is also the question of what Oakeshott described as the individual *manqué*

---

[151] *Ibid.*, p. 180.
[152] Oakeshott, 'The Rule of Law', p. 162.
[153] Oakeshott, *On Human Conduct*, pp. 200–1.
[154] *Ibid.*, p. 273.
[155] But see Terry Nardin's excellent book *Law, Morality, and the Relations of States*, Princeton, NJ: Princeton University Press, 1983, in which he argues that practices and non-instrumental rules are required even in inter-state relations.
[156] Oakeshott, *On Human Conduct*, pp. 276–7.

or the masses, people whose moral character is such that they do not welcome the morality of individuality.[157] Instead, they long for the warmth of community, the certainty of following a leader and the fellowship of a common good. Understandably, they resent the emergence of the state in the mode of civil association.

While circumstances and dispositions like these may be unavoidable at least for the present time, it is also true that

> in the light of thick darkness enveloping ancient times there shines the eternal never-failing truth beyond all doubt: that the civil condition is certainly a human invention and that its principles are therefore those of human intelligences.[158]

Rare though the realisation of this civil condition is, its appeal is that free agents can cultivate their unique individuality and enjoy civil, political and social freedoms of various kinds in a self-contained civilised association, in which each is equally related to the other under its authoritative, non-instrumental rules. This prospect is certainly morally appealing (though not morally neutral, for it does prescribe conditions unfavourable to the individual *manqué*), and has the attraction of encouraging the autonomous individuals to understand that each of their individual selves is 'a collected personality, autonomous on account of its self-understanding and its command of resources it has made its own. And the half of this self-understanding is knowing its own limits.'[159] It is to be hoped that Oakeshott is right when he assumes that such a prospect will continue to exert a powerful influence on human imagination.

---

[157] *Ibid.* See also 'The Masses in Representative Democracy', in *Rationalism in Politics and Other Essays*, 1991, pp. 363–83.
[158] Vico, *La scienze nuova*, quoted from *On Human Conduct*, p. 108.
[159] *Ibid.*, p. 237.

6
Conclusion

So, what emerges from these attempts to conceive the possibility of civil order in contemporary pluralistic societies? In concluding his examination of the civil condition in *On Human Conduct*, Oakeshott says: 'the most difficult feature of the civil condition to identify and get into place has been law'. This is so, according to Oakeshott, partly because law in civil association has always been mixed up with many ambiguous rules that properly speaking are not the non-instrumental kind required by civil association, and partly because theorists of law have been much more concerned with the 'sources', the 'purpose' or the 'contingent beliefs' of law than with the nature and authority of law as a system of non-instrumental rules regulating interpersonal conduct.[1]

The arguments laid out in these chapters appear to confirm Oakeshott's observation in this regard. Gellner's attempt to differentiate the realms of faith, power and production in civil society falls into incoherence mainly because of his failure to understand the constitutive role played by the rule of law in ensuring pluralism in contemporary democratic societies. A balance of power approach turns out to be conceptually and philosophically too unstable to support civil association. Hayek's market-centred social theory admittedly takes the idea of the rule of law more seriously than Gellner's, as he has rightly separated

---

[1] Michael Oakeshott, *On Human Conduct*, Oxford: Clarendon Press, 1991, p. 181.

the purposive type of rules from the end-independent type of rules in the system of laws in a free society. His failure, however, is to allow the coordinating and utilitarian function of abstract rules (such as the price mechanism) to take centre stage in his 'Great Society', the result of which is to risk subordinating the rule of law to market or social evolutionary forces at the expense of genuine pluralism in society.

Habermas is far more sceptical about market forces than Hayek, and rightly makes law the legitimate integrating bond in his proposed discursive democracy. The main problem with Habermas, however, is his over-ambitious faith in rationality, requiring all legitimate rules to be arrived at by a procedure that reflects (or at least does not contradict) unanimous consensus. This optimism about the power of rationality no doubt derives from the Enlightenment. Jeremy Waldron believes that projects of this kind are 'distinctively *liberal*', since it is liberals who insist 'that intelligible justifications in social and political life must be available in principle for everyone, for society is to be understood by the individual mind, not by tradition or sense of a community'.[2] This turns out to be untenable, and a much more modest concept of reason than Kantian rationality can allow is required here.

Oakeshott is more perceptive in this respect, fully grasping Pascal's observation that 'when we do not know the truth, it is well that there should be a common error to fix the minds of men', and turns instead to Hobbes' theory of law and government. This asserts, 'there is never anything but a common error, that truth itself is a common error, and that since what is important is that it should be genuinely common, it must be fixed by authority'.[3]

The key to making the authority of law generally acceptable in an age of individual liberty and diversity is respect

---

[2]   Jeremy Waldron, 'Theoretical Foundations of Liberalism', in *The Philosophical Quarterly*, Vol. 37, No. 147, April 1987, pp. 134–5, emphasis in the original.

[3]   Michael Oakeshott, 'Thomas Hobbes', in *Scrutiny*, Vol. 4, 1935–1936, p. 276.

for its non-instrumental nature, which separates law from any substantive ends and purposes, and allows it to reign only as a formal practice qualifying, not determining, interpersonal interaction and conduct. The need to recognise non-instrumental rules as authoritative within civil order perhaps becomes most compelling in the relations of states. In this connection, Terry Nardin displayed a genuine understanding of the relationship between civil order and the rule of law in the international arena when he said,

> The basis of international association lies in deference to practices that embody recognition of the fact that we must coexist on this planet with others with whom we sometimes share little beyond a common predicament. Such coexistence presupposes acknowledgement of certain common standards of conduct: that individuals and states are united on the basis of authoritative common rules and not merely by their possibly convergent desires.[4]

Civil orders, therefore, are always rule-following orders. 'In civility lies the difference between a well-ordered and a disordered liberal democracy', says Edward Shils.[5] This is so because civility denotes 'the condition of men living in society, living in accordance with rules'.[6] While civil order does not require universal rationality as its foundation, it does not follow that reason has no role to play in civil association. Oakeshott in his essay 'Political Discourse' argues that political questions, which inevitably involve open-ended judgements supported by practical reasoning, are essentially contestable.[7] Hayek's critique of Cartesian rationalism not only shows that synoptic planning and rationalistic state intervention in the market more often than not are both epistemologically arrogant and politically disastrous, but also points to the need to establish some fair

---

[4] Terry Nardin, *Law, Morality, and the Relations of States*, Princeton, NJ: Princeton University Press, 1983, p. 324.
[5] Edward Shils, 'The Virtue of Civil Society', in *Government and Opposition*, Vol. 26, No. 1, Winter 1991, p. 3.
[6] *Ibid.*, p. 7.
[7] See Oakeshott, 'Political Discourse', in *Rationalism in Politics and Other Essays*, 1991. For Oakeshott's arguments on the essentially contestable nature of political issues, see the section entitled 'Politics and Civil Association' in chapter 5 of this book.

and open, trial-and-error-type procedures for members of civil association to try out their separate and potentially contestable ideas, and to resolve conflicts in order to arrive at some common and revisable understanding.

Stripped of its over-ambitious quest for unanimous rational consensus, Habermas's communicative rationality and the related idea of the ideal speech situation can also be regarded as one very useful procedure to help to establish a non-coercive, fair, open and rational mechanism for decision-making and conflict resolution in civil association. In this connection Stuart Hampshire's following observation and modest proposal are to the point:

> The two elements in procedural justice — a universal rational requirement of two-sidedness and respect for locally established and familiar rules of procedure — are linked as two natural needs in our minds in their practical and political workings. If either the rational requirement or the respect for customs breaks down and cease to operate, we should expect catastrophe.[8]

In addition, Hampshire believes that civil order requires its members to develop institutional loyalties towards those locally established and familiar rules of fair procedure for conflict resolution. They should also possess 'deep-seated habits of living together and arguing together' (i.e. the rational but modest requirement of accepting two-sidedness in public deliberation) to help to knit the association together.[9]

The need to develop 'institutional loyalties' in civil order points to the problem of motivation that exists in the theory of civil association, particularly for the more formalistic interpretation of the Oakeshottian type. In his discussion of Oakeshott's relationship to Hegel and to Hobbes, Paul Franco argues that while Oakeshott's creative reading of Hegel's *Philosophy of Right* in *On Human Conduct* has largely assimilated Hegel's political philosophy to his own conception of non-purposive civil association and has avoided invoking controversial metaphysical hypotheses (such as the idealist's assumption of the real will of the individual,

---

[8] Stuart Hampshire, *Justice is Conflict*, London: Duckworth, 1999, p. 91.
[9] *Ibid.*, pp. 88–9.

and the Hegelian assumption of the state as the realisation of rational freedom) to support its theoretical coherence, 'it is not clear ... how civil association combats the atomism that Hegel associated with liberal *burgerliche Gesellschaf*, the problem Tocqueville, shortly after Hegel, would designate by the term "individualism": the problem of individuals in liberal democracy retreating into the private circle of their family and friends without connection or a sense of responsibility to the larger community around them. Unlike Hegel (and Tocqueville)', Franco goes on to say, 'Oakeshott has little to say about the crucial role that the intermediate institutions of civil society play in lifting individuals out of their isolation and identifying them with the political whole.'[10]

The reply to this may well be that since the cultivation of individuality in civil association is an undertaking that is inevitably both personal and social at the same time, the individual therefore has an implied duty to enrich his or her personal autonomy as best as he or she can by nurturing the conditions in favour of the development of civility and morality (see the section entitled 'Freedom, Diversity and Autonomy' in Chapter 5 in this book). The more republican-oriented Habermas is also correct to tackle this problem of motivation directly by proposing the idea of constitutional patriotism, in which citizens' loyalty is attached to their common allegiance to the shared constitutional principles rather than to cultural or national solidarity. The idea of constitutional patriotism in the age of globalisation will be further examined in this concluding chapter.

The essentially contestable nature of politics in civil association points to the fact that civil order is not conflict free. What is required is that such conflicts must be resolved within the context of the rule of law in a way which acknowledges the authority of its non-instrumental rules, the provisions of which can only be validly amended in accordance with the requirements provided for in a legal procedure itself determined by the rule of law. Habermas's

---

[10] Paul Franco, 'Oakeshott's Relationship to Hegel', in *The Intellectual Legacy of Michael Oakeshott*, eds Corey Abel and Timothy Fuller, Exeter: Imprint Academic, 2005, p. 131.

discursive democracy readily admits the necessity of compromise and bargaining about non-generalisable interests amongst members of civil society, but he goes on to insist, 'fair compromise formation does not stand on its own, for the procedural conditions under which actual compromises enjoy the presumption of fairness must be justified in moral discourses'.[11] O'Sullivan also thinks that a theory of political compromise is required in the civil model. When referring to Richard Bellamy's idea of constitutionalism he states, 'so far as compromise itself is concerned ... a politics which assigns a central place to it must not only take account of crucial differences in the kind of compromise to be made, but also of the need to situate compromise within the framework of a genuinely political form of constitutionalism', for different sorts of policies and different kinds of compromise may require different arrangements in terms of political representation and decision-making.[12]

The need to anchor political compromise and conflict within the context of constitutionalism and the rule of law cannot be over-emphasised in the civil model, for without the latter, political compromise and conflict may easily be conceived solely in the language of pure power. The need to distinguish the language of power from the language of authority is essential to any coherent theory of civil order, for what ultimately constitutes civil association can only be its own system of non-instrumental rules, the authority of which cannot depend on any extrinsic considerations like power, purpose or utility. If the language of politics can be completely reduced to the language of power, civil order will be neither possible nor necessary. That is why Gellner's

[11] Jürgen Habermas, *Between Facts and Norms: Contributions to a Discourse Theory of Law and Democracy*, Cambridge: Polity Press, 1996, trans. William Rehg, p. 167.
[12] See Noel O'Sullivan, 'The Quest for a Political Liberalism', p. 25. I only have a copy of the unpublished version of this essay by Professor O'Sullivan. References to this article are made to this manuscript instead of to its published version. For Richard Bellamy's ideas on this issue, see his 'Citizenship Beyond the Nation State: The Case of Europe' in *Political Theory in Transition*, ed. O'Sullivan, London and New York: Routledge, 2000, chapter 5.

idea of the balance of power between the political and the economic realms in civil society and Hayek's ideas about the dethronement of politics in a spontaneous order have fundamentally misconceived the nature of civil association. Likewise, even Habermas's ambiguous idea of creative communicative power, as shown in Chapter 4, is in danger of undermining his own conception of discursive democracy.

The insistence on the dimension of authority is not only conceptually important; politically, it also sensitises social and political theorists to the need to take the question of legitimacy seriously in this age of globalisation and multiculturalism. Habermas's contribution to the debate about globalisation is of particular interest here.[13] To Habermas, the challenges of globalisation, particularly in the realms of the economy and the environment, have threatened the ability of traditional nation-states to exercise legitimate political power over their national policies, as the free flow of international capital, the power of multinational corporations and the need to engage in 'locational competition' have undermined the ability of the nation-state to raise taxes to finance its social policy and to stimulate national growth, and environmental problems like acid rain and global warming have rendered national boundaries more or less irrelevant in many respects.[14] These 'disempowering effects of globalization' open up 'legitimation gaps' in the political world — since 'power can be democratised; money cannot'.[15] Such gaps call for a postnational political response. Habermas's proposed solution is to extend his central ideal of constitutional patriotism (in which citizens do not identify with each other via the idea of nation, but via the more abstract bond of a constitutional proceduralism that acknowledges equal human rights and equal political

---

[13] See his 'The Postnational Constellation and the Future of Democracy', in *The Postnational Constellation: Political Essays*, trans., ed. and with an intro. by Max Pensky, Cambridge: Polity Press, 2001, pp. 58–112.
[14] *Ibid.*, pp. 68–80.
[15] *Ibid.*, pp. 80, 71, 78.

participation) to supranational entities like the European Union.[16]

To Habermas, the essence of constitutional patriotism is that citizens pledge their ultimate political allegiance to a relatively abstract political framework that embodies equal human rights and fair political participation, in a process of deliberative politics in which all the citizens concerned participate. In the context of a multicultural state, Habermas believes that if this political framework successfully replaces different subcultures (including the majority's culture) as the common pillar of political allegiance for all citizens, it can establish civil order there.[17]

In the context of world society, Habermas does not believe that a 'cosmopolitan democracy' under a world government is either possible or necessary, since, as he points out,

> any political community that wants to understand itself as a democracy must at least distinguish between members and non-members ... [and] the political culture of a world society lacks the common ethical-political dimension that would be necessary for a corresponding global community.[18]

Nevertheless, he thinks that it is possible for the democratic deliberative requirement enshrined in the idea of constitutional patriotism to provide a thin normative framework to 'delimit the choice of rhetorical strategies' by players in an international negotiation system and to develop a functioning international public sphere to 'tip the balance, from the concrete embodiments of sovereign will in persons, votes and collectives to the procedural demands of communicative and decision-making processes' in the international arena,[19] so that 'global powers no longer operate in the state of nature envisioned by classical international law, but on

---

[16] For a more detailed discussion of Habermas's idea of constitutional patriotism, see the section 'Constitutional Patriotism as the Political Bond in the Age of Post-traditional Society' in chapter 4 of this book.
[17] See Habermas, 'The Postnational Constellation and the Future of Democracy', p. 74.
[18] *Ibid.*, pp. 107–8.
[19] *Ibid.*, pp. 109, 111.

the middle level [i.e. between a world government and the nation-states] of an emerging world politics'.[20]

However, views critical of Habermas's efforts to extend civic solidarity beyond the nation-state should not be discarded lightly, particularly with respect to the question of the motivational force behind political solidarity. As Margaret Canovan says,

> To make sense, democracy requires a 'people', and social justice a political community within which redistribution can take place, while the liberal discourse of rights and the rule of law demands a strong and impartial polity. The resounding silence of most of the thinkers concerned on the topics of boundaries, the generation of political solidarity and the sources of political power bears witness to their presuppositions.[21]

Habermas's admission of the need to distinguish between members and non-members of a democratic community demonstrates that even civil order theorists have to acknowledge the force of Carl Schmitt's idea of the political, in which the distinction between friends and foes is central, and this distinction, according to Schmitt, depends largely on the political *decision* (particularly at the time of national emergency) of a homogeneous people rather than on a set of commonly subscribed civil rules.[22]

To this, civil order theorists may reply that unless we are talking about a situation of permanent (civil) war in which the only acceptable result for the parties involved is the total eradication of one's enemies, some kind of common bond must exist even between the friends and the foes within and outside the political community. In this connection, it is interesting to note that Chantal Mouffe, who sympathises with Schmitt's idea of the political, nevertheless admits, 'Adversaries do fight—even fiercely—but according to *a*

---

[20] *Ibid.*, pp. 109–10.
[21] Margaret Canovan, *Nationhood and Political Theory*, Cheltenham: Edward Edgar, 1996, p. 2.
[22] See Carl Schmitt, *The Concept of the Political*, trans. with an intro. by George Schwab, Chicago and London: The University of Chicago Press, 1996. See David Dyzenhaus's *Law and Politics: Carl Schmitt's Critique of Liberalism*, Durham and London: Duke University Press, 1998, for an excellent collection of critical essays on Carl Schmitt.

shared set of rules, and their positions, despite being ultimately irreconcilable, are accepted as legitimate perspectives', for ultimately 'the fundamental question for democratic theory is to envisage how the antagonistic dimension—which is constitutive of the political—can be given a form of expression that will not destroy political association'.[23]

To be fair to Habermas, however, it should not be forgotten that his aspiration for a postnational civic solidarity remains, at the moment, a hope rather than a realised fact. Habermas believes that 'collective identities are made, not found'. He therefore finds no reason to support the claim that while it was possible to use the idea of nations in the nineteenth and twentieth centuries to create a mode of solidarity between persons who had until then remained strangers to one another, it is necessarily impossible for a postnational political identity to emerge within some increasingly unified context such as the European Union. Moreover, Habermas does not forget to point out that even when supranational citizens share a common political life in accordance with some democratic principles, 'each is entitled to *remain* an Other' *outside* the political realm so long as he or she does not break the commonly shared civil rules.[24] Even for those who do not share Habermas's optimism in this respect and find his reliance on universal human rights to support a supranational civil order problematic, Terry Nardin's observation should not be forgotten: that, contrary to some conventional wisdom, the arena of international politics is far from anarchical or in perpetual conflict. Indeed, durable international relationships, as Nardin observes, are made possible because in reality there exists some common customary international rules of the non-instrumental kind, which are subscribed to by most if not all states to maintain a certain level of civil order in inter-

---

[23] See Chantal Mouffe, *The Political*, London and New York: Routledge, 2005, p. 52, emphasis mine.
[24] Habermas, 'What is a People?', in *The Postnational Constellation*, p. 19, emphasis in the original.

national society and provide some minimal and general standards of international conduct for all states to observe.[25]

It should be clear by now that any one-sided emphasis on either the collective strength of the political community or the autonomy of the individual is not consistent with the idea of civil association. All civil order theorists surveyed in this study argue that the bond of civility not only provides a common political identity for citizens to engage in public affairs, but also creates the conditions for the individuals concerned to pursue their personal endeavours, jointly or severally, in as free and diverse a way as possible. It is the non-instrumental nature of law in civil association which makes this diversity amongst individuals possible.

On the one hand, these individuals have to perform the role of democratic citizens in order to preserve the conditions of civil order. On the other, they are free to develop their own autonomous selves, with their own conceptions of the good, their different dispositions and their capacity for imagination, so long as their undertakings are all qualified by the common moral and legal concerns of civil association. Michael Walzer calls this 'the paradox of the civil society argument', for while citizenship is only one of the many roles that members of civil society need to play, civil society also compels its members to look beyond their own individual goods to the common concern, for 'only a democratic state can create a democratic civil society; only a democratic civil society can sustain a democratic state'.[26]

In this respect, O'Sullivan warns against the danger of overstretching the arguments of the more republican oriented civil order theorists and tipping the balance too much towards democratic citizenship.[27] He issues this warning on

---

[25] Terry Nardin, *Law, Morality, and the Relations of States*, Part One, Princeton, New Jersey: Princeton University Press, 1983.

[26] Michael Walzer, 'The Civil Society Argument', in *Dimensions of Radical Democracy: Pluralism, Citizenship, Community*, ed. Chantal Mouffe, London and New York: Verso, 1992, pp. 103-4.

[27] Habermas certainly is the most republican oriented theorist of the four that are being studied here. See also Richard Bellamy's 'The "Right to Have Rights": Citizenship Practice and the Political Constitution of the EU', in *Citizenship and Governance in the European*

the ground that an ethics of active participation as required by civic republicanism 'is simply not shared by many people in the modern world', as politics rarely engages the full attention of the citizens and the values of citizenship are in competition with many of the individual goods pursued by the citizens concerned.[28] What O'Sullivan suggests, instead, is a more modest kind of 'non-transformative civic education' which identifies a core of civic commitments and competences. If there is a conflict between individual or group commitments and this civic core, the latter should prevail.[29]

While it may be difficult to determine the precise balance to be struck in this 'paradox of civil society' in practice, what appears clear is that the kind of individuality most favourable to civil association contains both a public and a personal aspect. To the extent that the civil bond can really claim to be a common concern identified with by all citizens, individuals have an indispensable role to play in determining what kind of non-instrumental rules should be adopted and what public decisions should be taken in the light of the civil ideal to create conditions facilitating all kinds of individual pursuits. As the Kantian approach rightly emphasises, an individual is truly autonomous only if he or she is able to take responsibility for his or her actions or conduct; public rules, political institutions and authoritative decisions regulating his or her interpersonal exchanges should therefore reflect this as far as possible, and the participation of the citizens in and their part-authorship of these decisions are in this sense necessary.

On the other hand, every individual is unique and distinctive. Like an artistic creation or an aesthetic experience, part of the value of one's individuality lies precisely in its irreplaceable uniqueness. To develop the autonomous self

---

Union, eds Richard Bellamy and Alex Warleigh, London and New York: Continuum, 2001, chapter 3. Chapter 5 of Ronald Beiner's *What's the Matter with Liberalism?*, Berkeley, Los Angeles and London: University of California Press, 1992, also contains a very good discussion of the idea of citizenship understood along the lines developed within the tradition of civic republicanism.

[28] O'Sullivan, 'The Quest for a Political Liberalism', p. 20.
[29] *Ibid.*, p. 26.

of the individual as much as possible under civil association would therefore require individuals to pay equal attention to their own undertakings of self-enactment and self-disclosure. Since everyone has a history, not a nature, the more unique or irreplaceable each of these histories is, the more interesting and rich our human civilisation becomes.[30] It goes without saying that one should not forget Shirley Robin Letwin's reminder that the cultivation of individuality is an undertaking that is by nature both personal and social at the same time. This is so mainly because the personal and unique style of any individual is made possible only when the individual concerned is capable of making use of the common resources of civilisation shared by all of us.[31]

The fact that civil association as an 'ideal character', and according to Oakeshott, exists only in a compromised form under realistic human condition, may lead some critics to deride the theoretical quest for civil order as utopian or idealistic.[32] This criticism, however, is unwarranted. As O'Sullivan rightly points out, the civil model does not claim to provide a complete account of all political relationships, and all serious theorists of the civil model readily admit the importance of the managerial dimension of the political and its implications for individual freedom, power and

---

[30] Stuart Hampshire has offered us an excellent account of the value of individuality in his 'Individuality and Memory', in *Innocence and Experience*, London: The Penguin Press, 1989, pp. 111–58.

[31] See chapter 4 'Virtue without Struggle' in Letwin's *The Gentleman in Trollope: Individuality and Moral Conduct*. Richard E. Flathman's following observation is also relevant here: 'Individuals would be incomprehensible to themselves and to others apart from traditions and societies, and individuality is difficult if not impossible in the absence of a plurality of practices and groups; but ensembles of these elements that lack a diverse and vigorous individuality are insipid, derisory, and often dangerous to themselves and to others; while those that are actively antagonistic to individuality are deserving of our scorn and may properly arouse our fears.' See his *Willful Liberalism: Voluntarism and Individuality in Political Theory and Practice*, Ithaca and London: Cornell University Press, 1992, p. 88.

[32] See the last section of chapter 5 of this book.

policy-making.[33] However, what is crucial is, to quote O'Sullivan again,

> ... that the two faces of the political—that is the civil and managerial faces—may in principle conflict with one another. What is no less important is the fact that, even when they do not overtly conflict, they nevertheless always stand in a condition of ineliminable tension. What follows from this is that the political art in the full sense consists, not in achieving a final resolution of the tension, but in maintaining a *balance* between the different faces of the political. But in preserving this balance, it is the civil face that must be given ultimate primacy, since it is this face alone that guarantees respect for human dignity by making explicit provision for diversity and minimizing (not eliminating) the role of arbitrary power in the sphere of the political.[34]

In the quest for civil order, Gellner, Hayek, Habermas and Oakeshott each make significant contributions to the debate. The analysis by Gellner of the separation of faith, power and production in complex industrial society clearly draws attention to the fact that neither religion nor hierarchal politics is in command any longer in a social order of the civil kind. The new and fluid division of labour presupposed by the modern world, according to Gellner, facilitates the emergence of the individual to take centre stage in civil society. Hayek's theory of spontaneous order goes further in arguing that pluralism in civil society is not underpinned by rational political interventions; instead, the beneficial, albeit unintended, results of spontaneous social interaction is made possible by the adherence of all to the abstract, end-independent rules found in his 'Great

---

[33] See his 'Power, authority and legitimacy', in *Political Theory in Transition*, p. 147.

[34] See Noel O'Sullivan, 'Difference and the Concept of the Political in Contemporary Political Philosophy', in *Political Studies*, Vol. 45, 1997, p. 754, emphasis in the original. Josiah Lee Auspitz, in his excellent memoir in honour of Oakeshott, has also made the following comment: 'That civil association as an "ideal character" can exist only in compromised form does not diminish the force of [Oakeshott's] argument. On the contrary, it suggests a program of fine discrimination among the varieties of state action, and renewed attention to the ideal and literature of the Rechtstaat.' See his 'Michael Oakeshott', in *American Scholar*, Summer 1991, pp. 336–7.

Society'. The centrality of the rule of law in civil order is taken seriously by Habermas, who goes on to attempt to demonstrate that civil rules are legitimate only if all citizens are entitled to participate in the enactment of these rules within a democracy. The fundamental insight derived from Oakeshott's idea of civil association is its clear-headed focus on the importance of the authoritative and non-instrumental nature of civil rules in civil order, without which the individualities of the moral agents in civil society may be greatly compromised.

Bibliography

Allen, R. T., *The Political Thought of F A Hayek & Michael Polanyi: Beyond Liberalism*, New Brunswick and London: Transaction Publishers, 1998.

Anderson, Perry, 'Science, Politics, Enchantment', in *Transition to Modernity: Essays on Power, Wealth and Belief*, eds John Hall and I.C. Jarvie, Cambridge: Cambridge University Press, 1992, chapter 8.

Anscombe, G. E. M., 'Murder and the Morality of Euthanasia', in *Human Life: Action and Ethics: Essays by G. E. M. Anscombe*, eds May Geach and Luke Gormally, Exeter: Imprint Academic, 2005, pp. 261-77.

Arendt, Hannah, *On Violence*, San Diego, New York and London: A Harvard/HBJ Book, 1969.

—, 'What is Authority?', in Arendt, *Between Past and Future*, New York: Penguin, 1977, reissued 1993, pp. 91-141.

Auspitz, John Lee, 'Michael Oakeshott', in *American Scholar*, Summer 1991, pp. 351-70.

Bellamy, Richard, 'Citizenship Beyond the Nation State: The Case of Europe', in *Political Theory in Transition*, ed. Noel O' Sullivan, London and New York: Routledge, 2000, chapter 5.

—, 'The "Right to Have Rights": Citizenship Practice and the Political Constitution of the EU', in *Citizenship and Governance in the European Union*, eds Richard Bellamy and Alex Warleigh, London and New York: Continuum, 2001, chapter 3.

Baynes, Kenneth, 'Democracy and the *Rechtsstaat*: Habermas's *Faktizitat und Geltung*', in *The Cambridge Companion to Habermas*, ed. Stephen K. White, Cambridge: Cambridge University Press, 1995, chapter 9.

Beiner, Ronald, *What's the Matter with Liberalism?*, Berkeley, Los Angeles, and London: University of California Press, 1992.

Calhoun, Craig ed., *Habermas and the Public Sphere*, Cambridge, Massachusetts and London: The MIT Press, 1999.

Canovan, Margaret, *Nationhood and Political Theory*, Cheltenham: Edward Edgar, 1996.

—, 'Patriotism Is Not Enough', in *British Journal of Political Science*, No. 30, 2000, pp. 413-32.

Chambers, Simone, 'Can Procedural Democracy be Radical?', in *The Political*, ed. David Ingram, Oxford: Blackwell, 2002, pp. 168–88.
Coats Jr., Wendell John, 'Michael Oakeshott as a Liberal Theorist', in *Canadian Journal of Political Science*, Vol. XVIII, No. 4, December 1985, pp. 773–87.
Connolly, William E., *Politics and Ambiguity*, Wisconsin: The University of Wisconsin Press, 1987.
—, *Political Theory and Modernity*, Oxford: Basil Blackwell, 1988.
Cristi, Renato, *Carl Schmitt and Authoritarian Liberalism*, Cardiff: University of Wales Press, 1998.
Crowder, George, 'Pluralism and Liberalism', in *Political Studies*, XLII, 1994, pp. 293–305.
Dahrendorf, Ralf, 'Socialism's Honourable Exit', in *The Times*, 25 November 1988.
—, *Reflections on the Revolution in Europe: In a Letter Intended to Have Been Sent to a Gentleman in Warsaw, 1990*, London: Chatto & Windus, 1990.
Dore, Ronald, 'Sovereign Individuals', in *The Social Philosophy of Ernest Gellner*, eds John A. Hall and Ian Jarvie, Amsterdam-Atlanta, GA: Rodopi, 1996, pp. 221–36.
Dyzenhaus, David ed., *Law and Politics: Carl Schmitt's Critique of Liberalism*, Durham and London: Duke University Press, 1998.
The Economist, 28 February 2004 and 9 October 2004 editions.
Eisenstadt, Shmuel, 'Japan: Non-Axial Modernity', in *The Social Philosophy of Ernest Gellner*, eds John A. Hall and Ian Jarvie, Amsterdam-Atlanta, GA: Rodopi, 1996, pp. 237–56.
Ferguson, Adam, *An Essay on the History of Civil Society*, ed. Fania Oz-Salzberger, Cambridge: Cambridge University Press, 1995.
Flathman, Richard E., *Willful Liberalism: Voluntarism and Individuality in Political Theory and Practice*: Ithaca and London: Cornell University Press, 1992.
—, 'Citizenship and Authority: A Chastened View of Citizenship', in *Theorizing Citizenship*, ed. Ronald Beiner, Albany: State University of New York Press, 1995, pp. 105–51.
Fleetwood, Steve, *The Political Economy of Hayek: The Socio-economics of Order*, London: Routledge, 1995.
—, 'Hayek III: The Necessity of Social Rules of Conduct', in *Hayek: Economist and Social Philosopher*, ed. Stephen F. Frowen, London and New York: MacMillan/St. Martin's Press, 1997, pp. 155–78.
Forsyth, Murray, 'Hayek's Bizarre Liberalism: A Critique', in *Political Studies*, 1988, Vol. XXXVI, pp. 235–50.
Franco, Paul, *The Political Philosophy of Michael Oakeshott*, New Haven and London: Yale University Press, 1990.
—, 'Oakeshott's Relationship to Hegel', in *The Intellectual Legacy of Michael Oakeshott*, eds Corey Abel and Timothy Fuller, Exeter: Imprint Academic, 2005, pp. 117–31.
Fraser, Nancy, 'Rethinking the Public Sphere: A Contribution to the Critique of Actually Existing Democracy', in *Habermas and the*

Public Sphere, ed. Craig Calhoun, Cambridge, Massachusetts and London: The MIT Press, 1999, chapter 5.
Friedman, Richard, 'Oakeshott on the Authority of Law', in *Ratio Juris*, Vol. 2, No. 1, March 1989, pp. 27–40.
—, 'Michael Oakeshott and the Elusive Identity of the Rule of Law', in *The Intellectual Legacy of Michael Oakeshott*, eds Corey Abel and Timothy Fuller, Exeter: Imprint Academic, 2005, pp. 160–80.
Galettoi, A. E., 'Individualism, Social Rules, Tradition: The Case of Friedrich A Hayek', in *Friedrich A Hayek: Critical Assessments*, eds John Cunningham Wood and Ronald N. Woods, Vol. IV, London and New York: Routledge, 1991, pp. 280–96.
Gamble, Andrew, *Hayek: The Iron Cage of Liberty*, Cambridge: Polity Press, 1996.
Gaus, Gerald F., 'Ideological Dominance Through Philosophical Confusion: Liberalism in the Twentieth Century', in *Reassessing Political Ideologies: The Durability of Dissent*, ed. Michael Freeden, New York: Routledge, 2001, pp. 13–34.
Gellner, Ernest, *Thought and Change*, Chicago: The University of Chicago Press, 1964.
—, *Legitimation of Belief*, Cambridge: Cambridge University Press, 1974.
—, *Selected Philosophical Themes: Vol. II Contemporary Thought and Politics*, eds I. C. Jarvie and J. Agassi, London and New York: Routledge, 1974.
—, *Nations and Nationalism*, Oxford: Basil Blackwell, 1983.
—, *Plough, Sword and Book: The Structure of Human History*, London: Collins Harvill, 1988.
—, 'Civil Society in Historical Context', in *International Social Science Journal*, Vol.43, No.3, 1991, pp. 495–510.
—, *Postmodernism, Reason and Religion*, London and New York: Routledge, 1992.
—, *Conditions of Liberty: Civil Society and its Rivals*, London: Penguin Books, 1994.
—, 'Reply to Critics', in *The Social Philosophy of Ernest Gellner*, Amsterdam-Atlanta, GA: Rodopi, 1996, pp. 623–86.
—, *Nationalism*, London: Widenfeld & Nicolson, 1997.
Gerencser, S. A., *The Skeptic's Oakeshott*, New York: St. Martin's Press, 2000.
Gray, John, 'Oakeshott as a Liberal', in *Post-Liberalism: Studies in Political Thought*, New York and London: Routledge, 1993, chapter 4.
—, *Hayek on Liberty*, London and New York: Routledge, 1998, 3rd edn.
Habermas, Jürgen, *The Theory of Communicative Action: Reason and the Rationalization of Society, Vol. 1*, trans. Thomas McCarthy, Boston: Beacon Press, 1981.
—, *Theory of Communicative Action: The Critique of Functionalist Reason, Vol. 2*, trans. Thomas McCarthy, Cambridge: Polity Press, 1981.

—, *Philosophical-Political Profiles*, trans. Frederick G. Lawrence, London: Heinemann, 1983.

—, *The Structural Transformation of the Public Sphere*, trans. Thomas Burger with the Assistance of Frederick Lawrence, Cambridge and Massachusetts: The MIT Press, 1989.

—, *The New Conservatism: Cultural Criticism and the Historians' Debate*, ed. and trans. Shierry Weber Nicholsen, Cambridge: Polity, 1989.

—, *Postmetaphysical Thinking: Philosophical Essays*, trans. William Mark Hohengarten, Cambridge, Massachusetts and London: The MIT Press, 1992.

—, 'Overcoming the Past', in *New Left Review*, No. 203, Jan/Feb 1994, pp. 1–16.

—, 'Three Normative Models of Democracy', in *Constellations*, Vol. 1, No. 1, April 1994, pp. 1–10.

—, 'Citizenship and National Identity: Some Reflections on the Future of Europe', in *Theorizing Citizenship*, ed. Ronald Beiner, Albany: State University of New York Press, 1995, pp. 255–81.

—, *Between Facts and Norms: Contributions to a Discourse Theory of Law and Democracy*, trans. William Rehg, Cambridge: Polity Press, 1996.

—, *The Inclusion of the Other: Studies in Political Theory*, eds Ciaran Cronin and Pablo De Greiff, Cambridge, MA: The MIT Press, 1998.

—, *On the Pragmatics of Communication*, ed. Maeve Cooke, Cambridge: Polity Press, 1998.

—, *The Postnational Constellation: Political Essays*, trans., ed. and with an intro. by Max Pensky, Cambridge: Polity Press, 2001.

—, *The Future of Human Nature*, Cambridge: Polity Press, 2003.

Hall, John A. ed., *The State of the Nation: Ernest Gellner and the Theory of Nationalism*, Cambridge: Cambridge University Press, 1998.

Hall, John A. and Jarvie I. eds, *Transition to Modernity: Essays on Power, Wealth and Belief*, Cambridge: Cambridge University Press, 1992.

—, *The Social Philosophy of Ernest Gellner*, Amsterdam-Atlanta, GA: Rodopi, 1996.

Hamlin, A. P., 'Procedural Individualism and Outcome Liberalism' in *Friedrich A Hayek: Critical Assessments*, eds John Cunningham Wood and Ronald N. Woods, Volume IV, London and New York: Routledge, 1991, pp. 16–29.

Hampshire, Stuart, *Innocence and Experience*, London: The Penguin Press, 1989.

—, *Justice is Conflict*, London: Duckworth, 1999.

Hart, H. L.A., *The Concept of Law*, Oxford: Oxford University Press, 1961.

Hayek, Friedrich, *The Road to Serfdom*, Chicago: The University of Chicago Press, 1944, renewed 1972.

—, *Individualism and Economic Order*, Chicago: The University of Chicago Press, 1948, reprint, 1980.

—, *The Sensory Order: An Inquiry into the Foundations of Theoretical Psychology*, Chicago: The University of Chicago Press, 1952, Midway reprint, 1976.

—, *The Constitution of Liberty*, London and Henley: Routledge & Kegan Paul, 1960, reprint, 1976.

—, *Studies in Philosophy, Politics and Economics*, Chicago: The University of Chicago Press, 1967.

—, *Law, Legislation, and Liberty: Rules and Order*, Vol. 1, Chicago: The University of Chicago Press, 1973.

—, *Law, Legislation, and Liberty: The Mirage of Social Justice*, Vol. 2, London and Henley: Routledge & Kegan Paul, 1976, reprint, 1979.

—, *New Studies in Philosophy, Politics, Economics and the History of Ideas*, London: Routledge & Kegan Paul, 1978, reprint by Routledge in 1990.

—, *Law, Legislation, and Liberty: The Political Order of a Free People*, Vol. 3, Chicago: The University of Chicago Press, 1979.

—, *The Fatal Conceit: The Errors of Socialism*, London: Routledge, 1988.

—, *The Collected Works of F A Hayek*, Vol. III, *The Trend of Economic Thinking*, eds W. W. Bartley III and Stephen Kresge, 1991.

Hobbes, Thomas, *Leviathan*, ed. John Plamenatz, Collins/Fontana, 1978 (9th impression).

Ignatieff, Michael, 'On Civil Society: Why Eastern Europe's Revolutions Could Succeed', in *Foreign Affairs*, March/April 1995, Vol. 74, No. 2, pp. 128–36.

Jones, David Martin, 'Democratisation, Civil Society and the Pacific Asian Nouveaux Riches', in *Political Development in Pacific Asia*, Polity Press, 1997, chapter 3.

Keane, John, *Civil Society: Old Images, New Visions*, Cambridge: Polity Press, 1998.

Kristol, Irving, 'Capitalism, Socialism, and Nihilism', in *Neoconservatism: The Autobiography of an Idea*, The Free Press, 1995, chapter 9.

Kukathas, Chandran, *Hayek and Modern Liberalism*, Oxford: Clarendon Press, 1990.

Larmore, Charles, 'The Foundations of Modern Democracy: Reflections of Jurgen Habermas', in Larmore, *The Morals of Modernity*, Cambridge: Cambridge University Press, 1996, pp. 205–21.

Lee Kuan-yew Interview by Fareed Zakaria in 'Culture Is Destiny', in *Foreign Affairs*, March/April 1994, Vol. 73, No. 2, pp. 109–26.

Lessnoff, Michael H., *Political Philosophers of the Twentieth Century*, Oxford: Blackwell, 1999.

Letwin, Shirley Robin, *The Gentleman in Trollope: Individuality and Moral Conduct*, London and Basingstoke: MacMillan, 1982.

—, 'Morality and Law', in *Ratio Juris*, Vol. 2, No. 1, March 1989, pp. 55–65.

Liddington, John, 'Oakeshott: Freedom in a Modern European State', in *Conceptions of Liberty in Political Philosophy*, eds Zbigniew Pelczynski and John Gray, New York: St. Martin's Press, 1984, pp. 289–320.

Loughlin, Martin, *Public Law and Political Theory*, Oxford: Clarendon, 1992.
MacFarlane, Alan, 'Ernest Gellner and the Escape to Modernity', in *Transition to Modernity: Essays on Power, Wealth and Belief*, eds John Hall and I. C. Jarvie, Cambridge: Cambridge University Press, 1992, chapter 5.
Mapel, David, 'Civil Association and the Idea of Contingency', *Political Theory*, Vol. 18, August 1990, pp. 392–410.
—, 'Purpose and Politics: Can There Be a Non-Instrumental Civil Association?', *Political Science Reviewer*, Vol. 21, Spring 1992, pp.63–80.
Meyer, Frank S., *In Defense of Freedom and Related Essays*, Indianapolis: Liberty Fund, 1996.
Michelman, Frank I., 'Family Quarrel', in *Habermas on Law and Democracy: Critical Exchanges*, eds Michel Rosenfeld and Andrew Arato, Berkeley, Los Angeles and London: University of California Press, 1998, pp. 309–22.
Miller, David, *Market, State, and Community*, Oxford: Clarendon Press, 1990.
Minogue, Kenneth, 'Ernest Gellner and the Dangers of Theorising Nationalism', in *The Social Philosophy of Ernest Gellner*, eds John A. Hall and Ian Jarvie, Amsterdam-Atlanta, GA: Rodopi, 1996, pp. 113–28.
Mouffe, Chantal, *The Return of the Political*, London and New York: Verso, 1993.
—, *The Political*, London and New York: Routledge, 2005.
Müller, Jan-Werner, *Another Country: German Intellectuals, Unification and National Identity*, New Haven and London: Yale University Press, 2000.
Nardin, Terry, *Law, Morality, and the Relations of States*, Princeton and New Jersey: Princeton University Press, 1983.
—, 'Private and Public Roles in Civil Society' in *Toward a Global Civil Society*, ed. Michael Walzer, Providence, Oxford: Berghahn Books, 1995, pp. 29–34.
—, *The Philosophy of Michael Oakeshott*, Pennsylvania: The Pennsylvania State University, 2001.
Oakeshott, Michael, *Experience and Its Modes*, Cambridge: Cambridge University Press, 1933.
—, *The Social and Political Doctrines of Contemporary Europe*, New York: Cambridge University Press, 1950.
—, *Rationalism in Politics and Other Essays*, London and New York: Methuen & Co. Ltd., 1962, rpt 1981.
—, 'The Vocabulary of a Modern European State', *Political Studies*, Vol. XXIII, July 1975, pp. 197–219.
—, 'The Vocabulary of a Modern European State (Concluded)', in *Political Studies*, Vol. XXIII, No. 4, 1975, pp. 409–14.
—, *On History and Other Essays*, Oxford: Basil Blackwell, 1983.

—, *The Voice of Liberal Learning*, ed. Timothy Fuller, New Haven and London: Yale University Press, 1989.
—, *Rationalism in Politics and Other Essays*, New and Expanded edn, ed. Timothy Fuller, Indianapolis: Liberty Press, 1991.
—, *On Human Conduct*, Oxford: Clarendon Press, 1991.
—, *Morality and Politics in Modern Europe: The Harvard Lectures*, ed. Shirley Robin Letwin, New Haven and London: Yale University Press, 1993.
—, *Religion, Politics, and the Moral Life*, ed. Timothy Fuller, New Haven and London: Yale University Press, 1993.
—, *What is History and Other Essays*, ed. Luke O'Sullivan, Exeter: Imprint Academic, 2004.
O'Sullivan, Noel, 'Difference and the Concept of the Political in Contemporary Political Philosophy', *Political Studies*, Vol. 45, 1997, pp. 739-54.
—, 'Visions of Freedom: The Response to Totalitarianism', in *The British Study of Politics in the Twentieth Century*, eds Jack Hayward, Brian Barry and Archie Brown, Oxford: Published for the British Academy by Oxford University Press, 1999, pp. 63-88.
—, 'Power, Authority and Legitimacy: A Critique of Postmodern Political Thought', in *Political Theory in Transition*, ed. O'Sullivan, London and New York: Routledge, 2000, chapter 7.
—, 'The Quest for a Political Liberalism', 2001, manuscript.
—, *European Political Thought Since 1945*, Hampshire and New York: Palgrave MacMillan, 2004.
Parekh, Bhikhu, 'Oakeshott's Theory of Civil Association', *Ethics*, Vol. 106, October 1995, pp. 158-86.
Polanyi, Michael, *Personal Knowledge*, London and Henley: Routledge and Kegan Paul, 1962.
Preuss, Elrich K., 'Communicative Power and the Concept of Law', in *Habermas on Law and Democracy: Critical Exchanges*, eds Michel Rosenfeld Andrew Arato, Berkeley, Los Angeles and London: University of California Press, 1998, p. 323-35.
Rawls, John, *A Theory of Justice*, Oxford, Melbourne and Cape Town: Oxford University Press, 1972.
Rehg, William, 'Against Subordination: Morality, Discourse, and Decision in the Legal Theory of Jurgen Habermas', in *Habermas on Law and Democracy: Critical Exchanges*, eds Michel Rosenfeld and Andrew Arato, Berkeley, Los Angeles and London: University of California Press, 1998, chapter 12.
Riley, Patrick, 'Michael Oakeshott: Philosopher of Individuality', in *Review of Politics*, Vol. 52, No. 4, Fall 1992, pp. 649-64.
Rosemont Jr, Henry, 'Why Take Rights Seriously? A Confucian Critique', in *Human Rights and the World's Religions*, ed. Leroy Rouner, Notre Dame, IN: University of Notre Dame Press, 1988, pp. 167-82.

Rosenfeld, Michel and Arato, Andrew eds, *Habermas on Law and Democracy: Critical Exchanges*, Berkeley, Los Angeles and London: University of California Press, 1998.
Ryle, Gilbert, *The Concept of Mind*, England: Penguin Books, 1963.
Scheuerman, William E., 'Between Radicalism and Resignation: Democratic Theory in Habermas's *Between Facts and Norms*', in *Habermas: A Critical Reader*, ed. Peter Dews, Oxford: Blackwell, 1999, pp. 153–77.
Schmitt, Carl, *The Concept of the Political*, trans. with an intro. by George Schwab, Chicago and London: The University of Chicago Press, 1996.
Schomberg, von Rene and Baynes, Kenneth eds, *Discourse & Democracy: Essays on Habermas's* Between Facts and Norms, Albany: The State University of New York, 2002.
Shearmur, Jeremy, *Hayek and After: Hayekian Liberalism as a Research Programme*, London and New York: Routledge, 1996.
Shklar, Judith N., *Political Thought & Political Thinkers*, ed. Stanley Hoffmann, Chicago and London: The University of Chicago Press, 1998.
Shils, Edward, 'The Virtue of Civil Society', in *Government and Opposition*, Vol. 26, No. 1, Winter 1991, p. 3–20.
Solinger, Dorothy J., 'China's Transients and the State: A Form of Civil Society?', An Occasional Paper Published by Hong Kong Institute of Asia-Pacific Studies of the Chinese University of Hong Kong, 1991.
Taylor, Charles, *Philosophical Arguments*, Cambridge, Massachusetts and London: Harvard University Press, 1995.
de Tocqueville, Alexis, *Democracy in America*, trans. Henry Reeve and Rev. Francis Bowen, abr. and with an intro. by Patrick Renshaw, Hertfordshire: Wordsworth Editions Limited, 1998.
Varty, John, 'Civic or Commercial? Adam Ferguson's Concept of Civil Society', in *Democratization*, Spring 1997, Vol. 4, No. 1, pp. 29–48.
Waldron, Jeremy, 'Theoretical Foundations of Liberalism', in *The Philosophical Quarterly*, Vol. 37, No. 147, April 1987, pp. 127–50.
Walzer, Michael, *Interpretation and Social Criticism*, Cambridge, Massachusetts and London, England: Harvard University Press, 1987.
—, 'The Civil Society Argument' in *Dimensions of Radical Democracy: Pluralism, Citizenship, Community*, ed. Chantal Mouffe, London and New York: Verso, 1992, chapter 4.
Winch, Peter, *The Idea of a Social Science and its Relation to Philosophy*, London, Melbourne and Henley: Routlege and Kegan Paul and New Jersey: Humanities Press, 1958, reprint, 1984.
—, 'Authority' in Anthony Quinton, *Political Philosophy*, Oxford: Oxford University Press, 1967, reprint, 1985, pp. 97–111.
Worthington, Glenn, 'Oakeshott's Claims of Politics', *Political Studies*, Vol. 45, 1997, pp. 727–38.

Index

Allen, R. T. 71 n.
altruism 90 and n.
Andorra 194
Anscombe, G. E. M. 191 n.
Arendt, Hannah 136 and n., 137 and n., 141 and n.
Aristotle 146 n.
Auspitz, Josiah Lee 210 n.
authority 3, 10, 14, 34, 38-41, 43-44, 73, 81, 136, 138-142, 144-146, 152, 161, 166, 168 n., 169, 172, 174, 175 n., 176, 178 and n., 183 n., 185, 193, 197-198, 201-203
autonomy 104, 158, 185-193
  co-originality of public and private, 112-120, 128
  individual, 130, 201, 207-208
  moral, 113
  political, 106
  private, 106, 118, 129-130, 135
  public, 106, 129-130, 135

Baynes, Kenneth 140 n.
Beiner, Ronald 208 n.
Bellamy, Richard 202 and n., 207 n., 208 n.
Berlin, Isaiah 2 n.
Burke, Edmund 4

Canovan, Margaret 111 n., 125 and n., 205 and n.
Cantor, Georg 59
capitalism 55, 91 and n., 92 n.
Cartesian rationalism 10, 21, 62, 82, 92-93, 199
Chambers, Simone 114 and n.
China 17 n.
Cicero 146 n.
cives 146 n., 170-173, 176, 178, 181-182
civic loyalty 91

civil association 1, 5, 145-155, 158, 161-163, 165-185, 187-190, 193-195, 197, 199-201, 207-209, 211
civil disobedience 137 n., 143
civil society 1-2, 7, 13-49, 51, 53-54, 78-79, 81, 84, 86, 94, 106, 135, 139 and n., 143-144, 197, 202-203, 207-208, 210-211
civility 6-7, 46, 161-165, 170, 177, 183-184, 187, 199, 201, 207
civitas 146 n., 162, 164-165, 167-170
Coats, Jr., Wendell John 176 n., 187 n.
coercion 71-72, 76, 86, 95n.
communicative action 9 n., 11, 98-101, 105, 112, 118, 122, 126, 128-130, 132, 138 n.
communicative reason 98-104, 119, 126, 128, 130, 132, 137, 144, 200
communism 1, 38, 47-48, 93
communist economy 37
competition 65-66, 80, 184
  locational, 203
  perfect, 66n.
Confucianism 48 n., 49 n
Connolly, William E. 3 n., 134 and n., 135, 139
conservatism 176-180, 185 n.
Constant, Benjamin 17
constitutional patriotism 111, 120-128, 139, 201, 203-204, 204 n.
constitutionalism 3, 115 n., 120, 124, 202
Cooke, Maeve 98 n., 99 n.
Cristi, Renato 85, 86 n.
Crowder, George 16 n.

Dahrendorf, Ralf 54 and n., 139 n., 140 and n.
De Tocqueville 11 and n., 201

democracy 81, 106, 121, 124, 151, 178, 205, 211
  cosmopolitan, 204
  deliberative or discursive, 1, 4, 97-98, 111, 115-116, 118-119, 126, 135, 141-145, 198, 202-203
  liberal, 178 n., 199, 201
  models of, 113-114
  radical, 180
  representative, 142
democratisation 94 n.
Descartes, Rene 75
disenchantment 3, 5, 8, 103
diversity 185-193, 198, 207, 210
Dworkin, Ronald 174 n.
Dyzenhaus, David 205 n.

East Asia 48
Enlightenment, the 28, 198
enterprise association 152-153 n., 154-159, 169, 178, 188, 194
equality 170
ethical life 108-110, 114
evolution 88-90, 94 and n.

fascism 3 n.
feminism 178
Ferguson, Adam 28-29, 35, 51-53, 55-61, 84 and n., 94 n.
Flathman, E. Richard 187 n., 209 n.
Fleetwood, Steve 63 n.
Forsyth, Murray 59 n., 91
Franco, Paul 145 n., 177 n., 200-201, 201 n.
Frankfurt School 144
Fraser, Nancy 142, 143 n.
Free agents 152-154, 157-158, 161, 169-170, 181, 185-188, 195
Freedom 124, 145, 185-193
  civil, 188, 190, 195
  economic, 184 n.
  individual, 6, 10, 17, 34, 47, 66-68, 72, 74, 76-77, 86-87, 92, 94, 115, 158, 176, 179, 189-190, 198, 209
  negative, 86-91, 95 n., 112, 118, 198
  political, 181-182, 195
  positive, 95n.
  rational, 201
  social, 195
French Revolution 121
Friedman, Richard B. 175 n.
friend and foe 84 and n., 205
Frobel, Julius 131

Fuller, Lon 175 n.
Fuller, Timothy 154 n., 175 n., 177 n.

Galeotti, A. E. 77 and n., 86, 87 n., 92 n., 94 and n.
Gamble, Andrew 53 n., 85 n., 94 n., 95 n.
Gaus, Gerald F. 53 n.
Gellner, Ernest vii, 1-2, 4-5, 7-8, 11, 13-49, 51-52, 74, 89 n., 122 n., 123-124, 197, 202, 210
genetic engineering 128 n.
gentleman 186
Gerenscser, Anthony, 146 n., 180 n., 182 n., 183 n., 192 n.
globalisation 111, 120, 126, 201, 203
Grant, Robert 185-186 and 186 n.
Gray, John 53 n., 91 and n., 176 n.
Great Society, the 51 and n., 53 n., 54, 61, 63-64, 66, 69, 71, 73-75, 77-79, 81, 86-91, 198, 210-211

Habermas, Jurgen viii, 1-2, 4-8, 10-11, 14, 33, 97-145, 198, 200-201, 203-204, 206, 210-211
Hall, John A. 32 n.
Hamlin, A. P. 77 n.
Hampshire, Stuart 26-27, 200 and n., 209 n.
Hart, H. L. A. 168 n., 173 n., 175 n.
Hayek, Friedrich vii, 1-2, 4-7, 9-11, 33, 51-95, 197-199, 203, 210
Hegel, G. W. F. 144 n., 146 n., 200-201
Hobbes, Thomas 6, 33-34, 38, 146 n., 149 n., 198 and n., 200
human action 62
  unintended consequence of, 52-53, 55-61
human conduct 159-161, 164, 169, 188, 192
human knowledge
  dispersal of, 61-68
  limitations of, 57-61, 67, 69-70, 74-75, 88, 92-93
Hume, David 18, 52 and n., 71

ideal speech situation 200
Ignatieff, Michael 47 n.
individual responsibility 66
Individual
  abstract, 128
  as an end, 128-130

autonomous, 119, 145, 176, 195
  manque, 194-195
individualism 22, 48, 75-79, 87 n., 92 n., 187 n., 201
individuality 3, 25, 146 n., 162, 185, 187-188, 195, 201, 208-209, 211
individuation 129
Islam 48

Jarvie, I. C. 20 n.
Jones, David Martin 94
justice 68, 71, 86-87, 100, 109-110, 117, 164, 200
  social, 68 n., 91, 205

Kant 117 n., 123
Keane, John 47 n.
Keynes, John Maynard 85 n., 86 n.
Khaldun, Ibn 29
Kristol, Irving 91 and n., 92 n.
Kukathas, Chandran 53 n.

Larmore, Charles 115 and n., 117, 118 n., 119 and n.
Law 72-73, 79, 81, 97, 100, 104-112, 116 and n., 120, 131, 138, 141, 143-144, 184, 188-190, 192-193, 197-199
  common, 80
  criminal, 189
  equality before the, 109
  inner morality of, 175 and n.
  Kantian conception of, 110, 144 n.
  legitimate, 135-138, 140, 142
  natural, 107, 175 n.
  nomos, 81
  physical, 150
  proceduralist understanding of, 106-107
  thesis, 81
Lee Kuan-yew 48 n.
legal positivism 72, 112, 175 n.
legitimacy 14, 39-40, 43, 73, 87, 95, 106-107, 134 n., 137 n. , 139, 141, 144, 203
Lessnoff, Michael H. 3 n., 8 n.
Letwin, Shirley Robin 175 n., 186 and n., 209 and n.
lex 146 n., 170-174, 178, 180 n., 181-183, 185, 188, 191
  jus of, 175 n.
liberalism 4 n., 44, 53 n., 91 n., 94 n., 198 n.
  Kantian, 178

Liddington, John 187 n., 188-190, 189 n., 190 n., 192
lifeworld 129, 138 n., 139 n.
Lincoln, Abraham 150
Locke, John 4, 183 n.
Loughlin, Martin 175 n.

Macfarlane, Alan 20 n., 24 n.
majority rule 130-135, 140
Mandeville, Bernard 52 and n.
Mapel, David 168 n., 174 n., 175 n., 182 and n.
market 10, 37, 53-54, 65-68, 73-74, 79-80, 87-88, 91 and n., 92 n., 93-95, 123, 143, 197-199
Marx, Karl 2 n.
Marxism 2 n., 48
Mead, George Herbert 129 n.
Meyer, Frank S. 5 n.
Michelman, Frank I. 114, 115 n., 117 n.
Miller, David 91 n.
mind 65, 88
  theory of, 56-61
  Cartesian, 57, 59
Minogue, Kenneth 27 n., 32 n.
mixed economy 41-42
modernity 3, 48, 89 n.
modular man 5, 13, 20-28, 41-42, 47
Montesquieu, C. de S. 80
moral beliefs 53, 71
morality 54, 90 n., 93, 97, 100, 106-112, 116 and n., 131, 161-165, 177, 187, 201
  Kantian conception of, 135
  non-instrumental nature of, 91, 161
  self enactment aspect of, 162-163
  self disclosure aspect of, 162-163
Mouffe, Chantal 48 n., 178 and n., 179 and n., 180, 182, 205, 206 n.
Muller, Jan-Werner 2 n., 120 n.
multi-culturalism 120, 125-127, 203
mutual respect 128-130

Nardin, Terry 42 n.,, 146 and n., 194 n., 199 and n., 206, 207 n.
nation 79, 83-84, 121-125, 203, 206
nationalism 31-32, 42-46, 89 n., 111, 121, 122 n., 123-124
naturalistic evolutionism 7
Nazism 1, 93
Nietzsche, Friedrich 3
nihilism 91 and n.

Oakeshott, Michael vi, 1-2, 4-7, 9, 11, 14, 33, 142 n., 145-195, 197-198, 200-201, 209-211
O'Sullivan, Luke 173 n.
O'Sullivan, Noel vi-vii, 2 n., 91 and n., 120 n., 128 n., 134 n., 137 n., 142 n., 180 and n., 202 and n., 207-208, 208 n., 209-210, 210 n.

Parekh, Bhikhu vi, 176, 178
Pascal, Blaise 198
paternalism 135
Peters, Bernhard 143
planning 61, 64, 67, 80, 199
plural society 15-16
pluralism 13, 17, 19, 23-24, 33, 35-42, 46-48, 54, 73-74, 78-79, 108, 131, 197-198, 210
Polanyi, Michael 62 n.
political identity 74, 83, 117, 120, 125, 127-128, 179, 206-207
political, the 55, 79, 83-87, 137 and n., 205-206, 209-210
politics 93, 106, 126, 134, 146, 177, 180-185, 201-202
  dethronement of, 54, 82-86, 93-94
  of recognition, 127, 130 n., 203
Popper, Karl 2 n.
power 136-139, 141, 155, 172, 184, 194, 197, 202-203, 205, 209-210
  administrative, 135-138
  communicative, 135-144
  social, 138
practice 150, 152-153 n., 159-161, 177-178, 181, 190, 193, 194 n., 199
price mechanism 64-68, 75, 198
private property 66, 189
progress 77
Protestant ethic 19-20, 29, 41 n.,
public opinion 138 n., 140
public sphere 116, 128, 136, 138 and n., 139 n., 140, 144, 204
purpose 159-161

radicalism 176-180, 185 n.
rational consensus 130-135, 139-140, 144, 200
rationalisation 8
rationalism 8-9, 52, 75-76, 98, 177
  evolutionary, 93
rationality 56, 144, 198-199
Rawls, John 68 n., 106 n., 107 n.
Rehg, William 1 n., 97 n., 118 n.

relativism 101
religious beliefs 89-91, 130, 177, 210
respublica 146 n., 180 n., 181, 183-184, 193
Richardson, Henry 168 n.
rights 71, 205
  human, 97-98, 114, 120, 126, 203-204, 206
  individual, 105, 113, 115-116, 118-119, 127
  legal, 108
  moral, 112
  natural, 112
  negative, 105
  political, 105, 114, 127, 135
  positive, 112
  pre-political, 113
  private, 104 n., 106, 112, 114
  social and cultural, 127
  subjective, 113, 135
Riley, Patrick 146 n., 187 n.
Rorty, Richard 100 n.
Rosemont, Henry 48 n.
Ross, W. D. 168 n.
Rousseau, Jena-Jacques 75
rule
  abstract, 53 and n., 61-69, 72-74, 76, 78-79, 93, 198, 210
  civil, 165-169, 206, 211
  end-independent, 64, 69, 72, 74, 79, 81, 198, 210
  following a, 193 n.
  legal, 64, 66-67, 72
  moral, 63, 66-67, 69-70, 72-73, 164-165
  non-instrumental nature of, 7, 29, 33-37, 39, 41, 46-47, 166, 169, 191, 194 n., 195, 197, 199, 201-202, 208
  of conduct, 53, 63, 71-73, 87, 120, 170
  of just conduct, 63, 72, 81
  of law, 7, 10-11, 35-36, 69 n., 79, 86, 93, 115 and n., 155 n., 171-175, 184, 185, 188, 197-199, 201, 205, 211
  of procedure, 200
  organisational, 157
  prudential, 63, 66-67
  unity of, 73-75
Ryle, Gilbert 62 and n.

Scheuerman, William E. 142 and n., 143-144

Index

Schmitt, Carl 84 n., 85 n., 86 n., 205 and n.
Shakespeare, William 148
Shearmur, Jeremy 53 n.
Shils, Edward 6 and n., 199 and n.
Shklar, Judith N. 93 and n.
Simons, Henry C. 184 and n.
Smith, Adam 51 n, 52 and n.
social cohesion 74, 88, 91
social integration 101-107, 116, 121, 126, 130-131, 135, 138
social practices 55-62, 76, 89, 91-92
socialisation 129
socialism 91 n.
societas 146 n., 172, 175-182, 194
solidarity 90 and n., 98, 121, 124-125, 127-128, 201, 205-206
Solinger, Dorothy J. 17 n.
sovereignty 38-39, 85, 97, 123
   popular, 81, 98, 112, 115, 117, 131 n., 141
speech acts 102
spontaneous order 1, 52 and n., 53-54, 63-64, 67-69, 71, 73-75, 77, 81-84, 86-94, 203, 210
Stalinism 3 n.
state 43-44, 48, 54, 83 and n., 84, 86, 93-94, 95 n., 145, 146 n., 152 n., 158, 172, 175, 185, 188, 190, 194-195, 199, 201, 207
   constitutional, 116, 121-122, 124, 137-138, 141
   democratic, 207
   intervention, 80, 86 n., 199
   multi-cultural, 204
   nation, 120-122, 126, 203-204
   non-instrumental conception of, 42
   separation of economy and, 28-34
   society distinction, 78-82, 94
   welfare, 113-114

Taylor, Charles 78 and n., 79
Thatcher, Mrs 146 n.
totalitarianism 1, 2 n., 54, 91 n.
tradition 88-90
transactional association 154-158
truth 100
   transcendental, 101

universal pragmatics 99
universalisability of moral claims 108-109, 130

universitas 146 n., 172, 188, 194
utilitarianism 70-71

Varty, John 94 n.
Vico, Giambattista 195 n.
Waldron, Jeremy 4 n., 8 n., 198 and n.
Walzer, Michael 42 n., 47 n., 164 n., 183 n., 207 and n.
Weber, Max 3 n, 8, 19, 136
Winch, Peter 168 n., 178 n., 192, 193 n.
Wittgenstein, Ludwig 168 n., 192
Worthington, Glenn 183 n.

Zakaria, Fareed 48 n.